21 September 83

# SLIM GOURMET SWEETS AND TREATS

# SLIM GOURMET SWEETS AND TREATS

## *Barbara Gibbons*

*1817*

**HARPER & ROW, PUBLISHERS, New York**
Cambridge, Philadelphia, San Francisco, London
Mexico City, São Paulo, Sydney

FIRST EDITION

*Designer: C. Linda Dingler*

---

Library of Congress Cataloging in Publication Data

Gibbons, Barbara.
　Slim gourmet sweets and treats.

　Includes index.
　1. Low-calorie diet—Recipes. 2. Desserts.
3. Snack foods. I. Title.
RM222.2.G52 1982　　641.5′635　　82-47737
ISBN 0-06-015057-2　　　　　　AACR2

---

82 83 84 85 86 10 9 8 7 6 5 4 3 2 1

# CONTENTS

1. You Can Have Your Cake and a Slim Figure, Too   **1**

2. Cakes, Cookies, and Other Calorie-Saving Baked Goodies   **19**

3. Bottomless Pies, Topless Tarts, and Other Trimmers   **47**

4. Breads, Biscuits, Muffins, and Bread-Based Sweets   **70**

5. Pancakes, Waffles, Crêpes, and Omelets   **83**

6. Gelatins, Puddings, Custards, Mousses, and Molds   **97**

7. Cheesecakes and Other Easy Cheesy Treats   **130**

8. Frostings, Fillings, Sauces, Glazes, Jams, Jellies,
   and Other Toppings   **153**

9. A Year-Round Harvest of Fruit-Based Favorites   **172**

10. Ice-Cream-Parlor and Soda-Fountain Treats: Drinking "Light"   **202**

11. Nonsweet Nibbles, Noshes, and Other Savory Snacks,
    Decalorized   **227**

*Index*   **247**

# SLIM GOURMET SWEETS AND TREATS

# 1
# YOU CAN HAVE YOUR CAKE AND A SLIM FIGURE, TOO

### What's for Dessert?

If you have to live on a limited calorie budget, dessert is usually the first thing to go. After all, if losing weight depends on cutting back to 1,200 or 1,400 calories (and it does!) who can afford to waste a third of their calorie allotment on junk food? And most desserts, no matter how carefully prepared, or how expensive or "wholesome" the ingredients, really *are* junk food in terms of nutrition. Cakes, cookies, pies, and pastries are primarily sugar, starch, and fat—nutritionally neutered calories with little redeeming value in the way of vitamins or minerals, or appetite-appeasing roughage or protein. Convention-ally-made sweets are frequently the most fattening part of the menu, often outweighing every other part of the meal in calories, even the main course. No wonder most sweets head the should-be dieter's forbidden list!

But most of us could-be chubbies are afflicted with an unreformed sweet tooth. And therein lie the seeds of dieter discontent. Unfortunately, unsatisfied cravings for familiar foods are the main cause of diet dropout. After the first blush of calorie-counting commitment wears thin, so to speak, the dieter is left with the grim realization that the real price of slimness appears to be a life of dessert denial. Inevitably, self-denial gives way to self-delusion: "Just this once won't hurt." And "just one" is followed by one more, and pretty soon the dieter has drifted back into his old, familiar eating pattern . . . and his original weight. But the defeated dieter is even worse off than before. His failure further convinces him that he's a spineless stuffgut who lacks the moral fiber for slimness. Worse yet, the temporary deprivation of dieting has served notice to his metabolism that hard times are here and that every calorie consumed should be stockpiled—as fat—to tide him over the apparent famine. And that's why diets don't work!

What does work?

Cooking the Slim Gourmet way! If you're a venturesome experimenter, you can put your kitchen to work. Learn to cut out the excess calories you don't need and won't miss while duplicating the taste and texture of fattening favorites—including such previously off-limits items as sweets and snacks!

## Snacks and Desserts Don't Have to be Fattening

Neither your stomach nor the scale knows the difference between calories consumed as part of an official, permissible "meal" or as part of a between-meals snack or after-meal dessert. If snacks and sweets are nonfattening, if they're made from ingredients that are filling and satisfying as well as nutrition-rich, there's no reason why calorie counters need to consider them off limits.

In fact, snacking has definite advantages for the waistline watcher. Experiments with both lab animals and human volunteers demonstrate that calories count *less* when they're divided among several small snacks instead of "three squares." Eating frequently, but lightly, helps your body turn calories into energy instead of fat.

## Editing out the Empty Calories: Refined Sugars, Starches and Fats

If desserts and snacks are to be both satisfying *and* nonfattening, they must be relatively free of the calories that don't count nutritionally—the empty calories that fatten without filling. Sugar is chief among the no-account ingredients that don't carry their weight, nutritionally, and contribute nothing to the bottom line of balanced eating. Sugar is pure calories and nothing but. What's more, sugar is so rapidly absorbed into the bloodstream that it actually *causes* hunger . . . and a craving for more sweets! Refined fats, on the other hand, are more slowly absorbed. But their caloric content is double that of sugar. In fact, fat is the most fattening ingredient there is! What's more, most fats—shortenings and oils, for example—have virtually no taste, so they add little to the *flavor* of snacks and desserts.

## Duplicating the Taste and Texture of Sweets and Snacks with Little or No Sugar or Fats

The recipes in this book, gathered over a decade of writing my three-times-weekly "Slim Gourmet" newspaper column, illustrate how desserts and snacks can be made from lean, nutrition-rich ingredients: foods like skim milk and low-fat cheeses, whole grains, naturally sweet fruits and juices—foods that should be part of your diet anyway. Many of these sweets are sweet enough without additional sweetening needed. In others, you may want to augment the sweetness with small amounts of sugar *or* substitutes; the choice is up to you. Most of these recipes are adaptable to a variety of sweeteners—now on the market or soon to be available.

## Answers to Your Questions about Sweeteners

Sweetness without sugar calories is the diet cheat's dream—a way to have your cake and a slim figure too! But substitutes that replace the sweetness of sugar don't necessarily duplicate its other functions. Most conventional cakes and cookies rely on sugar for bulk and browning as well as sweetness. Simply replacing one with the other can result in a disappointing failure. In fact, some baked goods won't even be sweet because some substitutes break down in heat. A sweetener that's 200 or 400 times sweeter than sugar can't equal the volume that sugar provides: you can't replace a pound of confectioners' sugar with a few tablespoons of sweetener and expect to frost a layer cake!

Sugar substitutes have other exasperating idiosyncrasies: they sweeten some ingredients more than others—strawberries more than chocolate, for example—thereby resisting attempts to come up with a universal table of equivalents that can cover all situations. Each sweetener has its own unique profile. The perception of sweetness may vary, depending not only on the sweetener and other ingredients but also on the cooking method and the temperature at which the dessert is served, on how long the dessert is stored, even on the person you serve it to. Individuals vary in their ability to perceive sweetness—not only in sugar substitutes but in different forms of sugar. And some people are genetically unable to taste any sweetness at all in the most commonly available sugar substitute. Some sweeteners are okay for some people and not others. Some are illegal in the United States but available abroad. Some are brand new. And some have just as many calories as sugar!

In this chapter I answer the most commonly asked questions about using sugars and substitutes in low-calorie cooking. The question I do not attempt to answer is whether you should use sugar substitutes at all. That's a question every individual must decide for himself (and, in my opinion, free of government interference).

# About the Recipes in this Book

Because some readers can't use sugar in any form, and others prefer not to use sugar substitutes, and still others will use any combination of sweeteners that results in good-tasting low-calorie desserts, most of the recipes in this book are designed to be flexible, with sweetener variations listed to suit your personal choice. Calorie counts at the end of each recipe were computed using U.S. Department of Agriculture data for common and generic ingredients, and data from the nutritional labels of the most commonly available brands of products. Ingredients vary, however, and products change. So the actual calories in the dessert you produce will reflect any difference. Keep in mind that, if you substitute higher-calorie ingredients for those listed, the calories will be higher.

Remember, also, that the calories listed for "one serving" of an eight-serving or four-serving dessert represents one-eighth or one-quarter of the total. If you're in the habit of taking double-size helpings, the calories will be double.

**Q. What is white sugar?**
**A.** Ordinary white table sugar, also known as sucrose, is refined from sugar cane or sugar beets. It's so refined that there's no difference between them. In fact, packagers are not even required to label the source. White sugar contains 15 calories a *level* teaspoon, 46 calories a level tablespoon and 770 calories a cup. Sugar is pure refined carbohydrate and contains no protein or fat, no vitamins, minerals, or fiber!

**Q. What about confectioners' sugar?**
**A.** Confectioners' sugar is simply powdered sucrose, made by grinding ordinary granulated sugar through mills, then passing it through fine mesh. Sometimes cornstarch is added, as much as 3 percent, to keep it from lumping. On a weight basis, granulated sugar and powdered sugar contain the same number of calories, 1,746 a pound, but there's a distinct caloric difference in measurements. Because powdered sugar is fluffy and takes up more room than granulated sugar, a tablespoon of confectioners' sugar is only 31 calories; a cup is only 385, sifted (462, unsifted). However, you would need more confectioners' sugar to provide the same sweetening level than you would granulated sugar —in fact, the same calories' worth. But there *is* a calorie-cutting trick with confectioners' sugar: undersweeten cakes and cookies and sprinkle the outside lightly with confectioners' sugar after the baked foods are cool. Because the confectioners' sugar dissolves instantly in the mouth, the perception of sweetness is immediate and undiluted, thereby increasing the sweet sensation.

**Q. What about brown sugar?**
**A.** Brown sugar is simply less-refined cane sugar, with some of the molasses residue remaining on the granules. It's the molasses that provides the distinctive dark color and flavor. Dark brown sugar contains more molasses residue

than light brown sugar. Because molasses is sticky, brown sugar tends to cake easily. It should be stored in an airtight container. The addition of a dampened paper towel will restore the proper moistness and texture to brown sugar. ("Brownulated" sugar is specially processed to coat each granule so that the sugar remains free-pouring.)

One cup of brown sugar is 821 calories firmly packed, 541 without packing. Because brown sugar is coated with molasses, which is less sweet than sugar, it has less sweetening power than white sugar. However, you will need the same calories' worth of brown sugar to create the same sweetening level, so brown sugar does not save you any calories. Nor are there any real nutritional advantages to brown sugar: the nutrients are so minute as not to matter in comparison to the caloric content.

One trick for adding the taste of brown sugar is to replace it with its sweetening equivalent in sugar substitute, then add a little molasses.

**Q. What is molasses?**
**A.** Molasses is cane syrup, made by boiling down the juice of sugar cane. Unlike table sugar, molasses contains some of the flavor of the sugar cane (and some of the nutrients as well, but the proportion in comparison to the calorie count is very small). Depending on its color and moisture, molasses has less sweetening power than sugar: you would need a cupful of medium molasses to replace the sweetness in ¾ cup sugar.

Light molasses is 50 calories a tablespoon and 827 a cup; medium is 46 a tablespoon and 761 a cup.

When replacing sugar with molasses it is important to remember that you are adding moisture as well: a cup of molasses contains about ⅓ cup fluid. Molasses also contains acid, which should be neutralized by baking soda in baked goods to provide the leavening gas. To avoid baking failures, it's best to use molasses in recipes specifically designed for its use. However, sweetening fruits, pie fillings, puddings, and mousses with molasses requires no special adjustments.

**Q. How about turbinado sugar? Or demerara sugar?**
**A.** Both are simply coarsely granulated forms of brown sugar with little nutritional value. It requires the same calories' worth of these "health-food" sugars to equal the sweetness of ordinary white sugar.

**Q. What about maple sugar?**
**A.** Maple sugar is the boiled-down sap of maple trees. The sap residue that provides the distinctive flavor and aroma also lowers the calories and the sweetening power. The actual calories in solid maple sugar or liquid maple syrup depend on the proportion of sugar to residue and moisture. As with the previously mentioned sugars, maple sugar will not save you any calories because you will need the same calories' worth to equal the sweetness of white sugar.

One trick for duplicating the taste of maple sugar or syrup is to combine sugar substitute with a few drops of pure maple extract. Here's a tip for making a lower-caloried "semi-maple" syrup: combine a small amount of pure maple syrup with either fructose syrup or low-calorie sugar-free "diet" syrup. Pure maple extract added to these lower-caloried syrups also heightens the maple taste.

**Q. Honey is a favorite of health-food fans. How does honey compare?**
**A.** Honey is a refined sugar processed by bees instead of men and machines; its vitamin and mineral values are very small compared with its calorie count. Honey contains more calories than sugar: about 64 per tablespoon, 1,031 per cup, depending on its moisture content. Despite its higher calorie content, honey *can* save you some calories because its high fructose content makes honey substantially sweeter than sugar. Depending on its use, you need fewer calories' worth of honey than sugar to provide equal sweetness. For example, it takes only 20 calories' worth of honey (about 1 teaspoon) to provide the sweetness level of a heaping teaspoon of sugar (25 calories) in lemon tea.

Because honey is sticky and adheres to the measuring spoon or cup, it's hard to measure. Honey also retains moisture, so baked goods made with honey will not stale as quickly as those made with sugar. In substituting honey for sugar, be sure to reduce the amount of liquid called for in a recipe, proportionally. For example, if a recipe calls for 1 cup of sugar and 1 cup of water, you could replace them with ⅔ cup of honey and ⅔ cup of water.

**Q. What is fructose or "fruit sugar"?**
**A.** Fructose or "fruit sugar" is a sweet substance normally found in fruit and honey. It has the same calories as ordinary white sugar but its sweetness level ranges from identical to ordinary sugar to nearly twice as sweet, depending on how it is used.

To understand fructose (or fruit sugar) we must first take a look at ordinary sucrose, or white sugar. Sucrose is a "double sugar" because it can be broken down into two components: glucose and fructose. Glucose, also known as "blood sugar," is the troublemaker for diabetics, hypoglycemia sufferers, and others whose metabolisms go awry after consuming sugar. But glucose isn't very sweet. Most of the sweetness in sucrose comes from the other half: fructose.

If you assign a "sweetness score" to sucrose, then the score for fructose would be 175 while glucose would be only 125.

**Q. Does fruit sugar come from fruit?**
**A.** Most of the fruit sugar on the market today is chemically produced by breaking down cornstarch and treating it with enzymes. Prior to the discovery of techniques to "bend" glucose molecules to the opposite direction (thereby changing it to fructose) fruit sugar was too expensive to produce. High sugar prices in the mid-1970s provided the impetus to step up the production of fructose and high-fructose syrups as a cheaper raw material in the manufacture of soft drinks.

**Q. Is fructose safe for diabetics?**
A. The debate over the appropriateness of fructose for diabetics continues. In 1974 the U.S. Food and Drug Administration conducted a nationwide recall of a product called Sweet 'n' Natural Fruit Sugar (distributed by Sugar Foods Corp. of Brooklyn, a subsidiary of the company that makes Sweet 'n' Low saccharin sugar substitute).

The FDA conducted the recall because the labeling promoted use of the product to diabetics, even though the label did advise diabetics to consult a physician before its use.

**Q. If fructose has the same calories as sugar, can it save you any calories?**
A. Yes and no. Like some other sugar substitutes, fructose is sensitive to temperature, and its performance varies with ingredients and circumstances. Like saccharin and aspartame, fructose is sweetest in cold foods: soft drinks, puddings, gelatins, frozen desserts, etc. The perception of sweetness is most notable in acid drinks and desserts (in other words, those made with fruit ingredients). You might need only a tablespoon of fruit sugar in cold lemonade to replace 1½ or 1¾ tablespoons of white table sugar. On the other hand, you would need the same calories' worth of fruit sugar as you would ordinary sugar to sweeten hot coffee, chocolate cookies, or vanilla poundcake. Unlike aspartame or saccharin, fruit sugar does not break down and lose sweetness in cooking. The difference is in the perception of sweetness.

**Q. I've read that fructose (fruit sugar) is sweeter than sucrose (ordinary white table sugar) and I'm wondering if I could save calories by using it in cakes and cookies. I've noticed that some commercial "diet" cake mixes contain it.**
A. Despite widening use in "diet" foods, fructose was found to be no sweeter than sugar in such baked foods as vanilla cake or in highly sweetened beverages, according to evaluations reported in the *Journal of Food Science*. However, when fructose (fruit sugar) and sucrose (white table sugar) were compared in slightly sweetened liquids—water or low-acid beverages—fructose was found to be anywhere from 1.6 to 1.9 times as sweet as the same amount (and same calories' worth) of sugar.

**Q. Does fructose have any other special properties?**
A. It's a hangover cure! Fruit sugar increases the rate at which alcohol is broken down by the body, even while you're asleep, but to double the speed of clearing alcohol, you'd need to consume enough fruit sugar to equal the amount of alcohol . . . and both are high in calories.

**Q. Are there any natural sources of fructose?**
A. Fruits and juice concentrates are natural sources of fructose sweetening. Adding fruit or increasing the amount of fruit in desserts is one way to add additional sweetness naturally.

**Q. Are fruit-flavored sodas lower in sugar than other kinds?**
A. Virtually all of the calories in soda pop come from sugar. Here's how they compare:

| Soda 12-ounce can | Calories | Sugar (tsp.) |
| --- | --- | --- |
| diet soda | 0 | 0 |
| club soda | 0 | 0 |
| quinine or tonic water | 113 | 7½ |
| fruit-flavored soda | 170 | 10½ |
| colas | 144 | 9 |
| cream soda | 160 | 10 |
| root beer | 152 | 9½ |
| gingerale | 113 | 7½ |

**Q. I have high triglyceride levels. Should I avoid foods containing fructose?**
A. Follow your doctor's advice. However, in one study reported in the *American Journal of Clinical Nutrition* six male volunteers with high triglyceride levels (two of them were also diabetic) went on diets containing fructose as 20 percent of their carbohydrate calories. The high fructose levels did not raise triglyceride levels.

**Q. Since both sugar and starch are carbohydrates, and carbohydrates are important in the diet, what difference does it make if you substitute sweet foods for starchy foods?**
A. A high-sugar diet had a much more harmful effect on glucose tolerance levels than did a high-starch diet, according to an experiment reported in the *American Journal of Clinical Nutrition.* In the study, 10 men and 9 women, aged 35 to 55, consumed a high-sugar diet for six weeks, then switched to a high-starch diet. Their insulin and blood-sugar levels were much higher on the sugar diet.

**Q. I have hypoglycemia and my doctor suggested that I eat an orange at breakfast rather than drinking orange juice. What's the difference?**
A. An article in the *American Journal of Clinical Nutrition* reports on a study comparing whole fruits and fruit juices. Whole oranges and apples were less likely than their juice to bring on hypoglycemia, the exaggerated insulin response to consuming sugars. The natural fiber in the whole fruit seems to help minimize the insulin response to the natural sugars found in fruit. But this fiber isn't present in apple and orange juice. One surprising exception: whole grapes caused more of an insulin response than grape juice.

**Q. Do sweeteners like xylitol, sorbitol or mannitol save calories?**
A. No. These three sweeteners (found in some dietetic products here and

abroad) are "sugar alcohols" that contain the same number of calories as white table sugar. Xylitol has the same sweetness level as sugar, but sorbitol and mannitol are only half as sweet. So you'd need double the calories' worth of sorbitol or mannitol to achieve the same sweetening as you would with sugar. Their use in "dietetic" foods is not to save calories but to avoid the heightened insulin response to sugar that diabetics experience. All three sweeteners are more slowly absorbed from the gut than sugar. However, most adult-onset diabetics are overweight, and cutting calories to lose weight is a prime concern in regulating diabetes, so sweeteners that cost more calories than sugar have little advantage to overweight diabetics.

**Q. Can "dietetic" candies sweetened with sorbitol be harmful if eaten to excess?**
**A.** According to an article in the *Journal of the American Medical Association*, a doctor had to be hospitalized after snacking on twelve "sugar-free" mints during a protein fast. He developed severe watery diarrhea, painful stomach cramps, light-headedness, and low blood pressure. Subsequent reading of the label showed that the mints contained the diabetic sweetener sorbitol, which can have a laxative effect when consumed in excess.

**Q. What technical problems are there in cooking with sugar substitutes?**
**A.** All the low-calorie sweeteners—cyclamate, saccharin and aspartame—lack the bulk that sugar provides in high-sugar baked goods like cakes and cookies.

For that reason, recipes that rely on large amounts of sugar for their bulk and texture cannot be duplicated merely by using equivalent amounts of sugar substitute in place of the sugar called for. However, it is possible to reduce the amount of sugar substantially in some desserts, and augment the missing sweetness with sugar substitutes. (In 1981, the government approved a reduced-calorie bulking agent, poly-dextrose, which will be available to the food industry to help get around the technical problems of creating low-calorie cakes and cookies without sugar. However, this ingredient is not available to home cooks.)

Sugar also has a preservative effect, most notable in such commercial products as jams, jellies, marmalades, and preserves. So sugar-reduced or sugar-free homemade alternatives should be made for the refrigerator or freezer, and used promptly.

A third problem unique to saccharin and aspartame is instability. Both sweeteners tend to break down when exposed to high heat, long cooking, or long storage in wet or liquid recipes. When saccharin breaks down, the sweetness is lost and a bitter metallic aftertaste remains.

But, when foods made with aspartame are exposed to high heat, long cooking, or storage, aspartame loses its sweetness slowly. The sweet taste gradually disappears, without any metallic aftertaste.

**Q. Some Slim Gourmet recipes suggest using both sugar and sugar substitute in the same recipe. What's the point of that?**

**A.** Combining sweeteners often results in a synergistic effect: in other words, the combined effect of two sweeteners working together is greater than would be expected. For example: sweetening a drink with one teaspoon of sugar and one saccharin tablet (equal to 1 teaspoon sugar) results in a drink that's substantially sweeter than it would be if you had used either two teaspoons sugar or just two saccharin tablets.

A generation ago food technologists discovered that they could greatly magnify the sweetening power of cyclamate sweeteners by combining it with small amounts of saccharin. As a result, most of the cyclamate sugar substitutes on the market when they were banned in the United States were actually combinations of both cyclamate and saccharin. More recently, observers have noted that the new sweetener aspartame has a synergistic (or magnification) effect on saccharin.

The sweetness-multiplying phenomenon is not limited to combinations of synthetic sweeteners. In a detailed study reported in the *Journal of Food Science* it was demonstrated that combining the natural sweetener fructose (fruit sugar) with saccharin could result in foods that taste as sweet as those sweetened with sucrose (white table sugar) but with no saccharin aftertaste—and with 40 to 70 percent fewer calories! By testing various concentrations and combinations at different temperatures, trained taste testers were able to discover that the most successful results came about when the fructose and saccharin were just about equal, in other words one teaspoon of fruit sugar combined with saccharin to equal the sweetness of one teaspoon of sugar. Good results were obtained at various temperatures, but the greatest gain in sweetness was at cold temperatures, where equal amounts of both sweeteners resulted in a combination that was 60 percent sweeter than would have been predicted simply by adding up sweeteners used.

**Q. What is the most stable sugar substitute?**

**A.** Of the no- and low-calorie products, the most stable choice is cyclamate, no longer legal in the U.S. but available in Canada and many foreign countries. Unlike saccharin and aspartame, cyclamate does not lose its sweetness in baked foods or heat-treated products like canned fruits, commercial toppings, bottled drinks, or syrups.

**Q. Some of my friends who travel a lot bring back cyclamate sugar substitutes from other countries. Is this legal?**

**A.** I have posed this question to the U.S. Customs Office in New York and was told that there is no regulation prohibiting individuals from returning to the United States with cyclamate sweeteners purchased in Canada or abroad for their own use. Importing cyclamate for resale would, of course, be illegal. (For that reason, attempting to go through customs with a quantity of sweeteners beyond what one individual might be expected to use within a reasonable amount of time might be inviting problems.)

**Q. What low-calorie sugar substitute is the most sugarlike in taste?**
**A.** According to taste-test panels, the one closest in taste to white table sugar is aspartame. Recently introduced, aspartame is sold as a tabletop sweetener under the trade name Equal, and as a sweetener in low-calorie foods under the name NutraSweet. Aspartame is indistinguishable from table sugar in taste. It provides the clean, clear one-dimensional sweetness of sugar with none of the metallic overtones, chemical flavor, or bitter aftertaste of saccharin-based sweeteners.

**Q. What effect does aspartame have on the flavor of foods?**
**A.** While aspartame adds no taste of its own, this sweetener provides the surprising bonus of intensifying the natural flavor of some fresh fruit, tart berries particularly. When used to sweeten out-of-season California strawberries, the berries are not only sweeter but "strawberrier," with a flavor more like home-grown or field-ripened fruit. Peaches are "peachier" and fruit punches are "fruitier"—with less fruit juice. The effect that aspartame seems to have on fruit flavors is similar to the flavor-potentiating effect that MSG (monosodium glutamate) has on meat flavors: it neither alters nor adds to the flavor. It simply makes the flavor more pronounced.

**Q. But does aspartame cook like sugar?**
**A.** I tested aspartame in recipes for three years before it was marketed, and my experience indicates that it's not a universal substitute for sugar in every form of cooking, but with adjusted techniques, its potential is far greater than currently presumed. Yes, you can "cook" with it, if you know how. The secret is to avoid or minimize its exposure to heat.

Unlike cyclamate, which is stable in high heat and therefore maintains its sweetness in canning and baking, aspartame is a combination of proteins that tend to separate when cooked in a liquid and gradually lose their sweet taste. Because saccharin also breaks down in high heat or prolonged cooking, the technical problems of creating recipes with aspartame are similar to those already encountered by dieters and diabetics attempting to cook with saccharin sweeteners: cold desserts and those sweetened after cooking work better than baked goods. Unlike saccharin, however, aspartame leaves no bitter aftertaste. So it's not necessary to undersweeten or overspice aspartame-sweetened desserts to mask bitterness. Another benefit: according to test reports, all volunteers seem to perceive aspartame as sweet, while certain individuals cannot taste the sweetness in saccharin, experiencing only the metallic bitterness.

Because aspartame is some 200 times as sweet as sugar, it is not "equal" to sugar in bulk. The tiny amount needed does not match the volume and physical properties of sugar in meringues, icings, cookies, and cakes, nor the thickening properties in syrups and sauces, nor the preservative effects in jams and jellies.

Packaging requirements further complicate sugarless cookery with aspartame. Initial marketing approval of aspartame under the trade name Equal is only in the form of single-serving packets equivalent to 2 teaspoons of sugar. The manufacturer, G. D. Searle, hopes to gain approval for marketing Equal in bulk packages that would be less expensive and more convenient for recipe use.

**Q. Are there any ways around the problems of cooking with artificial sweeteners?**
**A.** Here are some suggestions:

• Bury the sweetener between two layers of soft fruit (quick-cooking McIntosh apples instead of firm "baking apples," for example). Quick-bake the pie at high heat, 425 or 450 degrees for only 15 or 20 minutes, just until the crust browns. (Use a glass pan and put the pie on the bottom rack so the undercrust browns quickly by reflected oven heat.) The point of this technique is to protect the sweetener from heat.

Another advantage of this technique: most fruits and berries will have better texture if they're just barely cooked.

• Cook the pie shell and the filling separately. Bake an unfilled single crust until brown. Meanwhile cook a cornstarch-thickened unsweetened fruit filling in a saucepan, then remove it from the heat and sweeten the filling to taste after it is cooked. Then spoon the filling into the prebaked crust.

• Bake an unsweetened topless fruit pie (cover the fruit filling with a round of aluminum foil). After the pie is removed from the oven, sprinkle the filling with granulated sugar substitute.

• Bake an unsweetened pie with a latticework upper crust (or put several slashes in the top crust). After the pie is baked, make a sweetening syrup by dissolving aspartame or saccharin sweetener in a little fruit juice. Carefully spoon some of this through the crust into the filling.

• At serving time, top an unsweetened pie with a sweet topping or sauce: a sweet whipped-cream or yogurt topping, for example, or a custard sauce that has been sweetened after cooking.

• Make unbaked "raw" pies: fresh berries in a graham-cracker shell.

**Q. Is it true that aspartame sweetener is 200 times sweeter than sugar?**
**A.** Yes, but the "200 times sweeter than sugar" claim is only an average. Actual sweetness depends on how and with what it is used. My experience indicates that you need relatively more Equal to sweeten chocolate-based desserts than desserts flavored with fruit. Tea requires more sweetening than coffee. Iced tea or tea with lemon needs less than hot tea.

In general, bitter flavors are less responsive to aspartame and require more of the sweetener, proportionally, than they would sugar. The use of sour ingredients, such as the acid in fruit, decreases the proportional need for aspartame sweetener. Cold foods and drinks need less, while warm or hot drinks need more.

**Q. Why does the label on aspartame-based sweeteners like Equal state "not for use in baking and cooking."**

**A.** Because that packaging statement was part of the original application for government approval made back in 1974. When approval was finally granted in 1981, the label wording was part of the final approval. In the meantime, however, recipe testing has disclosed that aspartame sweeteners are somewhat more flexible than originally believed and that, with some alterations in technique, aspartame can be used in cooking.

Here is what I have found:

CAKES: Because of the high heat and the lack of bulk, Equal is not a substitute for sugar in conventional cake recipes. But you will be able to make a less-sweet or nonsweet cake (sweetened with sugar or unsweetened), and apply an Equal-sweetened fruit-based topping or filling; strawberry shortcake, for example. No-bake cheesecakes are excellent, particularly if topped with aspartame-sweetened fruit.

COOKIES: The same problems will rule out conventional sugar cookies and the like, but no-bake creations like rumballs, fruit-and-nut squares, and mix-and-chill cereal-based concoctions will work. It's also possible to make less-sweet cookies, then roll them in sugar substitute, or sprinkle them after cooling.

PIES, TARTS: With some adjustments to conventional recipes, some types of baked fruit pies are possible, particularly with soft, quick-cooking highly acid fruits (berries, for instance). Apple pie is possible using soft, fast-cooking McIntosh apples, quick-baked at a high temperature so the crust browns quickly without subjecting the filling to high heat. For best results, the sweetener should be buried between two layers of fruit, where it will be most insulated from oven heat, rather than mixed with the filling. But the types of pies that are most successful are prebaked pie shells or no-bake graham-cracker pie shells with raw fruit or chilled pudding-type fillings. Yogurt fillings are very effective.

PUDDINGS, GELATINS, MOUSSES, CHILLED DESSERTS are the best types of desserts to make. Those made with fruits or juices are particularly good—and taste even better with aspartame than they do with sugar.

ICE CREAMS AND FROZEN FRUIT DESSERTS will be very successful, especially those flavored with fruit. Unlike sugar, Equal does not draw moisture out of frozen fruit.

JAMS, JELLIES, PRESERVES, SPREADS would need to be made for freezer storage, rather than shelf storage, since high-heat sterilization methods cause Equal to lose sweetness.

COFFEE, TEA, BEVERAGES: Equal stirred into hot coffee or tea does not lose its sweetness; hot cocoa requires more of the sweetener to overcome the bitterness of chocolate (using carob as a partial or total replacement for chocolate reduces the amount of sweetener needed). Because of the tendency of aspartame to gradually lose sweetness in long-stored liquids, commercial soft drinks present technical problems that bottlers are working on. However, homemade "diet soda" will be a simple matter: club soda, fruit-juice concentrate, and Equal mixed to order!

FRESH FRUITS, BREAKFAST CEREALS represent ideal uses for Equal; the sweetener can be applied at the table. Cooked fruits like baked apples, applesauce, and poached pears can be made unsweetened and then sweetened at the table. Sweetening at the table allows both dieters and nondieters to share the same foods; the nondieters simply sweeten theirs with ordinary table sugar.

**Q. I'm allergic to MSG. I've read that the new aspartame sweeteners have the same sort of flavor-enhancing effect on fruit that MSG (monosodium glutamate) has on meat flavors. Is it likely that I would also be sensitive to aspartame?**
**A.** Not likely, according to an experiment reported in the *Journal of Clinical Nutrition.* Volunteers were chosen who had proven reaction to MSG. Some were given orange juice sweetened with large doses of aspartame and some orange juice sweetened with sugar. Neither the volunteers nor the researchers knew which orange-juice samples contained the aspartame. None of the volunteers showed any symptoms like the MSG syndrome with either the sugar or aspartame-sweetened drinks.

**Q. What is saccharin?**
**A.** A calorie-free crystalline substance derived from coal tar. It's intensely sweet, about 400 times sweeter than sugar. Until the recent introduction of aspartame, virtually all the sugar substitutes on the U.S. market were based on saccharin. A quarter-grain tablet or a single packet of Sweet 'n Low is equal to 2 teaspoons of sugar.

**Q. If saccharin is calorie-free why does a packet of Sweet 'n Low have 3½ calories?**
**A.** Because Sweet 'n Low also contains nutritive dextrose (also known as glucose or blood sugar) as a bulking agent.

**Q. Are saccharin-based sweeteners safe?**
**A.** By law, all products and foods containing saccharin must carry a warning on their labels: "Use of this product may be hazardous to your health. This product contains saccharin which has been determined to cause cancer in lab animals." However, saccharin has been in use in the United States since 1902 with still no evidence as of this writing of its ever having caused any harm. By virtue of its long and widespread use, it could be said that saccharin is the most "tested" sugar substitute.

**Q. Why did the U.S. Food and Drug Administration attempt to ban saccharin?**
**A.** By law, the FDA had no choice but to proceed on an attempted saccharin ban in 1972 under the provisions of the Delaney Amendment, the same law that brought about the ban on cyclamate sweeteners. Under the provisions of the Delaney Act, any food additive that can be demonstrated to cause cancer in lab animals must be outlawed, regardless of the risk/benefit ratio. As with

the cyclamate studies that preceded it, the saccharin research involved feeding massive doses to lab rats. Opponents of the saccharin ban claimed that it was the huge amounts of saccharin and the design of the experiments that caused the rat tumors and that there is no evidence to support the idea that saccharin can cause cancer in humans.

When the FDA banned cyclamate, saccharin was an available alternative. But when the government tried to ban saccharin—an act that would have outlawed what was then the only remaining low-calorie sweetener—public outrage was so great that Congress stepped in to prevent the FDA from acting. A moratorium on the proposed saccharin ban is expected to continue through 1983.

**Q. When I make saccharin-sweetened desserts for my diabetic husband, he claims that they don't taste sweet at all, yet they taste sweet to me. Can you explain this?**
A. Some people—your husband is probably one of them—have an inborn inability to perceive saccharin as sweet. Their tastebuds are "blind" to the sweetness. The only thing that they can taste is the metallic overtones that are masked by the sweet perception that the rest of the population experiences. For these people, such products as sugar-free diet soda taste like poison! They simply can't understand how anyone can drink it.

Oversweetening a dessert with saccharin or cooking a dessert so that the sweet taste disappears can also result in a bitter, metallic, nonsweet taste that *everyone* will experience as unpleasant.

**Q. I baked an apple pie with a granulated saccharin sweetener. The filling tasted very sweet before I baked it, but when I served it the pie wasn't sweet at all. Why?**
A. Conventional fruit-pie recipes are baked in a hot oven for a relatively long time, causing such heat-sensitive sweeteners as saccharin and aspartame to break down and lose their sweetness. These sweeteners aren't successful in conventional oven-baked desserts.

**Q. Are there any ways around this problem?**
A. Baked goods can be undersweetened or nonsweetened, then topped after baking with granulated sugar substitute. After they are cool, cookies can be rolled in granulated sugar substitute mixed with a little cinnamon or other spice. Cakes or loaves can be sliced and served with sugar-substitute-sweetened fruit. Or you could make a frosting sweetened with sugar substitute.

**Q. I made quick-baked sugarless "sugar" cookies, but they didn't brown. When I baked them longer to make them brown, they weren't sweet. Why?**
A. Cake and cookie batters with little or no sugar won't brown very well; the normal exterior browning of conventional cakes and cookies is due to the caramelization of the sugar in the batter. If you bake them until they are brown, they are overcooked. If you have used saccharin sweeteners, the overcooking will cause the sweetener to break down and lose sweetness.

**Q. I made a chocolate mousse, substituting saccharin tablets dissolved in hot water for the sugar, but no matter how much I added, I couldn't make it sweet enough. What did I do wrong?**
**A.** You probably attempted to oversweeten a very chocolate dessert. Saccharin is self-limiting: beyond a certain point additional saccharin will be perceived as bitter rather than sweet, so saccharin is not a good sweetener for ingredients that are very bitter or very sour. A rule-of-thumb guide: limit the saccharin content to no more than the equivalent of 2 or 3 teaspoons sugar per serving. In other words, if a dessert serves 8 people, it can contain about 16 or 20 saccharin tablets, maximum 24 (or 8 to 12 packets of sugar substitute).

A way around this problem is to decrease the bitter ingredients: use *less* chocolate, or substitute nonbitter carob, the taste-alike for chocolate.

**Q. I noticed that decaffeinated coffee needs less sugar substitute then regular coffee. Why's that?**
**A.** Because decaffeinated coffee is less bitter. To minimize the need for sweetness in coffee-containing dessert recipes, use decaffeinated coffee.

**Q. Throughout the 1960s and 70s the government emphasis was on banning sugar substitutes; now it seems to have switched toward making them legal. Why's that?**
**A.** The political pendulum seems to have swung in the opposite direction on all fronts—away from demanding government regulation and "protection," toward eliminating government "interference" in individuals' lives. Today people seem more intent on retaining the right to make their own decisions rather than having federal agencies make decisions for them.

**Q. Is it likely that cyclamate will ever be made legal again in the U.S.?**
**A.** Abbott Labs, the manufacturer of cyclamate, and the Calorie Control Council, a trade association of diet-food makers, are continuing legal efforts to reverse the cyclamate ban.

**Q. I have a sweet tooth. Isn't it healthier to satisfy it with real sugar?**
**A.** "Real sugar" is an artificial sweetener, too! Few foods exist in nature that are as sweet as the sweetened foods modern "civilized" people have grown accustomed to. Sugar is nothing more than pure, processed calories, used as an additive to make foods sweeter than they could or would be. Think of it this way: if you were to take a stalk of sugar cane or a sugar beet (or any sweet fruit) and strip away all the vitamins and minerals, all the complex carbohydrates and valuable fiber—in short, everything of value—and save only the calories, what you'd have left is sugar. Sugar *is* calories, in their simplest form.

Sugar is abused and overused just as salt is; however, salt is calorie-free. While salt does serve some valuable functions in the human body, there is no need for sugar in human nutrition. In fact, sugar is a relatively recent "refinement" in culinary history. The development of sugar had to wait until man learned how to separate the calories and sweetness from plants that Mother Nature intended as a total package.

The healthiest and most natural way to satisfy your sweet tooth is to snack on sun-ripened fruits, unaugmented by artificial sweeteners in any form, including sugar. Many of the recipes in this book can be made without any additional sweetness other than that naturally provided by fruits and juices. The advantages of using fruits and juices as sweeteners is that the sweetness is accompanied by the vitamins and minerals originally "packaged by the manufacturer": Mother Nature.

However, most Westerners (especially those with weight problems) have become so habituated to the sweet taste of sugared foods that their search for sweets is akin to an addiction. Even when weight and health problems dictate the curtailment of sugar use, dieting attempts fail because the sugarholic is unwilling to give up sweets. In that respect, low-calorie sugar substitutes are a bit like methadone for sugar junkies—pragmatic alternatives that help the addict get off the more harmful stuff!

In my opinion, the decision about using sugar substitutes is one that every individual is entitled to make for himself or herself.

**Q. How can I tell which sweetener is used in sugar substitutes and low-calorie products?**
**A.** All products containing sugar substitutes are labeled with a list of ingredients which will tell you whether the product contains saccharin, aspartame, fruit sugar (fructose), sorbitol, mannitol, or xylitol.

**Q. How can I sweeten desserts for my kids? I don't want them to get hooked on sugar *or* substitutes!**
**A.** The taste for excessively sweet foods develops in childhood, so avoiding the exposure to sweet drinks and desserts is a good idea. Encourage your youngsters to make their own soda pop by combining defrosted fruit-juice concentrates with club soda. Make gelatins with plain gelatin and fruit juice; make puddings with fresh-fruit purées. Make cookies with lots of raisins and little or no sugar; sweeten cakes and loaves with mashed ripe bananas. Make milkshakes with bananas or other mashed fruit. Encourage kids to avoid chocolate and snack on fresh fruit. When you *do* serve sugar-sweetened desserts—ice cream or cake for example—omit the sugary frostings or toppings and pile them high with fresh fruit—more fruit than cake. Most of all, get children to regard sweets as special-occasion treats, not a normal ongoing part of daily meals.

**Q. With the emphasis today on avoiding salty foods, wouldn't my kids be better off snacking on sweets than on salty pretzels and potato chips?**
**A.** Cakes, cookies, candy, pie, and other sweets contribute more sodium to the diet of teenagers than such salty snacks as chips and pretzels, according to a study of 1,434 families reported in *Cereal Foods World,* a trade publication.

A week-long tally of food intake revealed that boys average 396 mg. of sodium a day from snack foods while girls average 293 mg. However, it is advisable to limit the amount of both salt and sugar in your diet.

**Q. Many desserts call for eggs, and these are off limits because of my cholesterol count. Any suggestions?**
**A.** It's the yolk that contains all of the cholesterol and most of the calories. One large whole egg is 79 calories and contains 274 mg. of cholesterol—more than you'll find in any other food. Of this, the white part contains only 16 calories, and no cholesterol.

Luckily for calorie- and cholesterol-conscious cooks, egg whites can perform many of the functions of whole eggs, and save you calories, too. Trouble is, eggs are a nuisance to separate. And, if you can't eat the egg yolks, there's not a lot to do with them unless you're into daily shampoos. And then there's the matter of color: egg whites are, well, white!

One way to beat the bother while avoiding egg yolks is to use a commercial substitute. Most of these products are primarily egg whites, with a small amount of oil added to replace part of the fat of the egg yolk, plus yellow coloring and yolk-like flavorings. With the added fat, the substitutes are higher in calories than plain egg whites, but less than whole eggs (check the label to be sure). "Eggbeaters," for example, is 30 calories a quarter-cupful, the equivalent of one 79-calorie egg. So Eggbeaters saves you calories as well as cholesterol.

You can substitute either fresh egg whites or no-cholesterol products for whole eggs in many ways. For example: Use 2 egg whites or ¼ cup substitute in place of each egg called for in baked goods: cakes, cookies, muffins, etc.

Use 2 egg whites or ¼ cup substitute in place of each egg in pancake, waffle, crêpe, or fritter batter.

Dilute egg whites or liquid substitute with skim milk and use in place of whole eggs when making French toast. For yellow-colored egg whites, add a pinch of ground turmeric (or a few drops of bottled food coloring).

# 2
# CAKES, COOKIES, AND OTHER CALORIE-SAVING BAKED GOODIES

From the waistline watcher's point of view, all cakes are "devil's food" whether they're chocolate or not. That's because most conventional cakes are combinations of starch, fat, and sugar in varying proportions. And that's just the beginning. Despite its lack of redeeming nutritional value, naked cake is considered spartan by most sweet freaks. To be worthy of their attention, cake must also have a topping in the form of a sugary icing. And if there's anything more fattening and less nutritious than cake, it's frosting!

The secret to enjoying your cake and a slim figure, too, is to serve the slimmest slice of cake but lavish it with lots of juicy fresh fruit toppings.

## SLIMMER CHIFFON CAKE

This calorie-reduced chiffon cake is made with less sugar and oil than the store bought variety.

> 9 tablespoons sugar, divided
> Sugar substitute to equal ⅔ cup sugar
> 2¼ cups sifted cake flour
> 3 teaspoons baking powder
> 1 teaspoon salt
> 1 cup skim milk
> ¼ cup vegetable oil
> 1½ teaspoons vanilla extract or lemon, orange, or almond flavoring
> 2 egg yolks
> 4 egg whites

Sift together 2 tablespoons sugar, the sugar substitute, flour, baking powder, and salt. Pour in the milk, oil, and flavoring; beat 1 minute. Add egg yolks and beat 1 more minute.

In another mixing bowl, beat the egg whites until frothy. Gradually beat in remaining 7 tablespoons sugar, a tablespoon at a time, until stiff and meringue-like. Fold the meringue mixture gently but thoroughly into the cake batter. Spoon the batter into two 8- or 9-inch nonstick layer-cake pans, or a 12-inch round nonstick tube pan.

Bake layers 25 to 30 minutes in a preheated 350-degree oven. Or bake in the tube pan at 325 degrees for 50 to 60 minutes. Allow to cool and slice thin, top with strawberry-orange cake topping. *Sixteen servings, 125 calories each (cake only).*

**Strawberry-Orange Cake Topping:** Wash, hull and thinly slice 2 pints fresh ripe strawberries. Peel, seed and dice 2 eating oranges. Combine fruit with 4 tablespoons orange liqueur (or 6 tablespoons orange juice and sugar substitute to equal 2 tablespoons sugar). Marinate at least 6 hours. Spoon over cake slices. *Sixteen servings, 115 calories each.*

# SLIM SPONGECAKE

The leanest and least-fattening cake to bake is spongecake. Aptly named, spongecake drinks in the juices of berries or other toppings with delectable ease, making it a versatile base for a variety of less-fattening, more-nutritious cake desserts. The perfect partner for spongecake is fruit . . . not frosting!

Our slim spongecake is made with a minimum of sugar and no fat whatsoever. Its light and airy texture comes from all that no-calorie air beaten into egg whites.

Spongecake also freezes well, so we suggest you bake two layers at a time, and freeze the second layer for later use (unless you're making a fruit-filled layer cake). Here's how to make two layers:

⅔ **cup sifted cake flour**
¼ **teaspoon baking powder**
⅛ **teaspoon salt**
 2 **eggs, separated, plus 1 egg white**
¼ **teaspoon cream of tartar**
½ **cup sugar, divided**
¼ **cup cold water**
¼ **teaspoon almond flavoring**

Sift together flour, baking powder, and salt. Set aside.

Beat the 3 egg whites and cream of tartar until stiff but not dry. Sprinkle ¼ cup sugar over whites; beat in thoroughly. Set aside.

Beat the 2 egg yolks until thick and light, about 3 minutes. Beat in water, remaining sugar, and flavoring. Continue beating an additional 5 minutes.

Gently fold flour mixture into yolk mixture in several small additions. Then, gently but thoroughly, fold in beaten egg whites. Divide mixture between two 8-inch nonstick layer-cake pans lined with wax-paper circles. Bake at 350 degrees about 35 to 40 minutes, until cake is springy and done. Cool. Remove layers and peel off paper. *Makes 2 layers, 415 calories each layer.*

Or . . . try this:

## SLIM PEACH MELBA CAKE

**1 layer Slim Spongecake, baked (preceding recipe)**
**16-ounce can juice-packed sliced peaches, drained**
**10-ounce package frozen sweetened raspberries, undrained**

Put the cake layer on a platter and arrange the peach slices on top, facing in the same direction. Purée the raspberries in a covered blender and drizzle over the peach slices. *Eight servings, 110 calories each.*

## HONEY SPONGECAKE

Here's an airy treat that's a decalorized version of the cake traditionally served during Jewish New Year season:

**4 eggs, separated**
**Pinch of salt**
**½ cup sugar, divided**
**8 ounces honey**
**1 cup cold coffee**
**2½ cups flour, sifted**
**1 tablespoon baking powder**
**1 teaspoon ground cloves**

Beat egg whites and salt until stiff. Beat in ¼ cup sugar gradually. Set aside.

In another bowl, beat egg yolks and remaining ¼ cup sugar thoroughly. Beat in honey and coffee.

Combine flour, baking powder and cloves. Beat into coffee-honey mixture. Gently, but thoroughly, fold coffee-honey mixture into beaten whites.

Pour into ungreased 10-inch tube pan. Bake at 325 degrees 1¼ hours, or until cake tests done. Invert pan to cool. Remove from pan when completely cool. *Sixteen servings, 160 calories each.*

## LIGHT CARROT TORTE (SPONGECAKE)

This is Jewish in origin, a carrot spongecake that's distinctly different from the heavy spicy carrot cake that's become a familiar-but-fattening part of the health-food restaurant scene. Despite its lack of shortening or oil, this carrot cake is so moist and flavorful that it needs no sugary icing. It would be a good choice for Rosh Hashanah.

3 eggs, separated
⅔ cup sugar, divided
2 cups raw grated carrots
2 tablespoons orange juice (or orange liqueur)
1 teaspoon grated orange rind (optional)
¾ cup all-purpose flour
1 teaspoon baking powder
2 tablespoons chopped almonds
2 tablespoons flaked coconut

Beat egg yolks until light. Beat in ⅓ cup sugar thoroughly. Lightly mix in carrots and juice. Thoroughly stir together orange rind (if using) flour, baking powder, almonds, and coconut. Mix with egg and carrot mixture. Beat egg whites until stiff but not dry. Gradually beat in remaining sugar. Gently fold into carrot mixture.

Preheat oven to 325 degrees. Spray an 8-inch springform pan with cooking spray. Pour in cake batter. Bake 50 minutes, or until cake tests done. *Eight servings, 165 calories each (orange liqueur instead of orange juice adds 10 calories per serving); or 10 servings, 135 calories each.*

**Spicy Carrot Torte:** Add ½ teaspoon ground cinnamon and ½ teaspoon mixed pumpkin-pie spice.

## CARROT CHIFFON CAKE

Our Slim Gourmet carrot cake is much less fattening than the usual kind, because it has no fat or fatty ingredients, and barely a tablespoon of sugar and flour per slice. What's more, our carrot cake shortcuts more than calories. This easy treat is made with canned carrots instead of shredded—much less work.

Of course, this isn't the dense, heavy (and heavily caloried) carrot cake of conventional recipes. Our version is basically a spongecake made with lots of airy egg whites. Aside from being free, air is nonfattening!

8-ounce can sliced carrots, drained
4 eggs, separated
1 teaspoon orange liqueur
½ cup sugar, divided

1 teaspoon grated orange peel
  Pinch of salt
½ cup flour
1 teaspoon baking powder
¼ teaspoon pumpkin-pie spice (optional)

Put drained carrots in blender container with the 4 egg yolks, orange liqueur, ¼ cup sugar, and grated peel. Blend smooth. Combine egg whites and salt in an electric mixer bowl and beat until stiff. Gradually beat in remaining ¼ cup sugar. Fold carrot mixture into beaten egg whites gently but thoroughly.

Sift flour and baking powder together. Sprinkle over carrot-egg-white mixture in several additions, and very gently cut and fold in each addition (along with spice, if used).

Spoon into an ungreased 8- or 9-inch tube pan. Bake about 1¼ hours at 325 degrees, or until an inserted cake tester comes out clean. Invert pan to cool; cool completely before removing from pan. *Ten servings, 100 calories each.*

## YOGURT ENGLISH TRIFLE

English Trifle is an easy dessert that can be very trifling about calories if you're a Slim Gourmet cook . . . or fattening, if you're not. Traditionally, a trifle is simply layered spongecake spiked with wine and topped with fruit (usually raspberries) then slathered with a rich custard. And perhaps a sprinkling of nuts for crunch. If you're counting calories while we reel off ingredients, you can see that a trifle can readily tally up to several hundred calories or more. Hardly a trifle!

Our tampered-with "trifle" begins with packaged spongecake. Then we top it with sugar-free fruit (whatever's handy or in season) mixed with wine and fruit juice. The sour-cream-like topping is a tangy mixture of yogurt and whipped topping mix, which leaves enough caloric leeway for a sprinkle of slivered almonds, if you like.

Our Slim Gourmet Yogurt Cream is a trim way to top off any low-cal dessert, especially fruit. Or try it on gelatin or spicy baked apples.

FOR EACH SERVING
1 small packaged individual spongecake
½ cup unsweetened fresh, canned, or defrosted sliced berries or other fruit
2 teaspoons sherry
1 tablespoon water or fruit juice
¼ cup Yogurt Cream (recipe below)
1 teaspoon slivered almonds

Put the spongecake in a small dessert dish. Combine fruit, sherry and water or juice, and spoon onto spongecake. Chill well. Just before serving, top with Yogurt Cream and slivered almonds. *Only 195 calories each.*

YOGURT CREAM
2 cups prepared regular or sugar-free whipped topping mix
1 cup vanilla or plain low-fat yogurt

Prepare topping mix according to package directions. Fold in yogurt. Chill to thicken. (Use sugar-sweetened topping mix with plain yogurt, or sugar-free topping mix with sweetened vanilla yogurt. Or choose both products in the sugar-free version and sweeten to taste with sugar substitute.) *About 10 calories per tablespoon, depending on sugar content.*

## GUILDFORD STRAWBERRY TRIFLE

4 to 5 ounces spongecake (1 layer), cut in 1-inch cubes
2 tablespoons orange liqueur
  4-serving package regular or low-calorie strawberry- or raspberry-flavored gelatin
1 cup boiling water
½ cup cold water
¾ cup sliced fresh strawberries
1 ripe banana, sliced
  4-serving package vanilla instant pudding
2 cups skim milk

Arrange cake cubes in the bottom of a clear glass serving bowl. Sprinkle with liqueur; prick with a fork.
Dissolve gelatin in boiling water. Mix in cold water, then strawberries. Chill until syrupy. Spoon over cake layer. Chill until firm.
Arrange banana slices over gelatin. Prepare pudding mix with milk according to package directions. Pour over banana layer. Chill until firm. (Garnish with several whole strawberries, if desired.) Serve directly from bowl. *Twelve servings, 125 calories each with regular gelatin, 100 calories each with low-calorie gelatin.*

## PINEAPPLE CASSATA (ITALIAN LAYER CAKE)

8-ounce sponge loaf or single layer, split (homemade or purchased)
8-ounce can juice-packed crushed pineapple
1 cup part-skim ricotta cheese
  Pinch of salt
1 teaspoon vanilla extract
2 tablespoons shaved chocolate or miniature chocolate chips (optional)

Split the cake horizontally to form 2 thin layers (easier to do if the cake is frozen). Spoon the pineapple over the bottom layer, reserving the juice. Beat the ricotta fluffy in blender or food processor, adding the salt, vanilla, and 2 or 3 tablespoons of the pineapple juice. Spread ricotta frosting on top layer and sprinkle with shaved chocolate, if desired. Chill several hours before serving. *Six servings, about 190 calories each (chocolate adds about 20 calories per serving).*

## DOUBLE CHOCOLATE ROLL

Chocolate Roll is an elegant sweet that's usually very inelegant about calories. The cake part is fattening enough, but the filling is often more so: a thick concoction of cream, butter, sugar, and other roly-poly stuff.

Here we roll out a low-calorized chocolate roll made with no fat or fatty ingredients, and very little sugar. It looks and tastes as elegant as it is.

Here's how:

CAKE
 **4 eggs, separated**
   **Pinch of salt**
¾ **cup sugar, divided**
½ **cup self-rising cake flour, sifted**
 **2 tablespoons plain low-fat cocoa**
 **2 tablespoons plus 1 teaspoon sifted confectioners' sugar**

FILLING
   **4-serving package instant chocolate pudding mix**
 **1 cup skim milk**
½ **cup plain low-fat yogurt**

To prepare cake: Combine egg whites and salt; beat until stiff. Gradually beat in ½ cup sugar. Set aside.

Beat egg yolks until light; beat in remaining ¼ cup sugar; continue beating until thick, about 5 minutes. Fold yolks into beaten whites.

Sift flour and cocoa together. *Gently* fold into egg mixture a little at a time.

Line a 15-by-10-inch jelly-roll pan with wax paper. Spread batter evenly over paper. Bake 30 minutes at 325 degrees.

Sift 2 tablespoons confectioners' sugar over a cotton or linen dish towel on a flat surface. Turn the cake out onto the towel. While still warm, peel off the wax paper and roll towel and cake together lengthwise. Cool. Unroll to fill.

To prepare filling: Beat together the pudding mix, milk, and yogurt. Mixture will be thick. Unroll cake. Spread evenly with filling. Reroll. Sift the remaining teaspoon of confectioners' sugar over the top. Refrigerate until serving time. *Twelve servings, 150 calories each.*

**Black Forest Roll with Cherry Filling:** Prepare cake as directed. Combine 2 cups canned cherry-pie filling with ⅛ teaspoon cinnamon in blender; cover and puree. Spread filling on cake and roll up gently. Refrigerate until serving time. (Other fruit fillings can be substituted). *Approximately 150 calories per serving.*

**Pineapple-Filled Chocolate Roll:** Prepare cake as directed. Drain into a saucepan the juice from 2 cups canned crushed unsweetened pineapple. Sprinkle on 1 envelope plain gelatin. Wait 1 minute, then heat gently until gelatin melts. Combine with pineapple. Chill until thickened but not set. Spread filling on cake and roll up gently. Chill until serving time. *115 calories per serving.*

## NO-BOWL NO-EGG CHOCOLATE CAKE

¾ cup sugar
1½ cups all-purpose flour
 3 tablespoons plain cocoa
 1 teaspoon baking soda
¼ teaspoon salt
 1 tablespoon vinegar
 3 tablespoons orange liqueur
 2 tablespoons salad oil
 1 cup water

Sift first 5 ingredients together into a 9-inch nonstick cake pan, which has been sprayed with cooking spray. Stir in remaining ingredients until thoroughly blended. Bake 30 minutes in a preheated 350-degree oven. *Twelve servings, about 135 calories each.*

## SHORTER SHORTCAKE

This Slim Gourmet shortcake is short on shortening, sugar, and calories, but there's nothing abbreviated about its flavor or versatility. One of the nicest things about shortcake is that it encourages the enjoyment of Mother Nature's seasonal bounty of fresh fruit. Top it with berries or sliced peaches, or spoon on my luscious Crush Sauce.

 1 cup all-purpose flour
1½ teaspoons baking powder
 1 egg
 1 teaspoon vanilla extract
⅓ cup diet margarine
 2 tablespoons sugar (optional)

Stir flour and baking powder together. Blend in egg, vanilla, diet margarine, and sugar with a fork. Knead lightly just until dough takes shape. Pat out on a lightly floured board, then roll with a floured rolling pin until about ¼ inch thick. Cut into 8 circles, using the rim of a small drinking glass.

Arrange cakes in a single layer on a nonstick baking sheet that has been sprayed with cooking spray. Bake uncovered in a preheated 450-degree oven 12 to 14 minutes, until golden. Allow to cool before removing from pan. Split shortcakes and layer with sliced or crushed berries or peaches, or spoon on Orange-Strawberry-Crush Sauce. *Eight individual shortcakes; each shortcake is approximately 100 calories (110 with sugar).*

## ORANGE-STRAWBERRY-CRUSH SAUCE

**1 pint fresh strawberries**
**2 eating oranges**
**2 tablespoons honey, fructose, or sugar substitute to taste (optional)**

Wash and hull berries; leave whole. Peel oranges and cut into chunks. Combine berries and orange chunks in blender container, a little at a time. Cover blender and chop fruit coarse by quickly turning the blender on and off, until the texture is like a relish. Add sweetener to taste if desired. *Sauce: eight servings, approximately 30 calories each (45 calories per serving with honey or fructose).*

**Lady Finger Layer Cake:** Split 8 packaged ladyfingers and arrange half in a shallow pan. Spoon on half the Orange-Strawberry-Crush Sauce or any crushed fresh fruit mixture. Top with remaining ladyfingers and cover with remaining fruit. (Or layer split ladyfingers and fruit mixture in individual dessert dishes.) Chill until serving time. *Eight servings, approximately 70 calories each.*

**Some Other Easy Ideas:** Spoon Orange-Strawberry-Crush Sauce into small spongecake shells, or use it as a filling for thin cold crêpes. Spoon it over frozen yogurt or ice milk to make a sundae, or layer it with cottage cheese for a sundae kind of lunch. To make a chill-and-serve "trifle," layer Crush Sauce with broken-up graham crackers in individual dessert cups. Cover with plastic wrap and chill several hours. Top with a dollop of vanilla yogurt and a dusting of cinnamon before serving.

## SUGARLESS BUTTERMILK SHORTCAKE

This moist and flavorful nonsweet cake is the basis for an easy dessert. Serve warm from the oven with a topping of crushed berries, sliced peaches, or other fresh fruit, sweetened to taste (with sugar substitute, if desired).

**1½ cups buttermilk-biscuit baking mix**
**4 tablespoons diet margarine**
**1½ teaspoons vanilla extract**
    **Pinch of grated lemon or orange peel (optional)**
**1 whole egg**
**⅓ cup fresh skim milk**

Combine ingredients in an electric mixer bowl. Beat on low speed until blended. Scrape bowl, then beat on high speed 3 minutes. Spread the batter evenly in a 9-inch nonstick round or square cake pan which has been sprayed with cooking spray.

Bake in a preheated 375-degree oven 18 to 20 minutes, or until a knife inserted in the center comes out clean. (This cake does not brown; don't overbake or it will lose its moist, tender texture.) Cut into squares and top with crushed berries or sliced fruit, sweetened to taste, if desired. *Nine servings cake, 115 calories each.*

## SUGARLESS STRAWBERRY SHORTCAKE

Here's one way to make a skinny strawberry shortcake that's long on strawberries but short on cake . . . and calories! Boost the sweetness of the berries with the *natural* fructose found in grape juice . . . no refined sugar or other sweeteners added! In this recipe, the biscuit base is made with pancake mix instead of biscuit mix, with no fat added.

**1 quart fresh strawberries**
**½ cup bottled red or white unsweetened grape juice**
    **Skinny Biscuit Shortcakes (recipe follows)**

Wash and hull berries; slice in halves or quarters. Crush a few of the berries with the grape juice. Then stir in remaining berries and chill. Serve on top of biscuits.

## SKINNY BISCUIT SHORTCAKES

**1 cup plain pancake mix**
**½ cup water**

Spray a nonstick cookie sheet with baking spray. Fork-blend ingredients together. With oiled hands, shape dough into 6 balls. Flatten the balls onto the cookie tin, then bake in a preheated 450-degree oven.

To serve: Split the biscuits and layer with berries. *Six servings, about 130 calories each with berry topping.*

**Sugarless Blueberry Shortcake:** Substitute 2 cups fresh blueberries for the strawberries. Combine ½ cup blueberries with the grape juice in a saucepan. Cook and stir until mixture boils. Remove from heat and allow to cool. Sweeten to taste, if desired, with sugar substitute. Stir in remaining blueberries. Chill. Serve on biscuits. Top with Yogurt Crème Chantilly, if desired (see page 175). *Six servings, approximately 140 calories each, topping additional.*

## STIR-CRAZY LIGHT FRUITCAKE

**1 cup self-rising flour, or 2 cups all-purpose flour plus 2 teaspoons baking powder and 1 teaspoon salt**
**1 egg**
**½ cup skim milk**
**4 tablespoons granulated fructose**
**1 teaspoon pumpkin-pie spice**
**½ cup fruit bits or mixed diced dried fruits**
**1 tablespoon brandy, rum, or orange liqueur (optional)**

Sprinkle unsifted flour into an 8-inch round or square nonstick cake pan. Add the egg, milk, fructose, and spice. Stir together with a spoon or rubber spatula until mixed. Stir in fruit and brandy, if desired. Level the surface with a rubber spatula.

Bake uncovered in a preheated 350-degree oven 20 to 25 minutes until done (when a knife inserted in the center comes out clean). Serve warm or cold, plain or with Light Orange Frosting (recipe follows). *Eight servings, 115 calories each, cake only (brandy adds 5 calories per serving).*

**Light Orange Frosting:** Combine 7½ ounces farmer cheese with 5 tablespoons orange marmalade, low-sugar marmalade, or undiluted defrosted orange-juice concentrate in food processor (using the steel blade) or blender. Process until smooth and fluffy. Spread on cool cake. *Eight servings, 70 calories each (frosting only) with marmalade, 55 calories each with low-sugar marmalade or orange-juice concentrate.*

## LIGHT GINGERBREAD

Gingerbread calories depend on whether you make it from scratch or a mix. According to government figures, homemade gingerbread is 3,344 calories, or

372 for one-ninth of a cake baked in a 9-inch pan. Gingerbread from a mix is considerably less: 1,573 calories, or 175 for a one-ninth piece.

Homemade gingerbread is fattening because most contemporary recipes call for a whole cupful of molasses and ½ cup of sugar . . . and shortening!

Early gingercakes were sweetened with honey or fruit. So we've borrowed their idea and sweeten our slimmer "light" gingerbread with honey and bananas. The bananas make the cake so moist that no fat or shortening is needed.

3 very ripe bananas
2 eggs
¼ cup skim milk
6 tablespoons honey (or fructose syrup or equivalent sugar substitute)
2 cups self-rising flour, or 2 cups all-purpose flour plus 2 teaspoons baking powder and 1 teaspoon salt
1 teaspoon baking soda
1½ to 2 teaspoons ground ginger
1 teaspoon cinnamon
½ teaspoon cloves
½ teaspoon nutmeg

Combine bananas, eggs, milk, and honey or other sweetener in an electric mixing bowl; beat until creamy. Stir remaining ingredients together and add to batter. Beat on low speed 15 seconds. Scrape bowl with spatula. Beat on high speed 30 seconds. Spoon into a 9-inch square nonstick cake pan which has been sprayed with cooking spray.

Bake in a preheated 350-degree oven 30 minutes, until set. Serve warm or cold. Spread with low-sugar orange marmalade if desired, or top with Orange "Cream" recipe which follows. *Nine servings (cake only), 195 calories each; 155 calories each with sugar substitute.*

## ORANGE "CREAM" TOPPING

½ cup part-skim ricotta cheese
½ cup orange marmalade (regular or calorie-reduced)
½ teaspoon vanilla extract (optional)
   Pinch of salt or butter-flavored salt (optional)
   Sugar substitute to taste (optional)

Combine and beat with electric mixer until fluffy. (If you are using low-sugar marmalade and want a sweeter topping without extra calories, a packet or two of sugar substitute may be added.) *One cup, 35 calories per tablespoon with regular marmalade; 25 calories per tablespoon with low-sugar marmalade; and 15 per tablespoon with sugar-free marmalade.*

# GINGER SQUARES

2 tablespoons diet margarine
2 tablespoons brown sugar
1 egg
1 tablespoon maple syrup
1 cup sifted all-purpose flour
¼ teaspoon baking soda
¼ teaspoon salt
¾ teaspoon ground ginger
¼ teaspoon cinnamon
¼ teaspoon cloves
¼ cup raisins

Cream together margarine and sugar. Beat in egg and syrup. Stir together flour, baking soda, salt, and spices; beat into egg mixture (dough will be stiff). Stir in raisins.

Spread and pat in a nonstick 8-inch square cake pan, which has been sprayed with cooking spray. Bake 10 minutes in a preheated 375-degree oven. While still warm, cut into 2-inch squares. Cool in pan before removing. *Sixteen squares, 55 calories each.*

# GINGER-PEACH UPSIDE-DOWN CAKE

If you like the convenience of cake mixes, but not the calories, it's good to know that prepared gingerbread mix is about 20 percent lower in calories than most other cake mixes. (The only lower-calorie cake mix is angelfood, the least fattening of all.)

You can cut the calories of gingerbread by topping it with fruit instead of icing . . . lots of fruit. More fruit means more servings and less cake, and fewer calories per serving.

Another way to cut cake-mix calories in half is by baking only half the package of cake mix at a time. Here's a delicious peach-glazed upside-down gingerbread that makes its own topping while it bakes. Empty the package of mix into a 4-cup measuring bowl and use only half. Pour the remaining mix into a plastic bag and tuck it back into the box to make another dessert some other time . . . with a different fruit topping.

16-ounce can juice-packed sliced peaches, drained (reserve juice)
1¼ teaspoons cornstarch (or arrowroot)
1 tablespoon honey (optional)
1¾ cups dry gingerbread mix (half of an 18-ounce box)
1 egg
½ cup water

Arrange peach slices in the bottom of a 9-inch square or round nonstick cake pan, with all slices facing the same way. Combine reserved juice, cornstarch, and honey, if desired. Mix well, until all white lumps disappear. Pour over peaches.

Combine gingerbread mix, egg, and water and mix according to package directions. Spoon evenly over peaches and juice mixture (don't attempt to mix it in; the cake will spread and cover the juices trapped underneath). Bake in a preheated 350-degree oven for 30 minutes. Remove from oven and allow to cool 20 to 30 minutes before up-ending.

To serve: Place a cake plate over the cake pan and turn over. The cake will be topped with peaches and a thick peachy sauce. Serve warm or chilled. *Nine servings, 120 calories each (honey adds about 5 calories per serving).*

## HOT GINGER-PEACH WINTER "SHORTCAKES"

All fruits go well with gingerbread, but nothing goes better than peaches. Ripe, juicy fresh peaches, when available . . . or try this winter shortcake, using canned peaches or any other canned unsweetened fruit.

**4 slices warm gingerbread (\*Each slice is one-ninth of a whole cake pre-
    pared from a mix, approximately 175 calories per slice.)
    16-ounce can juice-packed sliced peaches
1½ teaspoons cornstarch or arrowroot
    Few drops almond flavoring (optional)
    Sugar substitute to taste (optional)**

Arrange the warm gingerbread in 4 dessert dishes or bowls. Combine remaining ingredients except sugar substitute, if using, in saucepan; stir to mix well. Cook and stir over low heat until mixture simmers and thickens. Sweeten to taste, if desired. Spoon over gingerbread and serve immediately. *Four servings, 230 calories each.*

## QUICK BANANA LAYER CAKE

**    Pinch of salt
  2 egg whites
1⅓ cups spice-cake mix
 ⅔ cup water
  1 envelope (½ package) diet topping mix
 ½ cup chilled vanilla low-fat yogurt
  3 very ripe bananas**

Add a pinch of salt to the egg whites and beat stiff. In another bowl, beat the cake mix and water according to package directions. Gently but thoroughly fold the egg whites into the batter. Spoon the batter into two 8-inch layer-cake pans. Bake in a preheated 325-degree oven 20 minutes, or until done. Remove from oven and cool thoroughly before removing from the pan.

Combine diet topping mix and yogurt in a deep bowl and beat until they reach the consistency of whipped cream. Chill.

To assemble the layer cake, peel the bananas and cut lengthwise into long, thin strips. Spread a thin coating of whipped topping on the bottom cake layer. Top with thin strips of banana and spread with more whipped topping. Add the top layer and spread it with remaining "frosting." (If topping is too thick, beat in a little cold water.) Serve chilled. *Sixteen servings, 115 calories each.*

## CINNAMON-BLUEBERRY CAKE

All fruits are relatively low in calories and high in appetite-appeasing fiber, but few can match blueberries for a favorable fiber-to-calories ratio. A whole cupful is only 90 calories, yet contains 2.27 grams of natural fruit fiber. The natural fruit sugar in blueberries means adequate sweetness with less of that vitamin-neutered white stuff, sugar. The moistness of blueberry baked goods means less fat is needed . . . no frosting or topping, either!

1½ **cups sifted cake flour**
  2 **teaspoons baking powder**
  ¾ **teaspoon salt**
  1 **teaspoon ground cinnamon, divided**
  1 **egg or 2 egg whites or equivalent egg substitute**
  3 **tablespoons skim milk**
  8 **tablespoons sugar, divided**
  5 **tablespoons diet margarine, at room temperature**
1½ **teaspoons vanilla extract**
1¼ **cups fresh blueberries**

Sift flour, baking powder, salt, and ½ teaspoon cinnamon together; set aside.

In a mixing bowl, beat egg (or substitute), milk, and 7 tablespoons sugar together until well blended (don't overbeat). Add the flour mixture in several portions, beating well after each addition. Beat in diet margarine and vanilla until well blended. Fold in blueberries. Pour batter into an 8-inch square nonstick cake pan which has been sprayed with cooking spray. Combine remaining 1 tablespoon sugar and ½ teaspoon cinnamon; sprinkle over the top.

Bake in a preheated 400-degree oven 25 to 30 minutes, until golden. (Cake is done when a knife inserted in the center comes out clean.) Cool briefly before serving from the pan. Cut in 9 squares and serve warm or cold. *Nine servings, 165 calories each (10 calories less per serving with egg whites or substitute).*

*(continued)*

**Blueberry-Pineapple-Crush Cake:** Prepare Cinnamon-Blueberry Cake according to preceding recipe. Cut into squares and place in individual serving bowls. Top each serving with 3 tablespoons canned crushed juice-packed pineapple (sweetened to taste with granulated sugar substitute, if desired). *Each serving (cake and topping), 190 calories.*

**Strawberries on Blueberry Shortcake:** Prepare Cinnamon-Blueberry Cake according to preceding recipe. Top the warm cubes with Fresh Strawberry Shortcake Topping: Wash and slice 1 pint fresh ripe strawberries several hours before serving. Combine with 1 tablespoon sugar or fructose (or sugar substitute to taste) and 2 tablespoons water or unsweetened grape juice. Cover and refrigerate several hours to permit juices to form. Spoon the fresh strawberries and juice over the blueberry cake. *Nine servings topping, 20 calories each.*

# APPLE PUDDING CAKE WITH SELF-MAKING SAUCE

This is a cake that makes its own topping. Solid ingredients are placed in the bottom of a cake pan or baking dish, then topped with a quick-mix batter. Before baking, a cupful of boiling liquid is poured over the batter—making a very unlikely-looking mess! However, after this catastrophic-looking concoction is baked 30 minutes, what emerges is a delicious dessert, an upside-down apple cake with an apple-flavored pudding sauce . . . delicious hot or cold!

- **2 large McIntosh apples, cored and sliced**
- **1½ teaspoons lemon juice**
- **5 tablespoons fructose or honey or equivalent sugar substitute**
- **½ teaspoon cinnamon**
  - **Pinch each of nutmeg and allspice (optional)**
- **1 cup self-rising all-purpose flour or cake flour or pancake mix**
- **1 large egg**
- **3 tablespoons brown sugar**
- **⅔ cup cold water**
- **1 cup boiling water**

Arrange the apple slices neatly in rows or concentric circles in a square or round 9-inch nonstick cake pan which has been sprayed with cooking spray. Sprinkle lightly with lemon juice, sweetener, and spices.

Combine the flour, egg, brown sugar, and cold water; beat smooth. Spoon the batter over the apples. Sprinkle the top of the batter lightly with additional spices. Pour the boiling water in a thin stream over the batter. Bake uncovered, in a preheated 375-degree oven, for 30 minutes.

To serve: Cut into squares or wedges; invert each serving on a dessert plate. Spoon on some of the apple pudding sauce that forms in the bottom of the pan. Refrigerate leftover cake and serve chilled; the sauce will form a puddinglike glaze. *Ten dessert servings, 110 calories each; 120 calories each with honey; 85 calories each with sugar substitute.*

## APPLESAUCE CUPCAKES

1¾ cups cake flour
1 teaspoon baking soda
1 teaspoon cinnamon
1 teaspoon pumpkin-pie spice (or ¼ teaspoon each nutmeg, cloves, ginger, allspice)
¾ cup diet margarine
1 egg
¾ cup unsweetened applesauce
1 tablespoon vanilla extract
7 tablespoons golden raisins

Stir cake flour, baking soda, and spices together; set aside. Combine diet margarine, egg, applesauce, and vanilla; beat until blended. Beat in flour mixture. Stir in raisins. Pour batter into 16 nonstick muffin or cupcake cups and bake in a preheated 400-degree oven 20 minutes or more, until golden. *Makes 16 cupcakes, 105 calories each.*

## LOW-CALORIE PEACHES 'N' CREAM CAKE

6 large round "milk lunch" crackers (Royal Lunch)
2 cups drained juice-packed peach slices (reserve juice)
½ cup low-fat cottage cheese
2 eggs
½ cup peach juice (from can)
4 tablespoons free-pouring brown sugar
12 teaspoons sugar or equivalent sugar substitute (optional)
   Pinch of salt or butter-flavored salt
1 teaspoon vanilla extract
   Cinnamon

Arrange the crackers in a single layer in the bottom of an 8-inch round nonstick cake pan (the crackers need not be touching). Drain the peaches and reserve the juice. (If using peach halves, cut in large chunks.) Layer the drained peaches on top of the milk crackers.

In a covered blender, beat smooth the cottage cheese, eggs, peach juice, brown sugar, sugar or sugar substitute, salt, and vanilla. Pour over the peaches. Sprinkle with cinnamon. Bake in a 325-degree oven for 1 hour or longer, until set (insert the tip of a knife in the center to check; if it comes out clean, the cake is set). Serve warm or chilled. *Eight servings, 140 calories each with extra sugar; 115 calories each without.*

## SLIM PEACH KUCHEN

1 tube bake-and-serve biscuits (10 biscuits)
2 cups drained juice-packed peach slices
12 teaspoons sugar or equivalent sugar substitute (optional)
   Few drops almond flavoring
½ teaspoon apple-pie spice
1 egg
1 cup vanilla low-fat yogurt

Remove biscuits from tube and lay them flat in a nonstick round or square 8-inch baking pan. Press the dough flat and press biscuits together. Turn up the edges to form a crust. Bake in a preheated 350-degree oven for 5 to 7 minutes. Drain the peach slices and combine with sugar or substitute, almond flavoring, and spice.

Spoon into the biscuit crust. Stir egg and yogurt together and pour over peaches. Return to the oven and bake at 350 degrees for 20 to 30 minutes, until set. Serve warm or chilled. *Eight servings, 185 calories each with sugar; 160 calories each without.*

## STRAWBERRY RUSSE FRIDGE CAKE

No time to bake? Can't afford the calories anyway? This quick and easy "cake" is made in the refrigerator. It begins with half a spongecake . . . str-r-r-etched to serve ten!

1 cup thinly sliced fresh strawberries
¼ cup orange juice or orange liqueur
1 envelope plain gelatin
1 cup boiling water
2½ cups ice-cold skim milk
   Pinch of salt
   Pinch of grated orange rind (optional)
   4-serving package instant vanilla pudding mix
½ of a round spongecake layer (see instructions below)

Slice berries and set aside. Put orange juice in blender container and sprinkle on gelatin. Wait 1 minute, until gelatin is soft, then add boiling water. Cover and blend on high speed until all gelatin granules are dissolved. While blender runs, add the milk slowly through small opening. With blender running, add the salt, orange rind, if desired, then the pudding mix; process until well blended. Chill until slightly thickened.

Take 1 layer from a 2-layer package of spongecake. With a long sharp bread knife, carefully split the layer in half to make two layers out of one. Put the thin cake layer in the bottom of a round 8- or 9-inch cake pan. (Carefully rewrap the unused cake and freeze for future use. This recipe uses only half of a single layer.) Spread the sliced berries on top of the cake. Spoon the pudding mixture over the berries and cake, completely covering the contents of the cake pan. (Garnish with additional whole berries, if desired.) Chill several hours, until set. *Ten servings, 105 calories each; orange liqueur adds 15 calories per serving.*

**Yogurt Strawberry Cake.** Instead of the 2½ cups milk, use 1 cup plain low-fat yogurt, and 1½ cups skim milk. *Adds 5 calories per serving.*

## DEVIL'S FRIDGE CAKE

1 envelope plain gelatin
½ cup cold water
1 teaspoon instant coffee
    4-serving package chocolate-fudge instant pudding mix
    Pinch of salt
3 cups cold skim milk
4 thin slices chocolate pound cake

Combine gelatin, cold water, and instant coffee in small saucepan. Wait 1 minute, until gelatin is softened, then heat gently over very low heat until gelatin melts. Remove from heat and set aside.

Beat instant pudding mix, salt, and cold milk until well blended. Stir in gelatin mixture and mix well.

Cut cake into cubes. Put half the cake cubes in a single layer in the bottom of a loaf pan. Pour on half the pudding mixture. Add a layer of the remaining cake cubes. Pour on remaining pudding. Chill several hours, until set. To serve, cut in thin slices and serve from pan. *Ten servings, 150 calories each.*

**Chocolate Sour-Cream Icebox Cake.** Follow preceding recipe. Use 1 cup low-fat vanilla yogurt, 1 cup skim milk, and 1 cup cold water in place of the 3 cups skim milk. *45 calories less per serving.*

## SPICED APRICOT CUPCAKES OR MUFFINS

When all the seasonal fruits have fled (perhaps they go to Australia for the winter), that's the time to think dried apricots, one of our favorite fruits.

Their sunny color, cheerful disposition, and sweet-tart taste add adventure to lots of low-cal dishes. They're no slouch nutritionally, either. When you think apricots, think "A" for the vitamin of the same name. It's nonsense to call dried apricots fattening, since a dried apricot half has the same calories as a wet one: 10.

2 cups sifted all-purpose flour
3 teaspoons baking powder
1 teaspoon salt
¾ teaspoon apple-pie spice
5 tablespoons sugar or fructose
½ cup granulated sugar substitute
2 eggs
⅔ cup skim milk
2 tablespoons vegetable oil
1 cup crushed cornflakes or high-protein cereal flakes
½ cup finely chopped dried apricots

Stir flour, baking powder, salt, spice, and sweeteners together. Beat eggs, milk, and oil together, then stir into dry ingredients. Stir in cereal flakes and chopped apricots.

Spray nonstick muffin tins with cooking spray. Fill two-thirds full. Bake in a preheated 400-degree oven for 12 to 15 minutes, until golden. Serve warm (may be lightly "buttered" with diet margarine). *Twelve muffins, 180 calories each.*

## SLIM CINNAMON STREUSEL

BATTER
1½ cups biscuit mix
4 tablespoons diet margarine
1 teaspoon vanilla extract
1 whole egg
5 tablespoons cold water

TOPPING
3 tablespoons biscuit mix
2 tablespoons brown sugar
2 teaspoons ground cinnamon
1 tablespoon cold butter or regular margarine
Granulated sugar substitute to equal 2 tablespoons sugar (optional)

Combine batter ingredients in an electric mixer bowl. Beat on low speed until blended. Scrape bowl, then beat on high speed 3 minutes. Spread the batter evenly in a 9-inch square nonstick cake pan that has been sprayed with cooking spray.

Combine topping ingredients (except sugar substitute), and fork-blend until crumbly. Sprinkle crumb mixture on top of cake.

Bake in a preheated 400-degree oven until cake is done and topping is browned, about 18 to 20 minutes. Remove from the oven and allow to cool. Sprinkle with granulated sugar substitute, if desired. Cut into squares to serve. *Nine servings, 145 calories each.*

## EXTRA-EASY APPLE STREUSEL

This recipe is a cross between an apple crumb pie that makes its own bottom crust, and a streusel-topped apple cake that's more apples than cake. The same crumb mixture makes the bottom cake layer and the streusel topping. It is quickly baked, in only 20 minutes, and further saves calories by using diet margarine—only half the calories of butter, shortening, or regular margarine.

1 cup biscuit mix
3 tablespoons plus 1 teaspoon diet margarine, divided
    20-ounce can unsweetened pie-sliced apples, undrained
6 tablespoons granulated sugar substitute, divided (see note)
    Pinch of grated lemon or orange peel (optional)
¼ teaspoon cinnamon
2 tablespoons confectioners' sugar (optional)

(NOTE: Use the type of sugar substitute that can be used spoon-for-spoon in place of sugar—examples: Sprinkle Sweet or Sugar Twin—*not* concentrated artificial sweeteners such as those found in single-serving packets.

Spray a 9-inch glass pie pan with cooking spray. Combine biscuit mix with the 3 tablespoons diet margarine in blender or food processor, using the steel blade. Process until blended to fine crumbs (mixture will not form a batter; it will have the consistency of a heavy flour). Sprinkle half the flour mixture on the bottom of the pie pan. Spoon half the apples on top of the flour mixture. Sprinkle on 4 tablespoons of the sugar substitute. Spoon on the remaining apples, including any juice in the can. Sprinkle on the grated peel, if desired.

Add the cinnamon and the remaining 1 teaspoon diet margarine to the remaining flour mixture and process into crumbs. Sprinkle the crumbs evenly over the apples. Place on the bottom rack of a preheated 400-degree oven and bake 20 minutes, just until crumbs are lightly browned (don't overbake or sugar substitute will lose its sweetness). Remove from oven and allow to cool completely.

Stir remaining 2 tablespoons of granulated sugar substitute with confectioners' sugar, if desired, until blended; sprinkle over the top of the crumbs. Or omit confectioners' sugar and simply sprinkle the top of the cooled pie with sugar-free sweetener. *Eight servings, 120 calories each; 10 additional calories per serving with confectioners' sugar.*

**With Fructose:** If you prefer, granulated fructose (also known as fruit sugar) may be used instead of sugar-free sweetener. Substitute 1 teaspoon lemon juice for the lemon peel. *150 calories per serving.*

**With Other Canned Fruits:** Three cups canned unsweetened sliced peaches, diced pears, pineapple tidbits, fruit cocktail, or other juice-packed fruits may be substituted for the apples. If other fruits are used, drain them and reserve ½ cup of the juice to pour over the fruit before adding the final topping of crumbs.

# PASSOVER NO-BAKE FRUIT CAKE

No leavening—no fat, sugar, salt, eggs, or additives, either—a matzoh is simply flour and water, bread in its purest form. *One ounce is only 109 calories.*

**1 envelope unflavored gelatin**
**1 cup cold water**
**2 tablespoons honey, sugar, or fructose**
**3 apples, peeled, cored, sliced**
**1 tablespoon sweet red wine (optional)**
   **16-ounce can apricot halves in light syrup or juice**
**6 fresh strawberries (optional)**
**3 matzohs**
   **Pinch of salt**
   **Mint leaves (optional)**

Sprinkle gelatin over water in saucepan; wait 2 minutes until softened. Add honey or sugar and apple slices. Heat, stirring occasionally, until gelatin is completely dissolved and apples are tender. Stir in wine, if desired. Chill until partially set.

Meantime, drain apricots; reserve liquid. Blot with a paper towel to remove moisture. Cut a circle of wax paper to fit the bottom of a nonstick casserole or baking dish. Spray the dish with cooking spray; fit in wax paper. Place apricots (and strawberries, if desired) on the wax paper, upside down, in a decorative pattern. Spoon partially set apple mixture evenly over the apricots.

Break matzohs into small pieces. Mix with reserved apricot liquid and salt. Place over apple layer. Cover with wax paper and chill several hours or overnight, until firmly set.

To remove from pan: Run a knife around the edge of pan. Invert onto cake plate. Peel off wax paper carefully. Garnish with mint leaves, if desired. *Eight servings, 115 calories each.*

**Sugar-Free Version:** Use unsweetened apricots packed in juice or water. Omit honey or sugar and sweet wine. If desired, sweeten gelatin mixture with sugar substitute equal to 2 tablespoons sugar, after the gelatin is melted and removed from heat. Sweeten the apricot juice with sugar substitute equal to 2 teaspoons sugar. *100 calories per serving.*

# CHRISTMAS SLIMMER STOLLEN

**2 cans (8 ounces each) refrigerator crescent rolls**
   **8-ounce package low-calorie ("light") cream cheese or Neufchâtel cheese**

1 **tablespoon granulated brown sugar**
1 **tablespoon plain low-fat yogurt or skim milk**
  **Generous pinch of cinnamon**
2 **tablespoons Amaretto liqueur or ½ teaspoon almond flavoring or vanilla extract**
3 **tablespoons raisins**
1 **large unpeeled apple, cored, diced**
  **Almond Glaze (optional; recipe below)**

On a nonstick cookie sheet which has been sprayed with cooking spray, unroll the crescent-roll dough into two side-by-side rectangles, slightly over-lapping the edges to form one big square of pastry. Press the sides and perfora-tions together to seal.

Combine cream cheese, brown sugar, yogurt, cinnamon, and Amaretto (or flavoring); beat until fluffy.

Fold in raisins and apple. Spread the filling down the center of the pastry square. Fold edges of dough over filling, overlapping to cover filling. Pinch edges to seal.

Bake in preheated 375-degree oven 25 to 30 minutes, until golden. Cool before cutting. Serve plain or glazed. *Sixteen servings, 140 calories each without glaze (glaze adds about 15 calories per serving).*

ALMOND GLAZE
4 **tablespoons confectioners' sugar**
⅛ **teaspoon almond flavoring**
2 **or 3 teaspoons warm water or skim milk**
2 **tablespoons sliced almonds**

Combine sugar, flavoring, and liquid. Drizzle lightly over top of cooled stollen and sprinkle with almond slices.

# LOW-CALORIE ÉCLAIRS

Éclairs are admittedly trouble to make, but we think you will find this calorie-saving treat worth the effort.

4 **tablespoons diet margarine**
5 **tablespoons water**
8 **tablespoons flour**
¼ **teaspoon salt**
2 **eggs**

Combine diet margarine and water in a saucepan. Heat until margarine melts and water boils. Over very low heat, add the flour and salt. Beat until mixture leaves the side of the saucepan. Remove from the heat and beat in the eggs, one at a time.

On a nonstick cookie sheet, shape 9 éclairs about 3 inches long. Do this with a spoon, or put the éclair mixture into a pastry bag with a large plain tip and force out the filling in 3-inch lengths. Place the éclairs 3 inches apart.

Bake in a preheated 375-degree oven for 45 minutes. Remove from the oven and cool on a wire before splitting and filling. *Nine éclairs, 65 calories each.*

## LOW-CAL CHOCOLATE CREAM FILLING

Éclairs may be filled with low-fat ice milk and served immediately. Or fill with prepared diet pudding made according to package directions or with crushed fruit. Or try this chocolate filling.

**2 cups skim milk, divided**
**2 tablespoons cornstarch**
**¼ teaspoon butter-flavored salt**
**3 tablespoons unsweetened cocoa**
**4 tablespoons sugar or equivalent sugar substitute**
**1 egg, beaten**
**1 teaspoon vanilla extract**

Scald 1½ cups milk in a nonstick saucepan. Combine cornstarch, salt, cocoa, and sugar (not sugar substitute) with remaining milk. Stir into hot milk over low heat until mixture thickens.

Slowly stir some of the hot mixture into the beaten egg. Then gradually stir the egg mixture into the saucepan over low heat, stirring constantly until the mixture is thick and hot. Do not boil.

Remove from heat and stir in vanilla and sugar substitute if used. Chill until thick. Use to fill éclairs. *Each éclair with Low-Cal Chocolate Cream Filling, 125 calories (105 calories each with sugar substitute).*

### Cookies

A friend of mine—an ex-chubby—has discovered the ultimate no-calorie Christmas cookie: ceramics! A lady with great artistic skill and creativity, making, baking, and taking beautifully designed cookies on holiday visits used to be one of her greatest joys. Then she discovered the even greater joy of slimming down! She wasn't about to risk her new-found slimness by dabbling in gingerbread Santas and sugar icings, but she did miss her pre-holiday hobby. Until she discovered clay! Now she uses all her cookie-decorating skills and equipment to turn out the most enchanting-though-inedible colorfully glazed Christmas tree decorations in the shape of realistic-looking clay "cookies." If you have the time and talent to make pretty cookies, but disinclination to expose yourself to unneeded calories, that's a weight-wise way to channel your creativity.

On the other hand, most of us want something deliciously edible but less calorie-catastrophic than conventional sweets to fill our cookie jars around the holidays. And, because we lack the time or artistic talent (or patience!) to make fancy cookies, the type of recipe we look for is quick and easy.

## CHINESE FORTUNE COOKIES

18 homemade fortunes
1 egg white
4 tablespoons sugar
  Pinch of salt
2 tablespoons margarine, melted
¼ teaspoon vanilla
⅓ cup flour
1 teaspoon instant tea powder
2 teaspoons water

Make up funny fortunes or homemade Confucius sayings ("Confucius say too much junk food make Chinese sailor fat"). Type double space on white paper; cut into strips.

Mix the egg white, sugar, and salt in a bowl. Stir in all the other ingredients and blend thoroughly.

Spray a cookie sheet for nonstick baking. Spread the batter by the teaspoonful to make very thin 3-inch circles, leaving at least 2 inches between. (Do not bake more than 2 or 3 cookies at time.)

Bake 5 minutes in a preheated 350-degree oven, or until cookies are browned at the edges. Working quickly, while hot, remove cookies from the tin; insert a fortune message. Fold in half, keeping the side which was on top while baking as the outside, without pressing the fold. Then bend slightly, as if to fold in quarters. Allow to cool. (Propping hot cookies in muffin tins helps them to hold their shape.) *Eighteen cookies, 25 calories each.*

# RAISIN BARS

1 cup raisins
¾ cup unsweetened apple juice
2 tablespoons shortening
1 cup all-purpose flour
½ teaspoon salt
½ teaspoon baking soda
½ teaspoon baking powder
1 teaspoon cinnamon
¼ teaspoon nutmeg
¼ teaspoon ground cloves
¼ cup chopped nuts (optional)

In a small saucepan, bring raisins, apple juice, and shortening to a boil. Remove from heat and cool.

Mix remaining ingredients, except nuts. Stir into raisin mixture. Then mix in nuts, if desired.

Spray an 8-inch square nonstick baking pan with cooking spray. Spread dough evenly in pan. Bake in a preheated 350-degree oven 35 to 40 minutes. Remove from oven; cool. When cooled, cut into 2-inch squares. They may be stored in a tightly covered container. *Sixteen bars, 75 calories each (85 calories each with nuts).*

# RAISIN–CHOCOLATE CHIP COOKIES

Raisins add flavor and appetite-appeasing fiber to foods, along with sweetness, yet they have only half the calories of sugar: 26 calories a tablespoon instead of 46. When you add raisins to cookies you can cut down considerably on sugar.

1 cup plus 2 tablespoons all-purpose flour
¼ teaspoon salt
2 teaspoons baking powder
1 egg
  8-ounce container diet margarine
⅔ cup free-pouring brown sugar
2 teaspoons vanilla extract
½ cup raisins
½ cup miniature chocolate chips

Stir flour, salt, and baking powder together, and set aside. Combine egg, diet margarine, sugar, and vanilla in an electric mixer bowl; beat until fluffy. Add the flour mixture and beat well. Stir in the raisins and chocolate chips. Drop by teaspoonfuls on nonstick cookie sheets which have been sprayed with cooking spray. Bake in a preheated 400-degree oven 10 to 15 minutes, until lightly browned. Cool before removing. *Fifty small soft cookies, approximately 50 calories each.*

## RAISIN-BRAN DROP COOKIES

1 cup plus 2 tablespoons all-purpose flour
¼ teaspoon salt
½ teaspoon baking soda
1 teaspoon cinnamon or apple-pie spice
1 egg
1 cup diet margarine
⅔ cup free-pouring brown sugar
2 teaspoons vanilla extract
½ cup plain bran cereal
½ cup raisins

Stir flour, salt, baking soda, and cinnamon together; set aside. In an electric mixer bowl, beat the egg, diet margarine, brown sugar, and vanilla until fluffy. Add flour mixture and beat well. Stir in bran and raisins. Drop by teaspoonfuls on nonstick cookie tins sprayed with cooking spray. Bake 10 to 15 minutes in a preheated 375-degree oven, until lightly browned. *Fifty small soft cookies, 40 calories each.*

## CHOCOLATE MERINGUES

2 ounces unsweetened chocolate
1 tablespoon hot coffee
½ cup sifted cake flour
7 tablespoons white sugar, divided
4 egg whites at room temperature
¼ teaspoon salt
   Pinch of cream of tartar

Combine chocolate and coffee and allow to melt very slowly on a warming tray, or over very low heat. Meanwhile, sift flour with 3 tablespoons sugar; set aside.

In a glass or metal (not plastic) mixer bowl, combine egg whites, salt, and cream of tartar. Beat with an electric mixer until stiff. Gradually beat in remaining sugar, a tablespoon at a time. Beat in the flour mixture a little at a time. Fold in the melted chocolate.

Spray a nonstick cookie tin with cooking spray for no-stick baking. Drop the meringue mixture by the teaspoonful, 1 inch apart.

Bake in a preheated, 275-degree (slow) oven for 45 minutes, or until the cookies are dry. Cool before removing. *Two dozen meringues, 35 calories each.*

# CINNAMON-ALMOND MINI-MACAROONS

**1 egg white**
**Pinch of salt**
**5 tablespoons sugar**
**⅓ cup matzoh meal**
**⅓ cup ground almonds**
**1 teaspoon cinnamon**
**1 teaspoon confectioners' sugar (optional)**

Beat egg white and salt until stiff. Gradually, but thoroughly, beat in sugar. Fold in meal, almonds, and cinnamon. Drop by teaspoonfuls on nonstick cookie tin, sprayed for nonfat baking.

Bake in a preheated 275-degree oven for 30 minutes. Turn off heat; let cookies cool in oven 1 hour. When completely cooled, sprinkle with confectioners' sugar, if desired. May be kept in tightly sealed tins. *Makes about forty, under 20 calories each.*

NOTE: Best to bake meringue recipes on dry days.

**Protein Puffs:** For a delicious (but non-Passover) variation, substitute ⅓ cupful Special K or other high-protein cereal for the matzoh meal. *Makes forty, 15 calories each.*

# 3
# BOTTOMLESS PIES, TOPLESS TARTS, AND OTHER TRIMMERS

## Pies

Ten Ways You Can Cut the Calories

1. CUT PASTRY CALORIES IN HALF—SAVE 900 CALORIES: Make your pie topless . . . or bottomless! Spoon the filling into a single crust, then cover the filling with a smaller-size pie pan or a circle of foil cut 1 inch smaller, exposing the border of the crust. That way, the crust browns but the filling is protected. For a bottomless pie (a cobbler), spoon the filling into an unperforated piepan and cover with a single crust.

2. CUT SUGAR CALORIES IN HALF—SAVE 290 CALORIES: Use 6 tablespoons sugar instead of ¾ cup. Use sweet fruits—for example McIntosh instead of greening apples—and you'll be delighted to find that a less sugary pie is still sweet enough for adult tastes.

3. OR SWEETEN WITH FRUCTOSE OR HONEY . . . AND USE LESS: Both are sweeter than the same calories' worth of sugar. Replace ¾ cup sugar with 5 to 6 tablespoons of fructose or honey, and save from 195 calories with 6 tablespoons honey to 350 calories with 5 tablespoons fructose.

4. SWEETEN WITH FRUIT (OR JUICE)—SAVE 160 CALORIES: Replace part of the fruit with 1 cup raisins (golden raisins blend in with the fruit and are less noticeable than dark raisins). Or spoon 3 to 4 tablespoons undiluted frozen apple-juice concentrate into the fruit mixture. Mix and match fruits and juices for variety.

5. SWEETEN WITH SUGAR SUBSTITUTE—SAVE ABOUT 520 CALORIES: Use

the granulated type, and protect it from oven heat by sprinkling the substitute between two layers of fruit. Use quick-cooking fruit (eating apples rather than firm cooking types) and bake the pie at a higher heat for a shorter time: 425 degrees for 25 or 30 minutes. For best results, use a glass pan on the bottom rack of your oven.

6. THICKEN WITH ARROWROOT OR CORNSTARCH—SAVE 65 CALORIES: Use 1½ tablespoons arrowroot or cornstarch instead of ¼ cup flour. Arrowroot is available on the supermarket spice shelf, or in health-food stores, and has nearly 2 to 2½ times the thickening power of flour or cornstarch.

7. INCREASE SPICES—ADDS PRACTICALLY NO CALORIES: Cinnamon and nutmeg add to the perception of sweetness, cost next to nothing.

8. ADD VANILLA—ADDS VERY FEW CALORIES: The fragrance heightens the illusion of sweetness. (The alcohol and its calories evaporate.)

9. OMIT BUTTER OR MARGARINE—SAVE 200 CALORIES: Add a dash of salt instead.

10. MAKE A BIGGER PIE, MORE SERVINGS, SAVE CALORIES IN EACH SLICE: Use more fruit but the same amount of pastry. Here's how: Roll the pastry as thin as possible, and fit it into a 10-inch pie pan. Add 2 extra apples or other fruit (raisins, for example) and your pie serves 8 instead of 6, saving about 20 percent of the calories per serving.

## DOUBLE-CRUST PIE PASTRY
## WITH DIET MARGARINE

**1 cup all-purpose flour**
**½ teaspoon salt**
**½ teaspoon baking powder**
**½ cup diet margarine (at room temperature)**

Stir flour, salt, and baking powder together. Cut in margarine with a fork or pastry blender, until pastry leaves the sides of the bowl. Divide into two balls, one large, one smaller (two-thirds and one-third). Flatten, wrap, and chill.

Roll out the larger ball as thin as possible on a floured board, using a well-floured rolling pin. Line a nonstick 8-inch pie pan with the pastry. Add pie filling. Roll out the smaller ball and cut into ½-inch strips. Arrange the strips on top of the pie in a criss-cross diagonal pattern, placing the strips about an inch apart. (Strips which are too short may be stretched gently or rolled out lengthwise until long enough to span the pie.) Discard trimmings. *Calories: 855 (pastry only).*

## DOUBLE-CRUST PIE PASTRY WITH CORN OIL

**1 cup all-purpose flour**
**½ teaspoon salt (or butter-flavored salt)**
**½ teaspoon baking powder**
**¼ cup corn oil or other polyunsaturated oil**
**2 to 3 tablespoons ice water**

Stir flour, salt, and baking powder together (or use 1 cup self-rising flour, omitting salt and baking powder). With a fork or pastry knife, mix in the oil. Then cut in the ice water, a tablespoon at a time, only until the mixture leaves the sides of the bowl.

Shape into one larger and one smaller ball, wrap, and chill. Roll out as thin as possible on a well-floured board using a floured rolling pin. *About 935 calories.*

## SINGLE-CRUST LOW-CALORIE PIE PASTRY WITH OIL AND DIET MARGARINE

Stir ½ cup all-purpose flour with ¼ teaspoon salt. Add 2 tablespoons room-temperature diet margarine and 1 tablespoon vegetable oil. Mix lightly until pastry forms a ball. Flatten into a round on wax paper; cover with another sheet of wax paper and chill. Roll out on a lightly floured board with a floured rolling pin. Fit pastry into an 8-inch nonstick pie pan sprayed until slick with cooking spray. *About 470 calories.*

**Topless Pie:** Make pastry for a single crust. Omit top crust. Cover pie with a round of aluminum foil or an inverted pie pan as it bakes. *About 470 calories.*

**Bottomless Pie:** Make pastry for single crust. Put the filling mixture in a solid-bottom pie pan—no holes!—and cover with pastry. *About 470 calories.*

## ANGEL PIE SHELL

This heavenly pie crust is made with meringue—mostly egg whites and no-calorie air. When baked in the oven, the meringue turns into a crisp, sweet crust.

Use Double Berry Bavarian (see page 62) as a filling.

**2 egg whites**
**Pinch of salt**
**Pinch of cream of tartar**
**7 tablespoons sugar (not substitute)**

Have egg whites at room temperature. Beat in a nonplastic bowl until frothy. Add salt and cream of tartar and beat until stiff. Gradually beat in the sugar, a tablespoon at a time, until stiff peaks form.

*(continued)*

Spread the meringue mixture on the sides and bottom of a 9-inch nonstick pie pan. Bake in a 275-degree oven for 1 hour. Turn off the heat and leave in the oven an additional 30 minutes. Remove and cool.

Meanwhile, prepare Bavarian filling. Spoon filling into cooled pie shell. Chill 3 hours. *Ten servings, 85 calories each when filling is prepared with sugar; 70 calories each with sugar substitute.*

## SINGLE PIE CRUST

½ cup all-purpose flour
  Pinch of salt
2 tablespoons corn or safflower oil
4 or more teaspoons ice water

Fork-blend together, adding the ice water a little at a time, just until the pastry leaves the sides of the bowl. Form into a flat ball and chill thoroughly before rolling out thin on a floured board with a well-floured rolling pin. Spray an 8- or 9-inch nonstick pie pan with cooking spray for no-fat cooking, then line it with pastry. Crimp the edges. *470 calories total.*

## APPLE PIE, NATURALLY SWEETENED
## WITH RAISINS

  Pie pastry for 8- or 9-inch single crust, homemade or defrosted
6 cups peeled, thinly sliced apples
1 cup golden raisins
1 teaspoon cinnamon
½ teaspoon nutmeg
  Pinch of salt
2 teaspoons vanilla extract
1½ tablespoons cornstarch

Use a 10-inch pie pan with nonstick finish, sprayed with cooking spray. Roll pastry as thin as possible and fit into pie pan. (Or transfer defrosted commercial single crust into larger pan and press to fit with fingertips.) Combine remaining ingredients, mix well, and spoon into shell.

Cover filling with an inverted smaller pie pan, or use a circle of foil cut 1 inch smaller, exposing crust but covering apples. Bake in a preheated 425-degree oven 35 to 45 minutes, until crust is golden. Remove cover or foil and cool pie before cutting. *Eight servings, about 195 calories each.*

**Pear Pie:** Substitute ripe, thinly sliced peeled pears for the apples. Reduce raisins to ½ cup. *Eight servings, 195 calories each.*

**Apple Pie Sweetened with Sugar Substitute:** Use 6 cups sliced McIntosh apples; omit raisins. Use a glass pie pan. Put half the filling into the crust; sprinkle with 6 to 8 tablespoons granulated sugar substitute. Add remaining apple filling. Place glass pan on the bottom rack of a preheated 425-degree oven. Cover filling with inverted pie pan. Bake only 25 to 30 minutes, until bottom crust is golden. *Eight servings, 145 calories each.*

**Pear Pie Sweetened with Sugar Substitute:** Use 6 cups sliced peeled ripe pears and follow directions in preceding paragraph. *Eight servings, 175 calories each.*

## EASY UPPER-CRUST SUGARLESS APPLE PIE PLUS

No sugar . . . no sugar substitutes! Sweetened with raisins and concentrated apple juice. Save time with a frozen pieshell; save calories by stretching it to fit a larger pie!

**Small (8-inch) frozen single pie shell**
2¼ **pounds baking apples**
⅔ **cup white raisins**
 **6-ounce can defrosted undiluted unsweetened apple-juice concentrate**
2 **tablespoons cornstarch**
1½ **teaspoons apple-pie spice, or 1 teaspoon cinnamon and pinch each of nutmeg, ginger, allspice**
1 **teaspoon grated lemon rind**
 **Shake of salt or butter-flavored salt (optional)**

Set pie shell aside until completely thawed.

Peel and core apples; slice thin. Combine with remaining ingredients and mix well. Spoon into a larger, 9- or 10-inch, nonstick pie pan. Remove the pastry from its foil pan by gently folding it in quarters. Center the mid-point over the apple filling and unfold, so the pie is covered with a top crust. Press the edges of the pastry to the pie-pan rim with the tines of a fork. Make a few gashes in the crust to vent steam.

Place in preheated 450-degree oven and bake for 10 minutes. Reduce heat to 325 degrees and bake an additional 30 to 40 minutes, until crust is golden and apples are tender. Allow to cool completely before cutting in wedges to serve. *Ten servings, approximately 195 calories each.*

# RUBY APPLE COBBLER

Single 8-inch pie crust
20-ounce can unsweetened, pie-sliced apples (not pie filling)
4 purple plums, unpeeled, pitted, thinly sliced
1 cup crushed pineapple, juice-packed, undrained
6 tablespoons golden raisins
¼ cup rum (the alcohol calories evaporate)
3 tablespoons cornstarch
1½ teaspoons cinnamon or apple-pie spice
Pinch of salt
4 tablespoons fructose or equivalent sugar substitute

Defrost pie crust, if frozen, and set aside. Combine remaining ingredients, except fructose or substitute, and mix until blended. Spoon half of the apple-fruit mixture into a 9-inch nonstick cake or pie pan. Sprinkle evenly with fructose or substitute. Spoon on the remaining fruit mixture.

Arrange the pie crust on top of the fruit mixture (stretching gently, if necessary, to fit). Make 6 or 7 slits with the tip of a pointed knife. Bake in a preheated 425-degree oven until crust is golden, about 30 minutes. Serve warm or cold. *Nine servings, 180 calories each (20 calories less per serving with sugar substitute).*

# BRANDIED APPLE-APRICOT PIE

This topless treat is extra easy: use canned apricots and defrosted pie crust.

Frozen single 8-inch pie crust
16-ounce can unsweetened apricot halves, drained
2 apples, peeled, sliced
1 orange, peeled, seeded, cut in chunks
¼ cup golden raisins
¼ cup apricot brandy or liqueur
4 tablespoons free-pouring brown sugar
2 tablespoons arrowroot or cornstarch
¼ teaspoon cinnamon
¼ teaspoon nutmeg
⅛ teaspoon ground cloves
Sugar substitute to equal ¼ cup sugar (optional)

Defrost pastry and line an 8- or 9-inch shallow nonstick pie pan, gently stretching to fit, if necessary. Trim edges and discard excess pastry.

Combine remaining ingredients, except sugar substitute; mix well. Spoon half of the fruit mixture into pie crust. Sprinkle evenly with sugar substitute, if desired. Add remaining fruit filling. Cut a sheet of foil slightly smaller than the pie pan and use to cover the top of the pie, protecting fruit filling while exposing the crust border. (Or cover the pie pan with a slightly smaller pie pan.) Bake in a preheated 425-degree oven 25 to 30 minutes, until crust is browned. Remove from oven and cool. Serve warm or chilled. *Eight servings, 190 calories each.*

**With Yogurt, à la Mode:** Slice a half-size wedge of pie ($\frac{1}{16}$) and serve with a scoop of frozen vanilla yogurt. *145 calories per serving.*

# APPLE-PINEAPPLE-APRICOT LATTICE-TOP PIE

This is a "bottomless" pie, covered with lattice pastry.

  **8-inch single pie shell, thawed**
**4 eating apples, peeled and thinly sliced**
**¼ cup dried apricots, diced**
  **6-ounce can pineapple- or apple-juice concentrate, thawed**
**2 tablespoons cornstarch**
**1 teaspoon cinnamon**
**½ teaspoon nutmeg**
  **Granulated sugar substitute to equal 2 tablespoons sugar or equivalent fructose**

Flatten pie shell on a cutting board and slice it into ½-inch-wide strips. Combine remaining ingredients, except sugar substitute, and mix lightly. Spoon half the fruit mixture into a 9-inch nonstick deep-dish pie pan. Sprinkle evenly with sugar substitute. Add remaining fruit mixture.

Take the longest (center) strip of pie pastry and gently stretch it to fit across the middle of the cake pan or pie pan. Continue to stretch and arrange strips —¾ inch apart—until the pie is covered with a criss-cross lattice of pastry. Discard leftover pastry.

Bake the pie, uncovered, in a preheated 425-degree oven 25 minutes. Allow to cool before cutting. *Ten servings, 155 calories each; 10 calories more per serving with fructose.*

# OVEN-BAKED RUM-RAISIN-APPLE GRAHAM-CRACKER PIE

This dessert is really easy!

**1 ready-to-fill graham-cracker pie shell**
   **20-ounce can pie-sliced unsweetened apples (not pie filling)**
**1½ cups seedless raisins**
  **⅓ cup 80-proof rum**
  **6 tablespoons free-pouring brown sugar**
  **2 tablespoons cornstarch**
  **2 teaspoons vanilla extract**
  **2 teaspoons grated orange peel (or 1 teaspoon bottled peel)**
**1½ teaspoons pumpkin-pie spice (or ½ teaspoon each cinnamon, nutmeg, ginger)**
  **¼ teaspoon salt**

Unwrap piecrust. Drain apples and combine with remaining ingredients. Spoon into shell. Invert an aluminum pie pan over the filling to protect from drying out while baking, or cut a circle of aluminum foil and place over the filling. Bake in a preheated 425-degree oven for 35 to 40 minutes. Cool before cutting or serve chilled. *Eight servings, 230 calories each.*

**Sugar-Free Filling:** Omit brown sugar. Spoon half the filling into the pie shell. Sprinkle with sugar substitute (equal to 6 tablespoons). Add remaining fruit filling. Cover filling with foil. Reduce baking time to 25 to 30 minutes. *210 calories per serving.*

# QUICK AND EASY SPIKED FRUIT PIE

Another "bottomless" pie with a lattice top crust.

  **8-inch frozen pie shell**
  **20-ounce can unsweetened pie-sliced apples**
  **16-ounce can juice-packed pineapple tidbits**
  **6-ounce can undiluted defrosted unsweetened cider concentrate**
**3 tablespoons golden raisins**
**1½ teaspoons apple- or pumpkin-pie spice**
  **2 tablespoons orange liqueur or orange juice**
  **2 tablespoons cornstarch**

Set aside pie shell until thawed.

Combine remaining ingredients and mix well. Spoon into 9- or 10-inch nonstick pie pan; flatten the mixture with the back of a spoon. With a sharp knife, cut the pie pastry into ½-inch-wide strips. Put the middle (longest) strips over the middle of the pie filling. Continue to add the strips, spaced about ¾ inch apart, until the filling is covered in a criss-cross latticework of pastry. Press the edges to the pie pan with a fork. Trim off any overhanging pastry.

Bake pie in a preheated 425-degree oven 25 to 30 minutes, or until the pastry is golden. Cool completely before cutting. *Ten servings, 175 calories each.*

## DIETER'S MINCEMEAT WITHOUT PIE!

Commercial mincemeat can be as high as 345 calories for ½ cup, but our decalorized version is only 150.

    2 cups peeled cubed cooking apples
1½ cups raisins
    3 tablespoons orange juice
    1 teaspoon cider vinegar
    2 tablespoons brandy
    1 tablespoon cracker crumbs
    ½ teaspoon salt
    ½ teaspoon ground cloves
    ½ teaspoon cinnamon
    1 teaspoon grated orange rind
       Sugar substitute to equal ½ cup sugar (or to taste)

Combine ingredients, except sugar substitute, in a covered casserole. Bake at 350 degrees until tender, about 30 minutes. Remove from oven; stir in sugar substitute to taste. Serve warm or chilled. *Six servings, 150 calories each.*

**As Pie Filling:** Omit sugar substitute from the mixture. Spoon half the raw filling into a pie shell in a pie pan. Sprinkle with sugar substitute. Add remaining filling. Bake on the bottom rack of a 450-degree oven 25 to 30 minutes

## BAKED APPLE MINCE PIE

    2 cups cooking apples
1¼ cups raisins
    3 tablespoons orange liqueur
    1 tablespoon cracker crumbs or matzoh meal
    1 tablespoon arrowroot or cornstarch
       Pinch of salt
    ½ teaspoon ground cloves
    ½ teaspoon cinnamon
    1 tablespoon honey (optional)
       Pastry for single 8- or 9-inch pie pan

Peel, quarter, and core apples, then chop coarsely. (If you have a food processor, apples can be shredded, unpeeled, through coarse shredding disk.)

*(continued)*

Combine apples with remaining filling ingredients and spoon into pastry-lined 8- or 9-inch pie pan. Cover filling with a circle of foil cut to fit, or invert another pie pan over filling to keep filling moist. Bake in a preheated 350-degree oven 35 to 45 minutes. Cool. Serve slightly warm or chilled. *Eight servings, under 200 calories each (honey adds 5 calories per serving).*

## TOPLESS POLYNESIAN PIE

1 eating orange, peeled, seeded, and diced
   16-ounce can unsweetened crushed juice-packed pineapple, undrained
4 tablespoons golden raisins
2 tablespoons quick-cooking tapioca
   Pinch of salt
   Single 8-inch or 9-inch piecrust

Peel and dice the orange; pick out and discard any seeds with the tip of a sharp knife. Combine with the crushed pineapple, including juice. Stir in raisins, tapioca, and salt. Spoon into pie shell. Cover the filling with a smaller pie pan, or cut a round of aluminum foil and lay over the filling, so the crust will brown but the filling won't dry out. Bake in a preheated 425-degree oven for 35 to 45 minutes, until the crust is brown. Serve warm or chilled. *Eight servings, about 145 calories each.*

## BOTTOMLESS ORANGE SPICED FRUIT PIE

   8-inch pie shell, thawed
   20-ounce can pie-sliced apples
   16-ounce can juice-packed pineapple tidbits
6 ounces thawed orange-juice concentrate
3 tablespoons golden raisins
2 tablespoons cornstarch
1½ teaspoons allspice or pumpkin-pie spice
   Dash of salt
1 teaspoon grated orange peel (optional)
2 tablespoons honey or equivalent sugar substitute* (optional)

Thaw pie shell to room temperature and set aside. Combine remaining ingredients (except sugar substitute, if using) and mix well. Spoon into a large 9- or 10-inch deep-dish pie pan. If using sugar substitute, spoon half of the fruit filling mixture into the pie pan. Sprinkle evenly with sugar substitute; add the remaining fruit filling.

Gently remove pastry from its foil pie pan by inverting the pan on a large cutting board. Flatten it with your palms. Cut it into thin ½-inch strips. Arrange the strips over the fruit filling in a criss-cross lattice pattern.

Bake in a preheated 425-degree oven 35 minutes, until filling is bubbling and crust is golden. Cool before serving. *Ten servings, approximately 170 calories each. Honey adds 15 calories per serving.*

## HONEY PEACH DEEP-DISH PIE

Here's another "upper crust" pie

**Frozen 8-inch piecrust**
**5 cups thickly sliced peeled ripe peaches**
**2 teaspoons lemon juice**
**⅓ cup honey**
**2 tablespoons quick-cooking tapioca**
**¼ teaspoon cinnamon or nutmeg**

Defrost piecrust at room temperature. Use a rolling pin to roll out as thin as possible, so it will cover a 9-inch cake pan.

Combine remaining ingredients and mix well. Spoon into a shallow 9-inch nonstick cake pan. Fold crust in quarters for easy handling, then arrange over peaches. Trim off and discard excess pastry. Press border of pastry to the sides of the pan. Make several slits in the pastry to permit steam to escape. Bake in a preheated 425-degree oven about 35 to 40 minutes or more, until crust is golden. Serve warm or chilled. *Nine servings, 160 calories each.*

**With Fructose:** Substitute 4 tablespoons granulated fructose for honey. *140 calories per serving.*

**With Sugar Substitute:** Omit honey. Put half the fruit mixture in the pan. Sprinkle evenly with sugar substitute (equal to 5 tablespoons sugar). Add remaining fruit and pastry upper crust.

Reduce baking time to 25 to 30 minutes. *125 calories per serving.*

## HONEY NECTARINE PIE

**Pastry for double-crust pie**
**5 cups pitted, thinly sliced, unpeeled ripe fresh nectarines, or fresh peaches, peeled**
**⅓ cup honey or 5 tablespoons fructose**
**Pinch of butter-flavored salt**
**5 level teaspoons arrowroot or cornstarch**
**1 teaspoon vanilla extract**
**¼ teaspoon cinnamon or pinch of nutmeg (optional)**

Line an 8-inch pie pan with pastry. Stir nectarines with remaining ingredients until well-coated. Spoon into crust. Top with remaining pastry. Puncture top pastry several times with a fork. Bake in a preheated 450-degree oven 10 minutes. Reduce heat and bake an additional 30 minutes. Cool. Serve warm or chilled. *Eight servings, 230 calories each (30 calories less per serving with peaches; 15 calories less per serving with fructose).*

# HONEY BLUEBERRY TOPLESS TART

As far as I'm concerned, blueberries are the caviar of fruit. Unfortunately, each year they become more caviarlike in price. But one feature of blueberries remains constant: their low calorie count. A cup of fresh blueberries is only 90 calories. Few fruits are lower—or higher in fiber.

**Pastry for a single pie crust**
**3 cups frozen unsweetened blueberries, defrosted**
**3 tablespoons honey**
**2 teaspoons lemon juice**
**⅛ teaspoon salt**
**2 tablespoons cornstarch**
**¼ teaspoon cinnamon**
**Granulated sugar substitute to equal 3 tablespoons sugar**

Use a defrosted pastry crust (or prepare low-calorie version).

Transfer the pastry to a nonstick 9-inch round pie pan or straight-sided cake pan. Using your fingertips, spread the pastry up the sides of the pan, so the interior is thinly coated with pastry.

Mix blueberries with honey, lemon juice, salt, and cornstarch; spoon into the crust. Cover the cake pan with an inverted cake pan or pie pan, or cut an 8-inch circle of foil to cover the blueberries so they won't burn.

Bake in a preheated 375-degree oven on the lower shelf for 35 to 45 minutes. Remove from the oven and take off the cover. Stir cinnamon into sugar substitute and sprinkle over the blueberry filling. Cool before slicing. Serve warm or chilled. *Eight servings, 155 calories each.*

**Sugar-Free:** Omit honey. Increase sugar substitute to equal 5 to 6 tablespoons. *20 calories less per serving.*

# RAW BLUEBERRY DESSERT (OR PIE FILLING)

This technique not only saves calories but keeps the blueberries' natural uncooked fresh flavor.

1½ teaspoons plain gelatin (½ envelope)
½ cup water, divided
3 cups fresh blueberries, divided
½ cup regular or low-sugar grape jelly
   Granulated sugar substitute to taste (optional)
   Ready-to-fill graham-cracker crust (optional)
   Yogurt Crème Chantilly (optional; recipe given)
   Cinnamon (optional)

Combine gelatin and ¼ cup cold water and set aside to soften. Combine ½ cup blueberries with remaining water and jelly in a saucepan. Cook and stir over low heat until boiling. Remove from heat and stir in softened gelatin until dissolved. Refrigerate just until slightly syrupy, then stir in remaining raw berries. Sweeten to taste, if desired.

Spoon into ready-to-fill graham-cracker crust or into 6 stemmed dessert glasses, and chill until set. Top with cinnamon-spiced Yogurt Crème Chantilly, if desired. *Six servings (filling only), 115 calories each with regular jelly; 80 calories each with low-sugar jelly.*

**With Other Fruit:** Substitute sliced hulled fresh strawberries and strawberry jelly. *100 calories per serving with regular jelly; 65 per serving with low-sugar jelly.*

Or use thinly sliced peeled ripe peaches and peach or apricot jam. *100 calories per serving with regular jelly; 70 calories per serving with low-sugar jelly. Or mix fruits and jelly flavors.*

# DECALORIZED PUMPKIN PIE

What would Thanksgiving be without pumpkin pie? Less fattening, that's what! Commercial pumpkin pie can be 350 calories per portion or more, depending on the ingredients. Yet pumpkin itself is low in calories, only 80 a cupful. Nutritionally, pumpkin is no slouch. It's so nutrition-rich that one cupful of pumpkin provides nearly 16,000 units of vitamin A—twice an adult woman's daily requirement.

Pastry to line an 8- or 9-inch pie pan
1 cup cooked or canned pumpkin
2 eggs
1¼ cups fresh skim milk
4 tablespoons granulated fructose
4 tablespoons brown sugar or granulated sugar substitute
2 teaspoons cornstarch
¼ teaspoon salt
½ teaspoon ground cinnamon
Pinch each of allspice, nutmeg, ginger, and cloves

Roll pastry as thin as possible; line an 8- or 9-inch pie pan (or use a ready-to-fill pie shell, thawed). Beat remaining ingredients together until completely smooth. Pour into pie shell. Bake, uncovered, in a preheated 350-degree oven 1 hour, or until filling is set. Refrigerate. *Eight servings, 180 calories each.*

## QUICK-BAKE SUGAR-REDUCED
## PUMPKIN CUSTARD PIE

To keep the sugar substitute from breaking down and losing sweetness, this pie is baked in a glass pie pan on the bottom shelf of a very hot oven. The filling is made with fresh skim milk instead of evaporated milk. Cornstarch is added to help the filling thicken in high heat and prevent breakdown of the custard.

Frozen 8-inch single pie shell, thawed
2 eggs
1½ cups fresh nonfat milk
1¼ cups cooked or canned plain pumpkin (*not* pie filling)
5 tablespoons free-pouring brown sugar
4 tablespoons granulated sugar substitute or equivalent of 4 tablespoons
    sugar
2 tablespoons cornstarch
1 teaspoon pumpkin-pie spice, or ¼ teaspoon each allspice, nutmeg, ginger,
    cloves
½ teaspoon cinnamon
½ teaspoon salt

Preheat oven to 425 degrees. Spray a 9-inch glass pie pan with cooking spray for nonstick baking. Carefully fold the defrosted pie shell in quarters and transfer to the pan. Gently stretch the pastry with your fingertips up the sides of the pan.

Combine remaining ingredients in blender or mixing bowl; beat or blend smooth. Pour the mixture into the pie shell. Place the pan on the bottom shelf of the oven, closest to the heat source. Bake 20 to 22 minutes, only until filling is set and underside of the crust is lightly browned. Remove from the oven immediately and cool on a rack. Transfer to the refrigerator. Serve chilled. *Ten servings, 135 calories each.*

## PUMPKIN MERINGUE PIE

Pastry for 9-inch pie
3 eggs, separated
1½ cups cooked or canned unsweetened pumpkin
⅓ cup honey or no-cal sweetener to equal ½ cup sugar
13-ounce can evaporated skim milk
1½ teaspoons pumpkin-pie spice
Pinch of salt
4 tablespoons granulated white sugar

Prepare pastry and line a 9-inch nonstick pie pan. Preheat oven to 475 degrees.

Separate egg whites into a nonmetallic electric mixer bowl and set aside.

Put the yolks in blender container or another mixing bowl. Add pumpkin, honey or sweetener, milk, spice, and salt to the egg yolks. Blend or beat until smooth. Pour into pie shell. Bake in hot oven 10 minutes. Lower heat to 350 degrees and bake 50 to 60 minutes more, until set. Remove from oven and cool.

Beat egg whites until soft peaks form. Beat in the sugar, a tablespoon at a time, until stiff. Pile on top of cooled pie. Bake in a preheated 350-degree oven about 12 to 13 minutes, until meringue is delicately browned. Chill before serving. *Ten servings, 120 calories each. No-cal sweetener reduces each serving by 20 calories.*

## PUMPKIN CHIFFON FILLING

For a prebaked pie shell, or ready-to-fill graham-cracker shell.

1 envelope plain gelatin
5 tablespoons cold water or fruit juice
1-pound can plain pumpkin
Granulated sugar substitute to equal ½ cup sugar
2 teaspoons pumpkin-pie spice, or 1 teaspoon cinnamon and ¼ teaspoon each
     ginger, allspice, nutmeg, cloves
2 egg whites, room temperature
Pinch of salt
Pinch of cream of tartar (optional)
4 tablespoons white sugar

Combine gelatin and water or fruit juice in a saucepan. Wait 1 minute, then heat gently until gelatin is melted. Remove from heat and stir in pumpkin, sugar substitute, and spice. In a nonplastic mixing bowl, beat the egg whites, salt, and cream of tartar, if desired, until foamy. Beat in the sugar a little at a time, until stiff. Fold into the pumpkin mixture. Mound into the pie shell. Chill until set, about 3 hours. *Eight servings, approximately 55 calories each (filling only).*

# PUMPKIN CREAM-CHEESE PIE

**8- or 9-inch ready-to-fill graham-cracker pie shell**

FILLING
**8 ounces low-calorie ("light") cream cheese or Neufchâtel cheese**
**3 large eggs**
**1 cup plain cooked or canned pumpkin (*not* pumpkin-pie filling)**
**2 tablespoons skim milk**
**1 tablespoon vanilla extract (right, 1 *table*spoon!)**
**2 teaspoons pumpkin-pie spice, or 1 teaspoon cinnamon and ¼**
**teaspoon each ginger, allspice, nutmeg, cloves**
**Pinch of salt**
**Sugar substitute to equal ¼ cup sugar**
**4 tablespoons brown or white sugar**

Combine all filling ingredients in blender and beat smooth. Pour into prepared crust and bake in a preheated 275-degree oven for 1 hour, until set. Chill. *Eight servings, 210 calories each (Neufchâtel cheese adds 20 calories per serving).*

# DOUBLE BERRY BAVARIAN

This rich-tasting concoction seems sinfully fattening yet is only 65 calories a serving—less, if you make it without sugar. Use as a filling for the Angel Pie Shell (see page 49).

**1 package (2 envelopes) low-calorie strawberry gelatin mix**
**1⅓ cups boiling water**
**4 tablespoons sugar or equivalent substitute**
**Pinch of salt**
**1 cup evaporated skim milk**
**1 cup fresh strawberries, thinly sliced**

Dissolve both envelopes of gelatin mix in the boiling water. Stir in sugar (or substitute) and salt. Chill in refrigerator until syrupy.

Pour the evaporated milk into a metal mixing bowl. Chill it in the freezer until ice crystals form around the edges. (Chill your beater blades, too.) Beat the chilled milk on high speed until the consistency of whipped cream (this may take 8 to 10 minutes).

Gently fold the gelatin mixture and sliced berries into the whipped milk. Chill 3 hours or more, until set. Spoon filling into pie shell. Garnish with additional berries, if desired. *Eight servings, 65 calories with sugar; 45 calories with sugar substitute.*

## BURIED BERRIES BAVARIAN

This also makes a wonderful filling for the Angel Pie Shell (see page 49).

**1 envelope plain gelatin**
**1 egg**
**½ cup boiling water**
**2 cups ice cubes and water**
**1⅓ cups nonfat dry milk powder (envelope to make 1 quart)**
    **Pinch of salt**
**2 tablespoons honey, fructose, or equivalent sugar substitute**
**1 teaspoon vanilla extract**
**2 cups sliced fresh strawberries (or other berries)**
    **Pinch of cinnamon (optional)**

Stir gelatin and egg together in blender jar. Wait 1 minute, until gelatin softens, then cover the blender and turn it on. Add the boiling water slowly through the small opening in the lid. Blend on high speed, scraping often, until gelatin granules are dissolved. Fill a 2-cup measure with ice cubes, then add tap water to fill. Add ice and water to blender; cover and blend until ice cubes melt. Add dry milk powder, salt, sweetener, and vanilla, and blend smooth.

Divide sliced berries among 4 cups. Pour gelatin mixture on top. Or spoon into pie shell and sprinkle with cinnamon, if desired. Chill until set. *Four servings, 170 calories each with honey or fructose; 140 calories each with sugar substitute.*

# CONTINENTAL COFFEE PIE

COOKIE CRUST
½ cup vanilla-wafer crumbs
1 tablespoon butter or margarine

FILLING
1 tablespoon plain gelatin
¼ cup cold water
3 eggs, separated
1 cup hot espresso coffee
   Sugar substitute to equal 10 teaspoons sugar
¼ teaspoon cinnamon
½ teaspoon vanilla extract
   Pinch of salt
2 tablespoons sugar

To prepare cookie-crumb crust: Crush cookies in covered blender container on high speed until you have ½ cup. (Sugar-free dietetic cookies may be substituted.) Blend crumbs and soft butter; press onto the sides and bottom of an 8-inch pie pan. Chill well before filling.

To prepare filling: Sprinkle gelatin over cold water to soften. Beat egg yolks well in the top of a double boiler over hot water. Beat in hot coffee a little at a time. Cook over hot water, stirring frequently, until mixture is slightly thickened (don't overcook or it will separate). Then stir in softened gelatin until dissolved. Remove from heat and stir in sugar substitute, cinnamon, and vanilla. Set aside until cool.

Meanwhile, add a pinch of salt to the egg whites. Beat with electric mixer in a nonplastic bowl until soft peaks form. Gradually beat in sugar until thick. Gently but thoroughly fold in the coffee mixture. Spoon into the pie shell and chill 5 hours or more. *Eight servings, 85 calories each.*

# FRESH-FRUIT WINDOWPANE PIE

One of the nicest and most delectable summer desserts is also one of the easiest: Windowpane Pie. The fresh fruit shimmers like jewels under glass, dewy-fresh and color-bright, sealed under a clear cover of unsweetened apple juice and plain gelatin. You can create your own variations with any favorite combination of fruit (except fresh pineapple).

White grape juice also can be used for a clear glaze. (Orange, grape, cranberry, or pineapple juice may be used, but they will add their own color.)

2 teaspoons plain gelatin
1 cup chilled unsweetened apple juice, divided
  Honey, fructose, or sugar substitute to equal 5 tablespoons sugar
1 cup sliced fresh strawberries
1 cup sliced fresh peaches
1 cup fresh blueberries
  Prepared graham-cracker pie shell

Combine gelatin and ½ cup apple juice. Wait until gelatin is softened, then heat gently until dissolved. Stir in sweetener and remaining cold apple juice. Chill in freezer 8 to 10 minutes, until syrupy. Meanwhile prepare fruit.

Fill the pie shell with the fruit. Don't mix the fruit together, but arrange it in random clumps of color (much prettier!). Gently pack fruit down. When gelatin mixture is syrupy, spoon it over fruit until completely glazed. Chill several hours until set. *Eight servings, 150 calories each; 130 calories each with sugar substitute.*

**Mock Mango Pie:** Use 3 cups sliced fresh peaches for the fruit and canned unsweetened pineapple juice for the glaze. Follow directions above. *Eight servings, 150 calories per serving (130 calories each with sugar substitute).*

## SLIMMED-DOWN KEY LIME PIE

Traditional Key Lime Pie recipes are often made with sweetened condensed milk as their base. This sugar-enriched canned milk is over 980 calories a cup. But my adaptation uses evaporated skim milk, only 200 calories a cup, with very little butterfat. This recipe is also made without eggs or egg yolks so is cholesterol-safe.

For the best flavor, make with freshly squeezed lime juice. Unsweetened bottled lime juice may be substituted. Don't be tempted to tint the filling with food coloring. Key Lime Pie is never served green.

This is a refrigerator-style pie, made with a packaged graham-cracker crust. For an even lower-calorie treat, skip the crust: serve Key Lime Parfaits.

1 tablespoon plain gelatin
⅓ cup lime juice
1 cup boiling water
  Sugar substitute to equal ¼ cup sugar
  13-ounce can cold evaporated skim milk
¼ cup cold water
  4-serving package instant vanilla pudding mix
  Pinch of grated lime rind (optional)
  Ready-to-fill crumb crust
  Thin lime slices for garnish (optional)
  Prepared diet whipped topping mix (optional)

In blender container, combine plain gelatin and lime juice. Wait 1 minute, until softened, then add boiling water. Cover and blend on high speed until all granules are dissolved. Add sugar substitute, evaporated skim milk, cold water, pudding mix, and lime rind, if desired. Cover and blend smooth.

Chill in the refrigerator about 20 minutes, until mixture is partially set. Spoon into prepared pie shell and chill several hours, until firm. Pie may be garnished with lime slices, and prepared low-calorie whipped topping, if desired. *Eight servings, 175 calories each (toppings additional).*

**Key Lime Parfaits:** Omit pie shell from preceding recipe. Prepare filling according to directions. Then, whip 3 egg whites and a pinch of salt until stiff and fold into prepared filling when partially set. Spoon mixture into parfait glasses and garnish with lime slices. Chill several hours. *Eight servings, 100 calories each.*

## PRONTO BANANA YOGURT PIE

  **1 envelope plain gelatin**
  **2 tablespoons cold water**
**½ cup boiling water**
   **Sugar substitute to equal 3 tablespoons sugar or to taste**
**¾ cup low-fat vanilla yogurt**
**¾ cup low-fat vanilla ice milk**
  **2 small bananas, thinly sliced**
   **Ready-to-fill crumb crust**
   **Cinnamon**

Combine gelatin and cold water in blender container. Wait 1 minute, then add boiling water and sugar substitute; cover and blend. Add yogurt; cover and blend. Add ice milk; cover and blend. Refrigerate blender container 15 minutes.

Layer half the chilled filling in the pie crust, then a layer of banana slices, then remaining filling. Sprinkle with cinnamon and chill until set. *Eight servings, 145 calories each.*

## BURIED-TREASURE CREAM-CHEESE PIE

  **16-ounce can juice-packed sliced peaches, or any unsweetened canned fruit**
  **Ready-to-fill graham-cracker pie shell**
  **8-ounce package low-calorie ("light") cream cheese or Neufchâtel cheese**
**2 eggs**
**3 tablespoons honey or fructose, or 5 tablespoons sugar or equivalent substitute**
**1 tablespoon vanilla extract**
  **Pinch of salt**

Strain juice from canned fruit into blender container. Arrange drained fruit in bottom of pie shell.

Add remaining ingredients to blender. Cover and blend smooth. Pour over fruit. Bake in a 325-degree oven 1 hour. Chill before serving. *Eight servings, approximately 210 calories each.*

**Peach and Apricot Cheese Pie:** Use an 8-ounce can sliced peaches and an 8-ounce can apricot halves, diced.

**Fruit Medley Pie:** Use a 16-ounce can mixed fruit cocktail.

**Peach Medley Pie:** Use an 8-ounce can sliced peaches and an 8-ounce can fruit cocktail.

**Peach-Pineapple Cheese Pie:** Use an 8-ounce can sliced peaches and an 8-ounce can pineapple tidbits.

**Sugar-Free:** Omit sugar, fructose, or honey. Sprinkle sugar substitute equal to 3 tablespoons sugar over fruit layer. Add unsweetened cheese layer and bake as directed. After baking, sprinkle the top of the pie lightly with additional granulated sugar substitute (and cinnamon, if desired). *Approximately 10 calories less per serving.*

## HIDDEN-PINEAPPLE CHEESE PIE

Juice-packed pineapple is so sweet it's hard to believe that there's any market at all for pineapple packed in syrup. Adding sugar to pineapple is sort of like dying cherries red (or oranges orange . . . but that's done, too!). In this recipe, the pineapple layer is buried under a creamy, nutritious, dairy-rich filling, with no fat added.

2 **cups canned juice-packed unsweetened crushed pineapple**
5 **teaspoons cornstarch, divided**
   **Prepared ready-to-fill graham-cracker pie shell**
4 **ounces (½ package) low-calorie ("light") cream cheese or Neufchâtel cheese**
¾ **cup skim milk**
1 **egg**
6 **tablespoons fructose or 4 tablespoons honey or equivalent sugar substitute**
1 **tablespoon vanilla extract**

Press pineapple into strainer and reserve juice. Stir drained crushed pineapple with 1 teaspoon cornstarch and mix well. Spread in the bottom of pie shell.

Combine reserved pineapple juice with remaining ingredients in blender; cover and blend smooth. Pour over pineapple. Bake in a preheated 350-degree oven until set, about 40 to 45 minutes. Turn off oven and cool pie in oven 1 hour. Chill before serving. *Eight servings, 200 calories each (170 calories each with sugar substitute).*

# DOUBLE CHOCOLATE CHIP PIE

12-ounce container low-fat pot cheese (dry cottage cheese)
2 eggs
½ cup skim milk
2 one-serving envelopes low-calorie hot cocoa mix
4 tablespoons sugar
Pinch of salt
3 tablespoons miniature chocolate chips
Ready-to-fill graham-cracker crust

Combine first 6 ingredients in blender; cover and beat smooth. Fold in chocolate chips. Spoon into crust. Bake in a preheated 300-degree oven 1 hour. Turn off heat and open oven door. Allow pie to cool in oven 1 hour. Chill in refrigerator before serving. *Eight servings, 190 calories each.*

# CRAZY PINEAPPLE PIE

2 tablespoons diet margarine
¼ teaspoon ground cinnamon
1 cup buttermilk-biscuit mix
20-ounce can juice-packed crushed pineapple, undrained
4 tablespoons granulated sugar substitute

Blend diet margarine and cinnamon into biscuit mix in mixer bowl, blender, or food processor (using the steel blade). Mixture will be loose, like cornmeal or heavy flour. Sprinkle half the mixture over the bottom of a 9-inch glass pie pan which has been sprayed with cooking spray. Spoon on half the crushed pineapple. Sprinkle evenly with sugar substitute. Spoon on remaining pineapple (including juice in the can). Sprinkle evenly with remaining flour mixture. Bake in a preheated 400-degree oven 20 to 25 minutes, until topping is golden. Serve warm or chilled. *Eight servings, 125 calories each.*

# APPLE-PINEAPPLE STRUDEL PIE

2 sheets phyllo pastry, thawed
3 apples, peeled, cored, thinly sliced
8-ounce can juice-packed crushed pineapple, undrained
1 tablespoon cornstarch
2 teaspoons apple-pie spice
1 teaspoon vanilla extract
3 tablespoons honey
2 teaspoons melted butter

With cooking spray, spray until slick the bottom of a nonstick 9-inch round or square cake pan or pie pan. Line it with torn pieces of phyllo pastry, reserving two-thirds of the pastry for the top crust.

Stir together remaining ingredients, except butter, and spoon into the pan. Cover the apple mixture with 2 layers of phyllo pastry, torn in pieces to fit. Brush each layer lightly with melted butter. Tuck the edges of the pastry into the pan. Bake uncovered, in a preheated 400-degree oven, 20 to 30 minutes, until pastry is flaky. *Six servings, 125 calories each.*

**With Sugar Substitute:** Omit honey. After spooning half the apple mixture into the pan, sprinkle with granulated sugar substitute to equal 3 tablespoons sugar. Add remaining apple mixture. Proceed as directed. *95 calories each serving.*

# 4
# BREADS, BISCUITS, MUFFINS, AND BREAD-BASED SWEETS

### Easiest Yeast Bread Ever

This extra-easy home-baked loaf has the rough, rustic texture you expect from homemade bread, coupled with delicious flavor. You can slice it for sandwiches, or toast a single slice for a snack or breakfast.

Please try this bread even if you normally punch out when you hear the word "yeast." Unlike conventional recipes, this bread requires no kneading, punching down, and double rising. It's almost as simple and quick as quickbreads made without yeast. You merely mix all the ingredients, put them in a loaf pan, and just wait 45 minutes for the bread to rise before you bake it. Believe me, that's a lot simpler than most bread recipes!

What results is a loaf that's full of nooks and crannies, unmistakably homemade. (Who wants to make bread that looks store-bought?) Once you've tried the basic recipe you'll want to personalize it with your own touches: herbs, raisins, fruit, nuts, cinnamon, or other spices.

Since this bread is so easy that it will attract absolute beginners, allow me to share some helpful information:

• Yeast is sold in ¼-ounce envelopes in the refrigerated case of your supermarket. It should be absolutely fresh (check the date) and stored in your own refrigerator until you get around to using it.

• Use ordinary all-purpose flour, not cake flour and not self-rising flour. No need to sift it.

• This bread is "sugarless" despite the teaspoonful called for in the recipe. The yeast "eats" the sugar, you don't. For that reason, don't omit it.

• And don't omit salt. The salt helps control the rising. There are recipes for salt-free bread, but this isn't one of them.

• Have the water boiling and the milk cold. When you combine them, they will be the proper temperature to wake up the yeast. If you alter the directions, the liquid could be too hot (and kill the yeast) or too cold (and put it to sleep!).

• A warm place means between 80 and 90 degrees Fahrenheit. How about on top of your refrigerator or cabinet (in an un-air-conditioned kitchen)? In case you're thinking about it, don't attempt to put the bread in a "warm" oven for 45 minutes . . . that's too warm! Sunny windows can be too warm, too.

## QUICK AND EASY COUNTRY TOASTING BREAD

1 package (¼ ounce) dry yeast
1 teaspoon sugar
1 teaspoon salt
3 cups unsifted all-purpose flour
¾ cup boiling water
½ cup cold skim milk

Stir dry ingredients together; set aside. Add boiling water to cold milk in bowl. Add half the dry flour mixture and beat well. Stir in the rest of the flour mixture to make a stiff batter. Turn batter into a nonstick loaf pan sprayed with cooking spray. Cover with a clean towel and let rise in a warm place 45 minutes.

Bake in a preheated 400-degree oven, uncovered, for 25 minutes. Remove from the pan and allow to cool. Toast, if desired. *Twenty thin slices, 70 calories each.*

### Self-Rising Flour

Self-rising all-purpose flour is the time saver: it already contains baking powder and salt thoroughly blended in the right proportion. If you don't have self-rising flour, or if it's unavailable in your market, it's a simple matter to mix up your own ahead of time and have it on hand in your kitchen cabinet. Here's how:

Stir all-purpose flour with a spoon to aerate it. Use a standard measuring cup to measure the flour. Dip the cup into the flour to fill it, then level it off with a knife. (Don't press or compact the flour into the cup.) For each cupful of "mix," stir in 1½ teaspoons double-acting baking powder and ½ teaspoon ordinary table salt. Use standard measuring spoons, and level them off with a knife. Stir the mixture *very* thoroughly. Label the container and store it in your cabinet. It is not necessary to sift the "self-rising flour" before measuring it for biscuits or muffins. Simply stir it again before measuring it with a measuring cup.

# SUPER-SPEEDY IRISH NO-KNEAD BISCUIT BREAD

Reminiscent of Irish Soda Bread, this version leaves out the unneeded sugar and shortening while retaining the distinctive flavor that comes from combining raisins, caraway seeds, and buttermilk. (Plain low-fat yogurt is a convenient substitute for buttermilk, and provides the same flavor.) This recipe is a super-speedy shortcut that can even be made in a food processor:

1 **egg**
¾ **cup plain low-fat yogurt**
¼ **cup water**
1 **teaspoon baking soda**
2 **cups self-rising flour or plain pancake mix**
½ **cup soft raisins**
1 **tablespoon caraway seeds**

Combine first 3 ingredients in food processor, using the plastic or steel blade. Process smooth.

Stir baking soda into the self-rising flour (or pancake mix), then add half the flour mixture to the yogurt mixture. Blend in with one or two quick on-off motions of the processor. Scrape the container with a rubber spatula. Add remaining flour mixture; process with on-off motions just until blended. Blend in raisins and caraway seeds. The batter will be thick and sticky.

Spray a shallow nonstick baking tray or cookie tin with cooking spray. Use a rubber scraper to remove the batter from the food processor. Mound it in the center of the baking tray to form a flat, round loaf. Bake uncovered, in a preheated 350-degree oven, for 25 to 30 minutes, until golden, crusty and cooked through. Allow to cool slightly.

To serve: Cut the loaf in quarters, then slice each quarter into thin slices. *Twenty slices, 65 calories each with flour (70 calories each with pancake mix).*

**To Mix by Hand:** In a bowl, stir egg, yogurt, and water smooth. In another bowl, combine baking soda and flour. Add flour mixture to yogurt mixture, half at a time, and stir just until blended and sticky. Mix in raisins and caraway seeds, just until distributed.

# BUTTERMILK BANNOCK (IRISH SODA BREAD)

4 cups all-purpose or bread flour
3 teaspoons baking powder
1 teaspoon salt
¾ teaspoon baking soda
1 cup raisins or currants
2 tablespoons caraway seeds
2 eggs
1½ cups buttermilk

Stir dry ingredients, raisins, and caraway seeds together. Fork-blend eggs and milk together, then add to dry ingredients. Stir until a sticky batter is formed. Scrape the batter onto a well-floured surface and knead lightly. Shape the batter into a ball, then place it in a round nonstick casserole which has been sprayed with cooking spray. Mark a cross in the center, using a sharp knife.

Bake uncovered, in a preheated 350-degree oven, about 1¼ hours. Wait 10 to 15 minutes before attempting to remove the bread from the casserole; then allow the bread to cool on a wire rack. (If desired, cut the loaf in quarters; wrap and freeze the extras for later.)

To serve: slice thin. *Forty slices, about 65 calories each with all-purpose flour (70 calories each with bread flour).*

**Whole-Wheat Bannock Bread:** Follow the preceding recipe, but use 3 cups white all-purpose or bread flour and 1 cup whole-wheat flour. *65 calories per slice.*

**Soy-Enriched Bannock Bread:** Follow the basic recipe, but use 3 cups white all-purpose flour and 1 cup defatted soy flour. *60 calories per slice.*

## Easy Biscuits and Muffins That Shortcut Calories

Biscuits and muffins are two of the easiest and most versatile quickbreads to make.

Muffin batter contains egg, and biscuit batter doesn't; that's the chief difference. Muffin batter is baked in muffin cups while biscuits are either rolled out and cut into rounds, or simply dropped free-form onto a baking tray. Drop biscuits are easier to make; they don't require a rolling pin and pastry board. The batter for drop biscuits is thinner and contains more liquid. The biscuit recipe given here is for drop biscuits rather than rolled.

The way to cut calories in muffins and biscuits is to cut down on the amount of fat: use skim milk instead of whole, less shortening, butter, or margarine. A convenient way to add buttery flavor to batters without a high fat content is to substitute diet margarine for the shortening called for in standard recipes.

*(continued)*

However, diet margarine—which is half water—can't be substituted spoonful for spoonful. It's necessary to decrease proportionally the amount of milk or other liquid to accommodate the moisture in the margarine. These recipes have been adjusted to work with diet margarine.

## EASY STIR-AND-BAKE LOW-CALORIE MUFFINS

**1 cup self-rising flour**
**1 egg, unbeaten**
**3 tablespoons diet margarine (at room temperature)**
**⅓ cup skim milk**

Combine ingredients in a mixing bowl. Stir vigorously until batter is blended but lumpy; don't overmix. Fill 8 nonstick muffin cups approximately half full. Bake in a preheated 425-degree oven 15 to 18 minutes, until golden. *Eight muffins, 80 calories each.*

## STIR-AND-BAKE LOW-CAL DROP BISCUITS

**1 cup self-rising flour**
**3 tablespoons diet margarine (at room temperature)**
**6 to 7 tablespoons fresh skim milk, divided**

Combine flour, margarine, and 5 tablespoons milk in a mixing bowl. Stir vigorously until batter is blended. Stir in additional milk until a soft batter is formed. Drop batter by tablespoonfuls onto a nonstick baking tray or cookie tin which has been sprayed with cooking spray. Bake in a preheated 450-degree oven about 10 minutes, until golden. Serve warm. *Eight biscuits, approximately 80 calories each.*

**Shortcake Drop Biscuits for Fresh-Fruit Topping:** Add 1 teaspoon vanilla extract and 1 tablespoon sugar (optional) to Drop Biscuit batter, and prepare as directed. To serve, split biscuits (warm or cold), and smother with ½ cup crushed fresh berries, peaches, or other fruit (unsweetened or lightly sweetened with honey, fructose, or granulated sugar substitute to taste). *Each serving, approximately 150 calories (unsweetened).*

## BISCUIT AND MUFFIN VARIATIONS

**Blueberry:** Stir in 5 tablespoons fresh berries. *5 calories more per biscuit or muffin.*

**Bran:** Stir in 3 tablespoons bran flakes. *5 calories more per biscuit or muffin.*

**Cheese:** Stir in ¼ cup (1 ounce) shredded extra-sharp cheese, a pinch of dry mustard, and a shake of cayenne pepper. *15 calories more per biscuit or muffin (with Cheddar).*

**Cinnamon-Raisin:** Stir in 3 tablespoons raisins and a pinch of cinnamon. *10 calories more per biscuit or muffin.*

**Italian Herb:** Stir in ½ teaspoon dried oregano or mixed Italian herbs. Add 1 teaspoon onion flakes, if desired.

**Savory Parmesan:** Stir in 3 tablespoons grated Parmesan cheese and ½ teaspoon dried savory (or mixed herbs). *10 calories more per biscuit or muffin.*

**Parsley-Chive:** Stir in 1 tablespoon minced fresh parsley and 1 to 2 tablespoons finely minced fresh chives.

## FOOD PROCESSOR WHOLE-GRAIN CORNBREAD

What gives this special cornbread its fresh flavor is *real corn,* puréed smooth in the food processor or blender. The result is a flavor much like the traditional water-ground cornmeal that's so perishable and hard to find. Yet this recipe is super simple, even easier than conventional cornbread. And it's nutritious and less fattening. Corn kernels make this a "whole-grain" high-fiber bread (even though the corn is puréed so smooth that the texture is the same as bread made from highly processed refined cornmeal). Corn also makes this bread so moist that no butter, shortening, oil, or other fat is needed in the batter.

One further point: this recipe and the two following contain no sugar. In the South, where cornbread comes from, the idea of adding sweetness is considered a Yankee corruption. I agree! If you don't, however, you could add 2 to 3 tablespoons to the batter. Remember, each tablespoon of sugar adds 46 calories to the total.

**1 cup cooked or frozen cut corn, defrosted**
**1 cup cold water**
**2 large eggs**
**2 cups self-rising all-purpose flour**

Combine corn, water, and eggs in the food processor, using the steel blade. Process until corn kernels are completely puréed. Add flour. Process briefly with quick on-off motions, scraping down the container, until blended. Use a rubber scraper to transfer the batter to a 9-inch nonstick square or round cake pan.

Bake uncovered, in a preheated 425-degree oven, 20 to 25 minutes, until a knife inserted in the center comes out clean. Caution: top will not brown; don't overbake. Serve warm, cut into squares or wedges. When cool, wrap in plastic or foil. Leftovers may be sliced and lightly toasted before serving. *Sixteen servings, 75 calories each.*

**In Blender:** Purée corn with water until smooth. Add eggs and blend smooth. Pour into a bowl and stir in self-rising flour, just until blended.

## WHOLE-KERNEL CORN MUFFINS

If you prefer the texture of whole corn kernels, try these delicious snack-size muffins:

    1 large egg
    1 cup skim milk
 ¼ cup cold water
    1 cup cooked or frozen cut corn, defrosted
 1½ cups all-purpose flour
    1 cup white or yellow cornmeal
 1¼ teaspoons salt
 3½ teaspoons baking powder

Beat egg, milk, and water together until well blended. Stir in corn. Combine remaining ingredients in another bowl and stir together; then stir into egg-corn mixture, just until batter is blended.

Spray nonstick muffin cups with cooking spray. Fill cups about one-half to two-thirds full. Bake in a preheated 425-degree oven about 15 minutes. *Eighteen small muffins, about 80 calories each.*

## NO-FAT-ADDED CORNBREAD

For a more traditional cornbread without added fat or sugar, try this.

 ½ cup all-purpose flour
 ½ cup white or yellow cornmeal
    3 teaspoons baking powder
 ½ teaspoon salt
    1 cup skim milk
    1 large egg

Stir flour, cornmeal, baking powder, and salt together. In another bowl, beat milk and egg together. Combine ingredients and stir just until blended. Turn into a nonstick round or square 8-inch cake pan which has been sprayed with cooking spray.

Bake in a preheated 400-degree oven about 20 minutes, or until a knife inserted in the center comes out clean. Cut into wedges or squares. Serve warm or lightly toasted. *Nine servings, 70 calories each.*

## BLUEBERRY CORNBREAD

**1 cup sifted all-purpose flour**
**2 tablespoons sugar (optional)**
**3 teaspoons baking powder**
**½ teaspoon salt**
**1 cup cornmeal (preferably yellow)**
**1 egg, lightly beaten, or 2 egg whites (or equivalent egg substitute)**
**¾ cup diet margarine, at room temperature**
**¾ cup skim milk**
**1 cup fresh blueberries**

Stir the sifted flour, sugar if using, baking powder, salt, and cornmeal together until well blended; set aside.

Combine the egg, diet margarine, and milk in an electric mixing bowl; beat well. Stir in the flour mixture, a little at a time, only until well moistened. Gently fold in blueberries. Spoon into an 8-inch square nonstick baking pan which has been sprayed with cooking spray. Bake in a preheated 375-degree oven 20 to 25 minutes, until golden. Serve warm or cold, cut into squares. *Nine servings, 195 calories each (10 calories more per serving with sugar; 5 calories less per serving with egg whites or substitute).*

## MOIST ORANGE BANANA BREAKFAST MUFFINS

If you prefer to eat your breakfast away from home, during your morning coffee break, for example, these breakfast muffins are the ideal solution. They're naturally fruit-sweet and moist, so they need neither butter nor jam to be satisfying. They freeze and pack well, so they're good for lunch, too. In fact, they make such a nice snack or dessert that you don't have to leave home to enjoy them.

6-ounce can orange-juice concentrate
2 large very ripe bananas
2 eggs or equivalent no-cholesterol substitute
2 cups self-rising flour
1 teaspoon baking soda
1 teaspoon cinnamon
1 teaspoon allspice
4 tablespoons raisins
4 tablespoons high-fiber breakfast cereal (optional)

Defrost orange juice, but don't dilute it; combine with soft peeled bananas and eggs in an electric mixing bowl. Beat until light and fluffy.

Stir flour, soda, cinnamon, and allspice together; add to banana-orange mixture. Beat until blended. Stir in raisins. Spoon into 18 nonstick muffin cups sprayed with cooking spray. Sprinkle tops with cereal, if desired.

Bake in a preheated 350-degree oven until a knife inserted in the center of one comes out clean. Cool in the cups before removing. (To freeze, leave muffins in cups. When cool, double wrap with foil. Muffins freeze well.) *Eighteen muffins, approximately 95 calories each. (Cereal topping adds about 2 calories, egg substitute subtracts about 5 calories per muffin).*

## FIBER-BREAD ORANGE MUFFINS

Here's a low-calorie way to turn high-fiber bread and oranges into delicious muffins.

1 orange
3 slices fresh high-fiber bread (white or whole-wheat)
1 cup instant nonfat dry milk powder or ¾ cup non-instant
2 eggs or equivalent defrosted no-cholesterol substitute
1 teaspoon vanilla extract
½ teaspoon cinnamon or apple-pie spice
  Pinch of salt
½ teaspoon baking powder
½ teaspoon baking soda

Peel orange and cut into chunks, retaining juice. Puree in blender or food processor, using steel blade. Add remaining ingredients, except baking powder and soda. Blend smooth. Blend in baking powder and soda last.

Fill 16 nonstick muffin cups nearly to the top. Bake in preheated 350-degree oven about 20 minutes, until golden. *Sixteen muffins, approximately 40 calories each.*

## GOLDEN FRUIT MUFFINS

2 Golden Delicious apples, chopped
2 large very ripe bananas
2 eggs or equivalent no-cholesterol substitute
⅓ cup skim milk
2 teaspoons vanilla extract
1 teaspoon cinnamon
½ teaspoon allspice
½ teaspoon nutmeg
3 tablespoons granulated fructose, or sugar substitute to equal 9 teaspoons
    sugar (optional)
2 cups self-rising flour
1 teaspoon baking soda
4 tablespoons golden raisins
4 tablespoons crushed cereal (optional)

If using yellow apples, don't peel. If using red apples, remove the peel. Shred the apples coarse, or slice thin, or chop fine by hand.

In blender, food processor, or electric mixer bowl: combine bananas, eggs, milk, vanilla, spices, and sweetener, if desired; beat smooth. Stir flour and baking soda together; add to banana mixture. Beat just until blended (use on-off switch with blender or food processor). Stir in chopped apples and raisins (mixture will be thick).

Spoon into nonstick muffin cups which have been sprayed with cooking spray. Sprinkle the tops with crushed cereal, if desired. Bake 16 to 18 minutes in preheated 350-degree oven, until golden. Cool in the pans. *Eighteen muffins, 90 calories each. Fructose and cereal add approximately 10 calories; egg substitute subtracts approximately 5 calories per muffin.*

## APPLE-RAISIN MUFFINS

1⅔ cups all-purpose flour
2½ teaspoons baking powder
 ½ teaspoon salt
 1 teaspoon cinnamon
 ¼ teaspoon allspice or nutmeg
 ½ cup skim milk
 1 egg
 6 tablespoons diet margarine
 2 medium apples, pared and chopped
 4 tablespoons raisins

Stir flour with baking powder, salt, and spices; set aside. Combine milk, egg, and diet margarine; beat until blended. Add flour mixture and mix until blended but lumpy. Stir in chopped apples and raisins. Spoon batter into 14 nonstick muffin cups (about two-thirds full) and bake in a preheated 400-degree oven 20 minutes or more until muffins are golden. Serve warm or cold. *Makes 14 muffins, 105 calories each.*

## ONE-A-DAY PRUNE BREAKFAST MUFFINS

  2 **cups all-purpose flour**
  2 **teaspoons baking powder**
 ½ **teaspoon cinnamon or apple-pie spice**
 ½ **teaspoon salt**
  2 **eggs, lightly beaten**
 ⅞ **cup skim milk (14 tablespoons)**
  3 **tablespoons diet margarine (room temperature)**
  1 **teaspoon vanilla extract**
  6 **tablespoons crushed bran cereal, divided**
  1 **cup diced pitted soft prunes (6 ounces)**

Stir flour, baking powder, spices, and salt together; set aside. Beat eggs, milk, margarine, and vanilla in an electric mixer bowl. Add flour mixture and 4 tablespoons cereal. Mix just until batter is moist. Stir in diced prunes.

Spoon into 18 nonstick muffin cups (sprayed with cooking spray) and sprinkle the tops with remaining crushed cereal. Bake in a preheated 425-degree oven about 15 to 18 minutes. *Eighteen muffins, under 100 calories each.*

## DOT'S LOW-CALORIE CRANBERRY BREAD

  2 **cups all-purpose flour**
 ¾ **cup sugar**
1½ **teaspoons baking powder**
 ½ **teaspoon baking soda**
   **Pinch of salt**
 ¾ **cup orange juice**
  1 **egg, beaten, or equivalent no-cholesterol substitute**
  1 **cup fresh or defrosted cranberries, chopped**
 ¼ **cup chopped nuts (optional)**

Stir together flour, sugar, baking powder, soda, and salt. Beat in juice and egg until well blended. Stir in cranberries and nuts, if desired.

Spray the bottom of a 9- by 5-inch nonstick loaf pan with cooking spray.

Spoon in batter. Bake in a preheated 350-degree oven about 1 hour or until bread tests done. Cool thoroughly before slicing. *Makes 20 thin slices, 85 calories each (nuts add 10 calories per slice).*

## ORANGE BANANA QUICKBREAD

Undiluted defrosted orange juice adds flavor and sweetness to my favorite fruitbread loaf, but be sure you use *real* unsweetened juice concentrate, not an imitation made with sugar and pulp. This recipe is made without added shortening or sugar.

**6 ounces orange-juice concentrate**
**2 large very ripe bananas**
**2 eggs**
**2 cups self-rising flour**
**2½ teaspoons pumpkin-pie spice**
**1 teaspoon baking soda**
**4 tablespoons golden raisins**

Thaw orange juice but don't dilute. Combine it with peeled bananas and eggs in an electric mixer bowl. Beat until fluffy.

Stir flour, spice, and baking soda together and add to mixing bowl. Beat 1 minute. Stir in raisins. Spoon into a nonstick 5- by 9-inch loaf pan. Bake in a preheated 350-degree oven 30 to 35 minutes, until a knife inserted in the center comes out clean. *Makes 20 slices, approximately 85 calories each.*

### Bananas in Bread Batter Add Moistness but No Fat

Bananas as a butter substitute? While bananas have no fat whatsoever, they do make it possible to create lower-calorie quickbreads with no fat added. Mashed soft banana added to a butterless batter provides the characteristic moistness that's usually associated with butter, margarine, shortening, or oil. A whole banana is only 100 calories, while 100 calories' worth of butter measures only 1 tablespoon. But wait, there's more! Bananas provide natural fruit sweetness, so less (or no) sugar is needed. And bananas replace part of the flour. If you have to be calorie-careful, banana in quickbread is a natural.

On the subject of bananas as a butter substitute, we've received letters from readers who really do use ripe mashed banana as a butter substitute: spreading it on toast, rolls, or English muffins instead of the other (fattening) spread. No jelly needed, either, because bananas are sweet!

You won't need butter *or* jelly on the following fabulous fruitbread because it is so moist that no spread is necessary. (To take advantage of the natural fiber and pectin content, use the apples unpeeled . . . easier, too!)

## FABULOUS HIGH-FIBER FRUIT BREAD

3 small or 2 large very ripe bananas
2 eggs
1 teaspoon vanilla extract or walnut flavoring
   Pinch of butter-flavored salt (optional)
2 teaspoons apple-pie spice, or 1 teaspoon cinnamon, plus ½ teaspoon each
   nutmeg and allspice
3 tablespoons honey or fructose syrup
   Granulated sugar substitute to equal 3 tablespoons sugar (optional)
⅓ cup skim milk
1 teaspoon baking soda
2 cups self-rising all-purpose flour, unsifted, or 2 cups regular all-purpose
   flour, 2 teaspoons baking powder, ½ teaspoon salt
4 tablespoons raisins
1 tablespoon chopped walnuts (optional)
2 unpeeled Golden Delicious apples, cored, shredded or minced

Use very soft bananas, with brown-speckled skins. Combine peeled bananas, eggs, vanilla, salt if used, spice, honey, sweetener if used, and milk. Beat smooth. Stir baking soda into flour and add to mixture; beat smooth. Stir in raisins, walnuts if desired, and minced or shredded apples.

Spoon batter into nonstick 5- by 9-inch loaf pan sprayed with cooking spray. Bake in preheated 375-degree oven 40 to 45 minutes. Serve warm or cold. Wrap in foil and store in refrigerator. *Makes 20 slices, 85 calories each.*

## BANANA FRUIT LOAF

2 eggs
2 very ripe large bananas
1 teaspoon vanilla extract
1 teaspoon cinnamon
1 teaspoon allspice
¼ cup honey
2 cups all-purpose flour
2 teaspoons baking powder
1 teaspoon baking soda
½ teaspoon salt
6 tablespoons raisins
2 apples, cored, peeled, chopped

Beat eggs, bananas, vanilla, spices, and honey together. Stir together flour, baking powder, baking soda, and salt; then add to banana mixture. Beat smooth. Fold in raisins and apples. Spoon into a nonstick loaf pan sprayed with cooking spray. Bake in a preheated 375-degree oven 40 to 45 minutes. *Makes 20 slices, approximately 95 calories each.*

# 5

# PANCAKES, WAFFLES, CRÊPES, AND OMELETS

  

## Some Pointers for Pancake Lovers:

For us weight-wary folks, pancakes are among the foods that have simply ceased to exist, along with Hershey bars and Mallomars. Not that pancakes are so calamitously calorie-laden. It's just that everything else they touch is! Butter, for example, has 100 calories per tablespoon.

By some evil magic a couple of hotcakes can easily make several hundred calories' worth of butter disappear before your very eyes, only to reappear around your waistline before next Tuesday.

Pancake syrup? It's nothing more than sugar—pure calories in a pourable state. You might just as well skip breakfast and pour it directly on your hips, where it's going to go anyway. Honey is little better despite its health-food image.

The space that's left on the plate is usually occupied by greasy sausage or even greasier bacon, both so fat-laden that there's little point in debating their relative demerits. (But, for the record, bacon is nearly twice as fattening as breakfast sausage!)

No wonder a "simple" order of pancakes and bacon can easily wipe out your calorie allowance for a whole weekend! Unless you're a Slim Gourmet cook.

Making pancakes from scratch instead of using a mix isn't any more work, since most of the "work"—mixing and cooking—has to be done anyway.

Plain pancake mixes are little more than self-rising flour, sometimes gussied up with added (and unwanted) fats and sugars, to which you add your own eggs and milk. Just-add-water mixes take away the trouble (and better taste) of added fats and sugars. Thaw-and-pour mixes are hardly convenient: they require defrosting before use. They too contain added fats and sugars, and have a somewhat gummy texture.

Of all the commercial varieties available, buckwheat-pancake mixes tend to be the most nutritious and least fattening, with more protein and fiber than other types.

Shoppers should take pancake "lightness" claims lightly! It may be a mistake to assume that "light" on the label has anything to do with a reduced calorie count.

When making pancakes, whether from a mix or from scratch, it's not necessary to add either fat or sugar to the batter, regardless of what the directions say.

Nor is oil needed to grease the griddle if it has a nonstick surface. Cooking spray for no-fat frying applied to a nonstick surface makes fat-free pancakes possible. If you feel you must use butter, wouldn't you rather put it *on* your pancake than *in* it?

But slathering butter (or margarine) on pancakes is just a habit, one that's easy to break once you realize that each level tablespoon has 100 calories, more than the pancake itself.

## BASIC LOW-CALORIE PANCAKES

**1 egg**
**½ cup fresh skim milk**
**½ cup water**
**½ teaspoon vanilla extract (optional)**
**1 cup all-purpose flour**
**2 teaspoons baking powder**

Beat together the egg, milk, water, and vanilla, if desired. Combine flour and baking powder and stir into the liquid, just until smooth but slightly lumpy. Don't overmix.

Spray a nonstick griddle with cooking spray until slick. Preheat it to 400 degrees (or until a drop of water will dance on the surface).

To make pancakes: Pour a little of the batter onto the hot griddle. Leave at least 2 inches of space between pancakes. Allow them to cook undisturbed until the tops of the pancakes are bubbled, then turn with a plastic spatula. Cook just until the underside is lightly browned.

To keep pancakes warm while additional ones are being made: stack them in a cake pan over a warming plate set at the lowest heat. Rearrange the pancakes to warm evenly. *Ten 4-inch pancakes, 60 calories each. Recipe may be doubled. Unused batter may be stored in the refrigerator. Thin with a little cold water if batter becomes too thick.*

**In Food Processor:** Using the plastic or steel blade, process together milk, water, egg, and vanilla, if desired. Combine dry ingredients and add to processor. Process with on-off switch just until almost smooth, but still slightly lumpy.

**Extra Low-Calorie:** Substitute water for the fresh milk. *55 calories per pancake.*

**Low-Cholesterol:** Omit the egg and add ¼ cup water *(50 calories per pancake)* or skim milk *(55 calories per pancake).* Or substitute equivalent defrosted egg substitute *(55 calories per pancake).*

**Buttermilk Batter:** Substitute buttermilk for the milk and substitute ½ teaspoon baking soda for the baking powder. *60 calories per pancake.*

**Yogurt Pancakes:** Substitute ¼ cup low-fat plain or vanilla yogurt and ¼ cup water for the milk. Substitute ½ teaspoon baking soda for the baking powder. (Omit vanilla if using vanilla-flavored yogurt.) *60 calories per pancake.*

**Whole-Wheat Pancakes:** Use ½ cup whole-wheat flour and ½ cup white flour. *55 calories per pancake.*

**Buckwheat Pancakes:** Use ½ cup buckwheat flour and ½ cup white flour. (To make home-ground buckwheat flour: Put toasted buckwheat groats or grits, also known as "kasha," in your blender or food processor, using the steel blade. Cover and process until powdered, about 3 minutes. Do ½ cup at a time.) *55 calories per pancake.*

**Cornmeal Pancakes:** Use ½ cup cornmeal and ½ cup white flour. *60 calories per pancake.*

**Fresh Corn Pancakes:** Combine ½ cup cooked or defrosted (uncooked) corn kernels with 1 egg and ¾ cup water or skim milk in blender or processor; process smooth. Combine corn mixture with ¾ cup flour, 2 teaspoons baking powder, and ½ teaspoon salt. Stir smooth. *55 calories per pancake.*

**Blueberry Pancakes:** Just before pouring, stir into batter ⅓ to ½ cup whole fresh or frozen unsweetened blueberries. If frozen blueberries are used, do not defrost them first. *65 calories per pancake.*

**Self-Rising Pancake Mix:** For each cupful of flour, stir in 2 teaspoons double-acting baking powder and ½ teaspoon salt. Mix well, then store in the pantry in a tightly covered container. Or buy self-rising flour. To make pancakes: use 1 cup of this mixture in place of the flour, baking powder, and salt.

# ORANGE-FLAVORED PANCAKES WITH APPLESAUCE

1 cup self-rising pancake mix, regular or whole-wheat (see page 85)
½ teaspoon baking soda
1 egg or equivalent egg substitute
¾ cup orange juice, unsweetened
½ cup water (approximately)
1 teaspoon vanilla extract
2 cups chunky, unsweetened canned or homemade applesauce (recipe follows)
1 tablespoon orange liqueur or 2 tablespoons orange juice (optional)
  Cinnamon or apple-pie spice

Stir pancake mix and baking soda together. Make a well in the center and add egg, ¼ cup juice, ¼ cup water, and vanilla. Stir until well blended. Add more water as needed.

Spray a nonstick griddle until slick with cooking spray. Heat over moderate flame. When hot, use a measuring cup to drop batter on skillet by scant ¼ cupfuls. Cook undisturbed until tops of pancakes are bubbled and nearly dry. Use a spatula to turn; briefly brown the other side. Keep warm.

Meanwhile, stir applesauce and orange liqueur or juice, if desired, together in a small saucepan over low heat until bubbling.

To serve, divide pancakes among 4 plates and spoon on hot applesauce. Sprinkle with spice. *Four brunch servings, 215 calories each; eight dessert servings, 110 calories each (liqueur adds under 10 calories per brunch serving; under 5 calories per dessert serving).*

(Extra pancakes can be stored in the freezer: allow to cool on wax paper, then wrap individually and freeze. Reheat in toaster, toaster-oven, oven, or microwave oven.)

**Fast Applesauce:** Peel, core, and thinly slice 3 or 4 large McIntosh apples into a heavy saucepan. Add ½ cup water (or juice: unsweetened apple, white grape, or orange). Cover tightly and simmer 4 to 5 minutes. Fork-stir until chunky or whip smooth. Sweeten to taste, if desired, with granulated sugar substitute. *Four servings, about 100 calories each.*

Some variations:

**Pineapple Pancakes:** Substitute unsweetened pineapple juice for the orange juice. (Or use apple juice or any other unsweetened fruit juice.) *220 calories per brunch serving; 110 calories per dessert serving.*

**Pineapple Topping:** Stir ½ teaspoon cornstarch and 3 or 4 tablespoons water into 1 cup undrained unsweetened juice-packed crushed pineapple. Cook and stir in a small saucepan until bubbling. Add a pinch of pumpkin-pie spice, if desired. *5 calories per tablespoon.*

# BANANA PANCAKES

Here's a pancake batter that needs no oil or shortening—in the batter or on top of the pancakes. Instead of syrup, why not use warmed unsweetened applesauce and a pinch of cinnamon? Double the recipe for additional quantities.

**1 very ripe banana, peeled**
**½ cup self-rising pancake mix**
**1 egg**
**¼ cup skim milk**

Combine in blender or food processor and blend smooth. Cook on preheated nonstick griddle well sprayed with cooking spray, no fat added. *Six small pancakes, 75 calories each; or four large pancakes, 110 calories each.*

# YOGURT–COTTAGE CHEESE PANCAKES

**¾ cup low-fat plain or vanilla yogurt**
**½ cup low-fat cottage cheese**
**2 eggs**
**¾ cup all-purpose flour**
**½ teaspoon baking soda**
**1 teaspoon salt**
  **Pinch of grated lemon or orange peel (optional)**

Combine yogurt, cottage cheese, and eggs in blender or food processor. Cover and blend until completely smooth and the texture of cream.

Stir together flour, baking soda, salt, and peel, if desired; add to the yogurt mixture. Blend only until mixed.

Spray a griddle, large nonstick skillet, or electric frypan liberally with cooking spray. Heat until a drop of water dances on the surface. Pour the batter onto the hot surface in rounds. When the pancake tops are bubbled, turn them and brown the other side. Serve hot with puréed peaches, crushed strawberries, applesauce, or low-calorie syrup. *Ten pancakes, 70 calories each; 5 calories more per pancake with vanilla yogurt.*

**Pancake "Shortcakes":** Allow Yogurt–Cottage Cheese Pancakes to cool, and reserve them for desserts. For each serving: Top the pancake with ½ cup sliced fresh strawberries or other fresh fruit (lightly sweetened with honey, fructose, or sugar substitute to taste). Top with a squiggle of pressurized light whipped cream or a blend of low-fat vanilla yogurt and light whipped cream folded together. *Approximately 120 calories per serving, complete.*

# OVEN-BAKED GERMAN PANCAKE

This puffy German pancake is much too spectacular to face at breakfast. Better at brunch or as an after-hours meal-size dessert. Despite its dramatic appearance, German pancakes can be low-calorie. Our recipe serves 6, yet calls for only ½ cup flour and no fat at all.

In case you're not familiar with it, a German pancake is baked in the oven. If your oven has a window, it's a show worth watching: the batter spreads up the sides, puffs up, then sinks in the middle to make the ideal "container" for fresh fruit or other nonfattening filling. You slice it in wedges to serve.

Since it's cooked in the oven at high heat, the ideal gadget is an all-metal slope-sided skillet or omelet pan with a metal handle—not wood or plastic. A nonstick 9-inch pie pan or other shallow slope-sided oven-proof casserole of similar size should work as well.

> 3 **eggs**
> ½ **cup skim milk**
>   **Pinch of salt**
> ½ **cup instant-blending flour**

Preheat oven to hot: 450 degrees. Spray pan well with cooking spray for no-fat baking. Use a fork or wire whisk to beat eggs well. Beat in milk and salt. Beat in flour just until blended. Pour into pan. Bake in oven 25 minutes. Remove and fill with one of the fruit fillings that follow. Slice into 6 wedges to serve. *Six servings, 85 calories each (without filling).*

## PEACH AMBROSIA FILLING OR TOPPING

> 1 **eating orange, peeled and chopped in chunks**
> 2 **large ripe peaches, peeled and thinly sliced**
> ½ **cup fresh strawberries, hulled and sliced**
> 3 **tablespoons honey or fructose or equivalent sugar substitute, or to taste (optional)**

Peel orange and dice coarse, retaining juices. Pick out and discard seeds, if any. Stir in remaining ingredients. Cover and store in refrigerator. (Orange juice will keep peaches from browning.) Use as filling for Oven-Baked German Pancake, or as topping on low-cal ice milk, frozen yogurt, or cottage cheese. *Six servings, 30 calories each; honey or fructose adds about 25 calories per serving.*

## PINEAPPLE FILLING OR TOPPING

> 20-**ounce can unsweetened crushed pineapple, undrained**
> 2 **teaspoons cornstarch or arrowroot**
> 3 **tablespoons honey or fructose or equivalent sugar substitute, or to taste (optional)**

Cook and stir pineapple and cornstarch or arrowroot until bubbling. Add sweetener, if desired. Use as filling for Oven-Baked German Pancake. *Six servings, 70 calories each (honey or fructose adds about 25 calories per serving).*

## HOT RUM-APPLE-RAISIN FILLING

The alcohol calories evaporate.

**3 large unpeeled apples, cored, diced**
**2 tablespoons raisins**
**1 tablespoon arrowroot or cornstarch**
**3 tablespoons rum or brandy**
**¼ teaspoon salt or butter-flavored salt**
**1 teaspoon apple-pie or pumpkin-pie spice, or ½ teaspoon each cinnamon and nutmeg**
**2 tablespoons honey or fructose or equivalent sugar substitute to taste (optional)**

Combine ingredients (except sugar substitute, if using) and simmer in saucepan just until sauce is thickened and apples are tender but not mushy. (Stir in sugar substitute after cooking. Or combine ingredients in a covered dish and bake in oven, separately, while pancake is baking.) Filling may be spooned onto pancake, over low-calorie French toast, or on top of vanilla ice milk or frozen yogurt. *Six servings, 65 calories each (honey or fructose adds about 25 calories per serving).*

## GERMAN FRESH-FRUIT PANCAKE

Here's one big pancake to fill with fresh fruit.

**1 cup all-purpose flour**
**½ teaspoon baking powder**
**Pinch of salt**
**1 cup skim milk**
**5 eggs**
**4 or 5 ripe peaches, peeled and sliced**
**2 tablespoons brown sugar**
**Cinnamon**

You will need a nonstick skillet with a metal (nonplastic) handle that can go into a hot oven.

*(continued)*

Stir flour, baking powder, and salt together. Beat in milk. Beat in the eggs, 1 at a time.

Spray the skillet liberally with cooking spray. Add the batter. Cook on top of the range over direct heat for 1 minute, then transfer the skillet to a preheated 425-degree oven. Bake uncovered 20 to 25 minutes, until puffed and golden. Remove from the oven. Fill with sliced peaches (or other fresh fruit) lightly sprinkled with brown sugar and cinnamon. *Six servings, 210 calories each.*

**Without a Skillet:** Use a nonstick pie pan. Preheat it in the oven while you make the batter. Spray the pie pan with cooking spray. Pour the batter into the heated pie pan and bake at 425 degrees for 20 to 25 minutes.

## HIGH-PROTEIN HIGH-FIBER-BREAD PANCAKES

This recipe takes advantage of the new low-calorie fiber-added breads that are becoming so popular among dieters.

FOR EACH SERVING
 1 large egg
¼ cup skim milk
½ teaspoon vanilla extract (optional)
   Scant teaspoon baking powder
 2 slices bread, low-calorie, high-fiber, whole-wheat or white

Combine ingredients in blender or food processor, using steel blade; cover and blend smooth. Spray a nonstick skillet with cooking spray until slick. Heat over moderate flame. Pour in ¼ cup batter. Rotate skillet slightly to spread batter in a larger circle. Lower heat a little. Cook undisturbed until top of pancake is lightly bubbled and slightly dry. Turn with a spatula and cook other side until golden. (If making only 4 pancakes, it's simpler to make them one at a time.) These pancakes are best if cooked at a little lower temperature, and a little longer, than conventional pancakes.

*Four large pancakes, 50 calories each. For smaller pancakes, use a coffee-measuring spoon; eight small pancakes, 25 calories each.*

Top with heated chunky unsweetened applesauce or juice-packed crushed pineapple . . . not syrup!

**Main-Course Pancakes:** Omit vanilla. Serve with "creamed" chicken, turkey, or tuna, using a white sauce made with skim milk and no fat.

### What to Serve with Pancakes and French Toast

In place of bacon, use the 30 percent leaner pork strips broiled until brittle-crisp and well rendered of fat, blotted on paper toweling.

Or thin slices of Canadian bacon, skillet-browned in a sprayed nonstick skillet with no fat added (only 980 calories a pound instead of 3,016 for regular bacon).

Or homemade sausage patties made by seasoning 1 pound lean fat-trimmed ground pork with ½ teaspoon poultry seasoning (857 calories per pound).

Or defrosted turkey sausage (880 calories a pound instead of 1,565 calories for regular pork breakfast sausage).

Or thin slices of heat-and-eat ham steak (lean only) at only 55 calories an ounce.

## SLIM SUNDAY FRENCH TOAST

French toast isn't fattening, . . . until you cook and serve it! The basic ingredients—bread, milk, and eggs—are filling and nutritious, particularly if the bread chosen is whole-wheat or protein-enriched diet bread. But the problems begin, and the calories mount up, once the cooking and serving take place.

French toast is fried in a skillet liberally larded with fat. When served, it's usually sprinkled with sugar, spread with butter, slathered with jam, or swimming in syrup, the empty-caloried additions that getcha! And we haven't even considered the fat-rich "go-withs" like bacon or sausage!

You can still enjoy a Sunday brunch of French toast if you're a calorie-careful cook. Choose a bread that's nutritionally redeeming, like whole-wheat, high-protein bread, or the new high-fiber brands. Use skim milk in place of whole. Use a nonstick skillet liberally coated with cooking spray for no-fat frying. Of course, you can replace butter or margarine with diet margarine, but even diet margarine is 50 calories a tablespoon, so why not omit butter or margarine altogether? A Slim Gourmet calorie-reduced topping (recipes given) is all you need.

3 **eggs**
½ **cup skim milk**
  **Shake of salt**
  **Few drops vanilla extract**
8 **slices white or whole-wheat bread**
  **Cinnamon (optional)**

Spray a large nonstick skillet, Teflon griddle, or electric frypan with cooking spray for no-fat frying, until the surface is wet and shiny. Meanwhile beat eggs, milk, salt, and vanilla together in a shallow dish. Dip the bread slices in this mixture a few slices at a time. Brown the egg-soaked bread in the skillet over moderate heat, turning once. Sprinkle with cinnamon, if desired. *Eight slices, 110 calories each with white bread; 95 calories each with whole wheat.*

**High-Fiber French Toast:** Substitute 8 slices high-fiber, calorie-reduced bread for ordinary bread. Follow preceding directions. *85 calories, per slice.*

*(continued)*

**French Toast Toppings:** Sugar-free or low-sugar preserves or orange marmalade (*8 to 25 calories per tablespoon,* depending on the brand) . . . Gently heated canned crushed juice-packed pineapple *(8 calories a tablespoon)* . . . Heated unsweetened applesauce *(about 7 calories per tablespoon).*

## CALORIE-REDUCED MAPLE SYRUP

*Real* **maple syrup (not maple-flavored pancake syrup)**
**Sugar-free diet pancake syrup**

Mix equal amounts. Store in refrigerator in a covered syrup bottle or container. Put bottle in saucepan of hot water to warm. *About 25 calories per tablespoon* (instead of 50 or 60).

## SLIM HONEY-MAPLE SYRUP

**1 cup sugar-free maple-flavored pancake diet syrup**
**⅓ cup honey**

Stir together in small saucepan over low heat to warm gently before serving. Omit butter from French toast or pancakes—not needed. *Approximately 40 calories per tablespoon.*

## LOW-SUGAR BLUEBERRY "SYRUP"

**1 pint fresh or defrosted blueberries**
**⅓ cup water**
**5 tablespoons fructose syrup or maple syrup**
**1 teaspoon lemon juice**

Combine ingredients in a heavy pan with a tight-fitting cover. Cover and simmer 3 to 4 minutes over low heat. Serve warm over pancakes, French toast, low-fat frozen yogurt or vanilla ice milk. Pour leftover syrup into a jelly jar; cover and refrigerate. Reheat the syrup by uncovering the jar and placing it in a pan of hot water. *Approximately 1⅔ cups, 20 calories per tablespoon.*

**Sugar-Free:** Omit syrup. Increase water to ½ cup. Remove from heat and stir in sugar substitute equal to 5 tablespoons sugar (or to taste). *Under 10 calories per tablespoon.*

# SLIM GOURMET BLINTZES

You don't have to be Jewish to love blintzes. But you'd better be skinny, because blintzes are plenty fattening, prepared according to usual Jewish-mother tradition.

What's a blintz? A pancake fried in fat, filled with a rich cheese mixture, then browned in butter and served with sour cream or jam (or both!). Sounds fattening? You better believe it.

If you don't believe in fattening recipes, you can still be a blintz freak, thanks to our Slim Gourmet version. Since our recipe is naturally high-protein and full of good dairy nutrition, even a Jewish mother would approve.

We've made our batter with more eggs and less flour, then cooked them— crêpe-style—in a nonstick skillet sprayed with vegetable coating for no-fat frying. Our filling is based on low-fat cottage cheese, and more egg—but no sugar. Then we bake our blintzes in the oven.

To top your blintzes, we suggest sugar-free preserves, drained juice-packed pineapple, or one of the low-fat sour cream substitutes (sour dressing) sold in some areas.

 3 cups flour
 1 teaspoon butter-flavored salt
 ½ cup skim milk
 ½ cup water
 3 eggs
 1 egg white
   Blintz Filling (recipe below)

Combine flour and salt, stir in milk and water gradually; add eggs and egg white, and beat smooth.

Spray a 6-inch nonstick skillet with cooking spray. Pour about 2 tablespoons batter into pan. Tip and roll pan to cover bottom. Cook about 1 minute, until top dries. Turn out on towel, browned side down. Repeat until all batter is used.

Put spoonful of Blintz Filling on each pancake. Fold in sides. Roll to make envelope. At serving time, reheat in oven. Serve topped with low-fat sour dressing or low-calorie preserves, if desired. *About 18 filled blintzes, 125 calories each.*

BLINTZ FILLING
 3 cups low-fat cottage cheese
 2 tablespoons granulated sugar substitute
 ½ teaspoon butter-flavored salt
 ¼ teaspoon bottled lemon rind
 1 egg yolk

Blend well; use to fill blintzes.

# SKINNY CRÊPES

You don't need special skill—or even a special skillet—to make crêpes! You don't need high-calorie ingredients, either.

Crêpes are nothing more than skinny pancakes, made so thin and flexible that they can be filled and rolled up. Like pancakes, the batter can be made with no additional fats or oil, and cooked on a nonstick griddle without grease. If the fillings and toppings are also lean, your crêpes will be low-calorie and suitable for waistline watchers.

Unlike pancakes, crêpes need to be made one at a time. Any small skillet or omelet pan can be used, if it has a nonstick surface. If the batter seems to become too thick, thin it with a tablespoon or two of skim milk or water.

 1 **large egg**
⅓ **cup skim milk**
⅓ **cup water**
½ **cup flour**
 **Pinch of salt**
½ **teaspoon baking powder (optional)**

Beat egg, milk, and water together. Combine flour and salt and baking powder, if desired, for extra lightness. Stir into batter until smooth.

Spray the inside of a small nonstick skillet, crêpe or omelet pan with cooking spray; heat over medium flame. (Pan is hot enough when a drop of water will bounce on the surface of the pan.) Use a coffee measure (2 tablespoons) to measure batter. Pour a small amount of the batter into the center of the pan. Rotate the pan so batter spreads evenly to form a single thin pancake.

Cook 30 to 45 seconds, until surface of the pancake is dry. Turn the thin pancake by flipping it, or lift it by the edges with your fingertips or a spatula. Briefly cook the other side 10 to 15 seconds, just until lightly browned. Continue making crêpes until all batter is used. Stack crêpes with wax paper between them. *Eight 6-inch crêpes, or ten 4-inch crêpes, enough for four servings, 85 calories each serving (crêpes only).*

# STRAWBERRY-FILLED DESSERT CRÊPES
# WITH SOUR CREAMY TOPPING

One plus two and three equals four. That's the easy-to-remember recipe for protein-rich, low-calorie crêpes! One egg plus 2 tablespoons flour and 3 tablespoons milk equals 4 crêpes. Need more? Simply multiply! For a dozen crêpes, triple the recipe: use 3 eggs, 6 tablespoons flour and 9 tablespoons skim milk (a little more than half a cup).

What makes this crêpe formula different from most recipes is the higher proportion of protein-rich ingredients, milk and eggs, and the lesser amount of flour. This egg-rich mixture is really a cross between an omelet and a skinny pancake.

Here's how to make eight delicious Strawberry-Filled Dessert Crêpes in a nonstick skillet or omelet pan, using no added fat or oil:

CRÊPES
**2 large eggs**
**Pinch of salt**
**4 tablespoons all-purpose flour**
**6 tablespoons skim milk**

FILLING
**1 pint fresh strawberries**
**3 tablespoons free-pouring brown sugar or fructose or equivalent sugar substitute**
**½ cup sour cream or low-fat sour dressing**
**½ cup low-fat vanilla yogurt**

Beat eggs, salt, flour, and milk together; set aside to rest. To make crêpes with no fat added, spray a 6-inch nonstick omelet pan with cooking spray for no-fat frying, then heat over moderate flame until a drop of water will bounce on the surface.

Pour in a little of the batter, about 2 or 3 tablespoons, just enough to cover the bottom of the pan thinly when rotated. (Don't add too much batter or you'll have a pancake instead of a crêpe.) Cook about 30 seconds, then turn and brown the other side. Flip out of the pan onto a plate. Continue making crêpes, one at a time, until all the batter is used.

To make filling: Wash, hull, and slice the berries and sweeten to taste. In another bowl, stir sour cream or dressing and vanilla yogurt together until well blended. Spoon 3 or 4 tablespoons sliced berries into the center of each crêpe and add some yogurt mixture. Fold up and arrange on plates. Top with additional yogurt cream. *Eight crêpes, 105 calories each with sugar, 85 calories each with sugar substitute and sour dressing.*

Any combination of fresh fruit can be made into low-calorie dessert crêpes.

## FRUIT AND CHEESE OMELET

Breakfast, brunch, lunch, dinner, supper, or a super-nutritious dessert . . . that's the versatility of a low-calorie Fruit and Cheese Omelet prepared the Slim Gourmet way, with no fat added. In fact, this delicious omelet is so adaptable it can even be prepared with no-cholesterol egg substitute and diet cheese. Cholesterol watchers take note!

This omelet is a cinch to prepare in a double-sided omelet pan.

FOR EACH SERVING
 **2 large eggs, lightly beaten, or equivalent egg substitute**
 **¾ ounce part-skim or diet cheese**
   **Pinch of grated nutmeg**
 **¼ unpeeled McIntosh apple, sliced**
 **6 or 7 seedless green grapes, sliced**
   **Salt and pepper to taste**

For easiest omelet making, use a double-sided, hinged omelet pan with a no-stick finish. Spray inside well with cooking spray. Heat the pan over moderate flame. Pour the egg equally into each side of the pan. Cook, undisturbed, until slightly set underneath, then use a heatproof plastic scraper or flexible spatula to lift the egg slightly so uncooked portion can run underneath.

Sprinkle julienne strips of cheese on the egg mixture in the right side of the omelet pan and sprinkle lightly with nutmeg. Arrange thinly sliced fruit over the egg mixture in the other half. When cheese begins to melt, close the cheese-filled side of the pan over the fruit. Turn off the heat and allow the omelet to remain in the closed pan for 2 to 3 minutes to heat the fruit through. Season to taste (and serve with soy-seasoned cooked brown rice, if desired, or whole-grain toast). *Each omelet, 230 calories.*

**In an Omelet Pan or Skillet:** Spray the pan well with cooking spray. Heat over moderate flame. Add the beaten eggs or substitute. When underside of egg is partially set, gently lift the omelet mixture with heatproof scraper or spatula. Arrange cheese on the right side of the mixture, sliced fruit on the left, sprinkle cheese with nutmeg. When cheese begins to melt, use a flexible plastic spatula to fold the cheese half gently over the fruit half. Leave the omelet in the pan. Cover the pan with a heavy china plate and turn off the heat. Leave pan covered about 2 to 3 minutes to warm the fruit (the plate will be heated, also).

**Larger Omelet, for Two:** Double the ingredients and follow the preceding directions, using a 10-inch nonstick skillet. When omelet is ready to serve, cut it in half. While it's possible to make even larger omelets in bigger skillets, it's not recommended because the oversize becomes unwieldy to handle. However, several single omelets can be made quickly in a small nonstick omelet pan and transferred to a larger covered skillet to keep warm. Omelets can also be made one at a time and transferred to a warm oven or reheated briefly in a microwave oven.

**Other Fruit Fillings:** Substitute thinly sliced banana, strawberries, unpeeled pears, apricots, pineapple, or any fruit that's not too wet.

# 6

# GELATINS, PUDDINGS, CUSTARDS, MOUSSES, AND MOLDS

### Fresh Fruit Gelatin Desserts

Why not turn the season's bounty of fresh fruits into real-fruit gelatin desserts? These sensational, naturally sweet treats are made with plain gelatin and real fruits and juices. The taste is so much superior to the chemically colored, bubble-gum-flavored stuff that's saturated with sugar. Healthier, too!

You can use almost any combination of fruits and juices, depending on your whim and what's available. The one exception is fresh or frozen pineapple or pineapple juice, which contains an enzyme that prevents gelatin from setting properly. (But canned pineapple or pineapple juice may be used.)

To glamorize gelatin for grownups, ¼ cup brandy, rum, wine, or fruit liqueur can replace part of the liquid.

## ALL-NATURAL SUGARLESS FRUIT JEL-LOW

1 envelope plain gelatin
¼ cup cold water
1 cup boiling water
   6-ounce can undiluted frozen fruit-juice concentrate, partially thawed (any variety except pineapple)

Sprinkle gelatin on cold water. Wait one minute, until gelatin is soft. Stir in boiling water until gelatin dissolves. Stir in undiluted fruit juice until completely melted. Chill until set. *Four servings, 95 calories each.*

# STRAWBERRY-ORANGE JEL-LOW

1 envelope plain gelatin
1¼ cups cold water
    6-ounce can undiluted orange-juice concentrate, partly thawed
    Fructose or sugar substitute to equal 2 tablespoons sugar (optional)
1 pint fresh ripe strawberries
1 ripe banana, peeled (optional)

Sprinkle gelatin on cold water in a small saucepan. Wait 1 minute to soften, then heat gently, stirring frequently, until gelatin dissolves. Stir in orange juice until defrosted and mixture is thoroughly blended. Sweeten to taste, if desired. Chill in refrigerator until syrupy.

Wash, hull and slice berries. Slice banana if used. Fold fruit into thickened orange gelatin. Spoon into a mold or 6 dessert cups and chill until completely set. *Six servings, 85 calories each; fructose adds 15 calories per serving. (To serve eight add sliced banana. 75 calories, each of 8 servings with banana.)*

**Orange-Peach Jel-low:** Reduce water to 1 cup. As directed, heat with gelatin, stir in orange juice and sweetener. Substitute 3 peeled, sliced, ripe, sweet peaches for the strawberries. *Six servings, approximately 100 calories each*

# BANANA-BLUEBERRY JEL-LOW

2 small ripe bananas
1 pint fresh blueberries
¼ cup cold water or sherry
1 envelope plain gelatin
1 cup boiling water
    6-ounce can undiluted frozen unsweetened apple-juice concentrate, partly thawed

Slice bananas into a glass bowl. Top with washed blueberries.

Put cold water or sherry in mixing bowl or blender container. Sprinkle on gelatin. Wait 1 minute, until softened, then add boiling water. Stir or blend until gelatin granules are thoroughly dissolved. Add apple-juice concentrate and mix or blend well. Pour over fruit. Chill until set. *Six servings, 120 calories each with water; 130 calories each with wine.*

## AMBROSIA JEL-LOW

1 envelope plain gelatin
¼ cup cold water
1 cup boiling water
   6-ounce can frozen orange-juice concentrate, partly thawed
1 ripe banana, peeled and sliced
1 red apple, cored and diced
2 tablespoons shredded coconut

Sprinkle gelatin on cold water in blender container. Wait 1 minute, until softened, then add boiling water. Blend, scraping frequently, until gelatin granules dissolve. Add partly frozen orange-juice concentrate; blend smooth. Refrigerate about 10 minutes, until mixture is slightly thickened. Then fold in banana and apple. Spoon into a loaf pan or individual dessert dishes and sprinkle with coconut. Chill until firm. *Six servings, approximately 100 calories each.*

## BRANDIED BANANA-PEACH JEL-LOW

¼ cup plain 80-proof brandy, or cold water and 1 teaspoon brandy flavoring
1 envelope plain gelatin
1¾ cups unsweetened undiluted white grape juice, divided
2 cups thinly sliced peeled ripe peaches or unpeeled nectarines
1 medium banana, thinly sliced

Put brandy in a saucepan. Sprinkle on gelatin. Wait 1 minute, until gelatin granules soften. Add ½ cup grape juice. Heat gently until gelatin melts. Remove from heat and add remaining grape juice. Pour over fruit arranged in a bowl. Chill until set. *Six servings, 115 calories each with brandy; 90 calories each without brandy; 20 calories more per serving with nectarines.*

## REAL STRAWBERRY JEL-LOW

Strawberries are such a favorite, it's easy to forget they're one of the least-fattening nutrition-rich fruits. A whole cupful is only 55 calories, yet strawberries are high in valuable food fiber and Vitamin C. Kids love them for their jewel-bright color and tangy sweet taste.

1 envelope plain gelatin
   Approximately 1 cup cold water
1 cup sliced ripe strawberries
   Honey, sugar, or sugar substitute to taste (optional)
1 cup bottled red unsweetened grape juice

Combine gelatin and cold water in a saucepan. (Add any very ripe or crushed berries to the pan.) Wait 1 minute, then gently heat, stirring until all gelatin is dissolved. Remove from heat and stir in sweetener, if desired. Stir in chilled grape juice. Refrigerate until syrupy. Stir in sliced berries. Spoon into a bowl or 4 dessert cups. Chill until set. *Four servings, 65 calories each without additional sweetener.*

## STRAWBERRY-ORANGE JEL-LOW

**1 pint fresh ripe strawberries, washed and hulled**
**1 envelope plain gelatin**
**¼ cup 60-proof curaçao (orange liqueur), or cold water and a pinch of bottled**
    **grated orange peel**
**1 cup boiling water**
    **6-ounce can undiluted unsweetened frozen orange-juice concentrate, partly**
    **thawed**

Put washed hulled berries in a round glass bowl. Use small berries, if available; otherwise slice them in half lengthwise.

Sprinkle gelatin on liqueur or cold water in a mixing bowl or blender container. Wait 1 minute, then add boiling water. Blend or mix until gelatin dissolves. Add orange-juice concentrate; blend smooth. Pour over fruit. Chill in refrigerator several hours. Serve from the bowl. Or dip the bowl briefly in warm water, then invert on a platter to unmold. *Six servings, 110 calories each with liqueur; 85 calories each without liqueur.*

**Strawberry-Banana-Orange Jel-Low:** Follow preceding recipe, but slice a small ripe banana on top of the strawberries. Use cold water instead of liqueur. *Six servings, approximately 95 calories each.*

## CRANBERRY-BANANA JEL-LOW

**4-serving envelope gelatin mix (strawberry, cherry, raspberry)**
**1 cup boiling water**
**1 cup ice cubes and water**
**1 cup raw cranberries**
**2 ripe bananas**

Put gelatin mix in blender. Pour on boiling water. Cover and blend until dissolved. Put ice cubes in a 1-cup measure and fill with tap water. Pour into blender. Cover and blend until ice is melted. Add cranberries, cover, and blend until coarsely chopped. Chill until syrupy. Layer with banana slices in a 6-cup mold, bowl, or individual dessert cups. *Six servings, 95 calories each with regular gelatin; 45 calories each with diet gelatin.*

*(continued)*

**With Fruit Juice:** Use plain unflavored gelatin instead of sweetened artificially flavored gelatin dessert mix. Use 2 cups red grape juice instead of water and ice cubes. Follow this procedure: Sprinkle gelatin on ¼ cup grape juice in blender. Wait 1 minute, then pour on 1 cup boiling grape juice. Cover and blend until dissolved. Add remaining ¾ cup cold grape juice and cranberries. Cover and blend until cranberries are chopped. Refrigerate until syrupy. Layer with banana slices, and chill until firm. *Six servings, 100 calories each.*

## SUGARLESS STRAWBERRY STRATA

This dessert makes its own pink fizzy topping. Use frozen berries.

**½ cup undiluted unsweetened red or purple grape juice, divided**
**1 envelope plain gelatin**
**¾ cup boiling water**
**1 cup frozen whole unsweetened strawberries**

Put 2 tablespoons grape juice in blender container and sprinkle on gelatin. Wait 1 minute, then add boiling water. Cover and blend on high speed, scraping down sides of container, until all gelatin granules are dissolved. Add remaining grape juice. Cover and blend. While blender runs, add frozen berries a few at a time through small opening. Pour into 4 clear parfait glasses and chill until set. (Dessert will separate into two layers.) *Four servings, 40 calories each.*

## THREE-LAYER LOW-CAL GELATIN
## WITH FRESH FRUIT

What better way to wind up a weight-wary dinner than with a jeweled confection of fresh fruit set like gemstones in a colorful three-layer gelatin creation?

Now that nearly every supermarket sells sugar-free gelatin mixes, these pretty concoctions are no longer off-limits to the calorie-wise. Ordinary gelatin mixes are mainly sugar; the gelatin and flavoring account for only a tablespoon or so. As a result, regular gelatins are a weighty 140 calories a cupful, while the sugar-free varieties are only 16!

Here's a favorite combination: peaches, strawberries, and oranges. Any fresh fruit can be substituted—except fresh pineapple (canned is O.K.)—and the gelatin flavors and colors can suit your artistic whim. The procedure is really very simple if you follow our suggested 15-minute waiting time in preparing each gelatin layer. Winter variations can include canned (unsweetened) fruit, cubes of unpeeled apple, chunks of grapefruit, or what-have-you.

3 four-serving envelopes low-calorie gelatin: lemon, strawberry, and orange
3 tablespoons sugar or equivalent substitute, divided
3 cups boiling water, divided
3 cups ice cubes, divided
2 ripe peaches, peeled and thinly sliced
1 cup sliced fresh strawberries
2 seedless oranges, peeled and sectioned
  Yogurt Crème Chantilly (see page 175)

Prepare each gelatin layer separately, 15 minutes apart: First, prepare the lemon layer by dissolving 1 envelope (½ box) diet lemon gelatin and 1 tablespoon sugar in 1 cup boiling water. Stir in 1 cup ice cubes until dissolved. Then set in the refrigerator to chill. Wait 15 minutes, then prepare the strawberry gelatin in another bowl the same way. Chill. Wait 15 minutes, then prepare the orange gelatin and chill.

By this time the lemon gelatin will be syrupy. Pour half the lemon-gelatin mixture in the bottom of a 9-by-13-by-2-inch rectangular pan (or any 8-cup container). Arrange the peaches evenly over the top of the lemon gelatin, then pour on the remaining lemon gelatin. Chill a few minutes in the refrigerator or freezer until partially set.

Then carefully spoon on half of the syrupy-thick strawberry gelatin. Top evenly with sliced strawberries and cover with remaining strawberry gelatin. Again, chill until partially set.

Now spoon on half of the orange gelatin layer. Arrange orange sections on top and spoon on remaining orange gelatin. Chill in the refrigerator all day or overnight. To serve, cut in cubes and top with Yogurt Crème Chantilly (see page 175), if desired. *Twelve servings, 70 calories each; 60 calories each with sugar substitute.*

## Frozen Cider for Naturally Sweet Treats

Did you know that apple juice and apple cider are really the same thing? The label depends on the season: what's called "cider" in fall is called "apple juice" the rest of the year.

A good way to combine fresh taste with convenience is to buy apple juice (or cider) in frozen-concentrate form. Small, 6-ounce cans are easy to keep on hand in the freezer; they take so little room.

Frozen cider concentrate (or apple juice) can also be the base of easy, naturally sweet, no-sugar-added desserts. One of the simplest is real apple "jel-low," cider concentrate (or apple juice) turned into a gel by combining it with plain unsweetened, uncolored, unflavored gelatin. By using partially thawed apple-juice concentrate (or cider) you speed the chilling and setting. The naturally flavored apple gel can also be used as a glaze for other healthy, less-fattening desserts. Here are some easy ideas to try:

## PEACH AND APPLE JEL-LOW

**6-ounce can apple-juice concentrate**
**1 envelope plain gelatin**
**½ cup cold water**
**3 or 4 ice cubes**
**2 peaches, peeled and sliced or cubed**

Defrost apple-juice concentrate until slushy. Sprinkle gelatin on cold water in a small saucepan. Wait 1 minute, until gelatin is soft, then heat gently until dissolved. Remove from heat and stir in apple-juice concentrate until thoroughly mixed. Stir in ice cubes until melted. Mixture should be syrupy. If not, refrigerate just until mixture is partially set.

Fold in peaches. Spoon into 4 dessert cups, a glass bowl, or a 3-cup mold. Chill until firm. *Four servings, 120 calories each.*

**Raw Peach Pie:** Fill a packaged graham-cracker shell with about 3 cups peeled, sliced peaches. Prepare apple gelatin mixture as directed above, but reduce water to ¼ cup. Spoon the partially set syrupy gelatin over the peach slices until glazed. Chill until set. *Ten servings, 135 calories each.*

## REAL APPLE JEL-LOW

**6-ounce can apple-juice concentrate**
**1 envelope plain gelatin**
**¼ cup cold water**
**1 cup boiling water**
**Pinch of cinnamon (optional)**

Defrost apple juice partially, just enough so the contents will slip easily from the can. Meanwhile, sprinkle gelatin over ¼ cup cold water. Wait a few minutes until it's softened, then stir in 1 cup boiling water, until gelatin granules are thoroughly dissolved. Add cinnamon, if desired, and partially defrosted apple juice, undiluted; stir until it's melted. Refrigerate until set. *Four servings, 95 calories each.*

## FRUIT UNDER GLASS

**Apple Jel-low (preceding recipe)**
**1 ripe banana, sliced**
**1 ripe peach, peeled, sliced**
**½ cup blueberries or sliced strawberries**
**1 large (or 2 small) unpeeled purple plums, thinly sliced**

Prepare Apple Jel-low and chill just until syrupy. Spoon a little of the partially set Jel-low into a shallow glass pie plate, covering the bottom. Arrange fruit attractively over Jel-low layer. (For an interesting arrangement, slice the banana lengthwise.)

Spoon the remaining Jel-low over the fruit, covering it completely. Refrigerate until firm. *Eight servings, approximately 70 calories each.*

**Apples Under Glass** Wash, core and quarter (but do not peel) 2 red and 2 yellow eating apples. Slice wafer-thin, using the slicing disk of a food processor, if available. Substitute for the mixed fruits in preceding recipe.

**Apples and Pears Under Glass:** Substitute ripe pears for the yellow apples. *90 calories per serving.*

## SUPERFRUIT GELATIN WITH GELATIN MIXES

In these quick recipes, we combine a four-serving package of gelatin dessert mix with four cups of fresh fruit. (That's right . . . four cups!) Our dessert is such a jampack of fruit you can hardly see the gelatin. And it serves eight instead of four, spreading the sugar twice as far.

Speaking of sugar, gelatin dessert mixes are mainly that and virtually nothing else nutritionally. Except, of course, salt. Gelatin does contain protein but the amount is so scant it barely counts. A half cup of prepared gelatin dessert contains less than 2 grams of protein; you need 50 or 60 grams minimum per day. Gelatin dessert mixes are primarily sugar and calories, no vitamins or minerals, nothing of value, so the more real fruit added, the better!

Try this simple trick with any combination of real fruit and gelatin:

**4 cups mixed cut-up fresh or canned unsweetened fruit (see below)**
**1 cup boiling water**
**4-serving package fruit-flavored gelatin dessert mix (any flavor)**
**1 cup ice cubes and water**

Wash, drain, and prepare fruit. Use a compatible mixture (for example, 1 pint each of fresh blueberries and sliced fresh strawberries. Or 1 peeled, diced, seeded eating orange, 2 peeled sliced peaches, and 1 cup canned—not fresh—unsweetened pineapple chunks). Put the fruit in a glass serving bowl.

In another bowl, pour the boiling water over the gelatin dessert mix; stir continuously until dissolved. Fill a 1-cup measure with ice cubes; then fill to the top with cold water. Pour into the gelatin mixture and stir continuously until all the ice is melted. Pour the mixture over the fruit. (With so much fruit, it's not necessary to wait until the gelatin mixture is partly set.) Cover and chill several hours until completely set. *Eight servings, approximately 75 calories each.*

**Sugar-Free:** Substitute any 4-serving package of sugar-free gelatin dessert mix. *Eight servings, approximately 40 calories each (depending on the brand).*

**Superfruit N Yogurt Gel:** Follow directions in basic recipe, but substitute an 8-ounce container of plain low-fat yogurt for the cup of ice cubes and cold water. Chill yogurt in freezer 10 minutes before adding to fruit. (Additional 20 calories per serving.)

**Superfruit Molds:** Follow directions in basic recipe, but use only 1½ cups liquid. Dissolve gelatin mix in ¾ cup boiling water and add ¾ cup ice cubes and cold water. Pack a mold with 4 cups cut-up fruit. Pour gelatin mixture over fruit.

Cover loosely with plastic wrap. Set a heavy saucer or other weight on top of the plastic wrap to keep fruit submerged while the mold sets in the refrigerator several hours. To unmold, dip the mold very quickly in a larger bowl of warm water, then invert onto a serving plate.

## REAL PEACH-BANANA JEL-LOW

Here's a natural treat you can make with really ripe peaches, good not only for waistline watchers, but also for hyperactive youngsters who must avoid fake flavors and colors usually found in commercial gelatins.

Be sure peaches are really ripe. They rarely are in the store; ripen them in a brown paper bag to let the natural sweetness develop, so you won't need to sweeten them artificially with sugar.

**3 tablespoons cold water**
**1 envelope plain gelatin**
**¾ cup boiling water**
**2 large, ripe peaches, peeled, pitted, cut up**
**1 large ripe banana, peeled and sliced**

Put cold water in blender or food processor container. Sprinkle on gelatin. Wait 1 minute, then add boiling water. Cover and blend on high speed until gelatin is dissolved. Add peaches. Cover and blend smooth. Pour into bowl and chill until syrupy. Fold in sliced banana and chill until firm. *Four servings, 90 calories each.*

## QUICK PINEAPPLE YOGURT BLENDER "PUDDING"

What's almost as easy as instant pudding, yet has only half the sugar? Our Slim Gourmet pineapple pudding—an easy, no-cook sweet that uses packaged instant pudding mix as a base. We stretch it with healthy goodies like low-fat yogurt and unsweetened pineapple, and come up with a tangy treat that's not so sticky-sweet as conventionally prepared pudding mixes. It's lower in calories, too—only 125 calories a serving instead of 175. There are no artificial sweeteners in this dessert, and it's something both kids and adults will enjoy.

    20-ounce can juice-packed unsweetened crushed pineapple, undrained
1 envelope plain gelatin
¾ cup boiling water
1½ cups plain low-fat yogurt
    Pinch of salt
    4-serving envelope instant vanilla pudding mix
    Cinnamon (optional)

Measure ¼ cup juice from pineapple into blender container. Sprinkle gelatin on juice and wait 1 minute to soften. Add boiling water. Cover, and blend until gelatin granules dissolve (scrape sides of blender). Add crushed pineapple, including remaining juice; cover and blend smooth. Add yogurt and salt; cover and blend smooth. Add instant pudding mix; cover and blend smooth. Spoon into 8 dessert cups or a big bowl and chill several hours, until set. Sprinkle with cinnamon, if desired. *Eight servings, 125 calories each.*

## CHEESECAKE-FLAVORED PINEAPPLE PARFAITS

Here's another easy sweet with pudding mix and pineapple.

2 tablespoons fresh lemon juice
    20-ounce can juice-packed unsweetened crushed pineapple, drained
2 tablespoons pineapple juice from canned pineapple
1 envelope plain gelatin
¾ cup boiling water
1½ cups plain low-fat yogurt
1 cup low-fat uncreamed cottage cheese
    4-serving envelope instant vanilla pudding mix
    Pinch of salt or butter-flavored salt
1 tablespoon grated (or scant teaspoon bottled) lemon peel
6 small crushed graham crackers

Combine lemon juice and juice from canned pineapple in a blender. Sprinkle on gelatin and wait 1 minute to soften. Add boiling water; cover and blend until gelatin dissolves (scrape blender bowl). Add yogurt and cottage cheese; cover and blend smooth. Add pudding mix, salt, and lemon peel; cover and blend smooth. Put container in refrigerator 20 minutes, until thickened but not set.

Layer mixture with drained pineapple in 10 parfait glasses. Top with graham-cracker crumbs. Chill several hours before serving. Or layer pudding mixture with pineapple in a 1½-quart bowl and sprinkle top with crumbs. Chill until set; portion out servings as needed. Store, covered, in refrigerator. *Ten servings, 135 calories each.*

## RUM-RAISIN-APPLE BREAD PUDDING

If Eve really tempted Adam with apples, she must have had some rum and raisins handy! Because nothing makes apples more tempting than the scent of rum and raisins.

Here are some unforbidden treats you can make. They're calorie-shy: the alcohol calories evaporate from the rum, and the natural sweetness of the raisins minimizes the need for sugar.

10 to 12 slices completely dried-out high-fiber bread
½ cup golden raisins
2 apples, unpeeled, very thinly sliced
3 cups skim milk
4 eggs
½ cup rum
1 tablespoon vanilla extract
2 teaspoons apple-pie spice
¼ teaspoon salt
2 tablespoons honey or fructose (optional)

Bread slices should be thoroughly dry and hard (leave uncovered on a rack in an unheated oven for a few days).

Break up bread and layer in a loaf pan with raisins and apples. Press down. Beat remaining ingredients together and pour over bread. Cover pan with foil and bake in a 300-degree oven 1¼ hours. Uncover pan and raise temperature to 400 degrees. Bake 15 to 20 minutes more, just until top is crisp. Serve warm or chilled. *Eight servings, 195 calories each (210 calories each with honey).*

## ORANGE-RAISIN HIGH-FIBER BREAD PUDDING

With a number of brands of special low-calorie high-fiber breads now available in most parts of the country, an old-fashioned treat like bread pudding takes on new appeal.

4 slices high-fiber bread
6 tablespoons raisins
½ teaspoon cinnamon or pumpkin-pie spice
3 eggs
¼ cup honey
1½ cups orange juice
1 teaspoon vanilla extract
¼ teaspoon salt

Spray a small nonstick loaf pan with cooking spray. Dice bread (can be slightly stale). Combine bread with raisins in loaf pan, mixing well. Sprinkle with spice. Combine remaining ingredients in blender, processor, or electric mixer bowl, and beat until blended; pour over bread.

Set the loaf pan in a larger pan; add boiling water to the larger pan. Slide the pan into a preheated 350-degree oven. Bake 35 to 45 minutes, just until set (when a knife inserted in the center comes out clean). *Six servings, 170 calories each.*

## MIRIAM'S ORANGE PUDDING

Here's a quick and easy sugarless sweet made with fresh oranges.

**2 cups orange juice**
**2 tablespoons cornstarch**
**2 sweet oranges, peeled and sectioned**

Cook and stir juice and cornstarch until thickened. Cool slightly. Stir in orange sections. Chill in individual dessert cups or 1 large bowl. *Four servings, 105 calories each.*

**Grapefruit Pudding:** Substitute grapefruit juice and grapefruit sections for orange; sweeten to taste with granulated sugar substitute. Or combine grapefruit sections with orange juice and sweeten to taste.

## SPICED CHOCOLATE BREAD PUDDING

**4 slices high-fiber bread, diced**
**6 tablespoons golden raisins**
**½ teaspoon cinnamon or pumpkin-pie spice**
**2 cups cold water**
**3 eggs, separated**
**6 tablespoons honey**
**1 teaspoon vanilla extract**
**3 envelopes low-fat cocoa or chocolate milkshake mix**
**1 cup boiling water**
**¼ teaspoon salt**

Combine bread, raisins, and spice; stir together.

Combine cold water, egg yolks, honey, vanilla, and cocoa mix in blender, mixer bowl, or processor. Beat on high speed until well mixed; slowly add boiling water while beating. Stir into bread-raisin mixture.

Combine egg whites and salt in a clean nonplastic electric mixer bowl, with clean beaters; beat egg whites until peaks form. Gently fold egg whites into bread mixture. Turn into a 6-cup casserole which has been sprayed with cooking spray. Set the casserole in a larger pan partly filled with hot water. Put the pan in a preheated 350-degree oven and bake 50 to 60 minutes, until set. *Six servings, 200 calories each.*

## For Calorie-wise Candy Fans

Are you a candy snacker?

These sugarless treats are kidstuff-sweet, but very grown up about calories and nutrition. They're easy to make, too, using fruit-juice concentrates and dried or canned fruit, combined with gelatin. *Plain* gelatin, not the sugar-saturated stuff with phony fruit flavors!

Once you've tried a few of the recipes, you'll want to experiment using other juice concentrates, chopped nuts, or whole-grain cereals.

These "candies" can be eaten at room temperature, but because they're real food instead of sugar and chemicals, they should be kept in the refrigerator.

# PHRUIT PHUDGE

**2 six-ounce cans apple-, orange-, or grape-juice concentrate**
**7 envelopes plain gelatin**
**¾ cup boiling water**

Use any unsweetened juice concentrate *except* pineapple.

Allow juice to defrost and reach room temperature; do not dilute. Combine gelatin in a saucepan with the contents of 1 can of concentrate. Wait 1 minute, until gelatin is soft. Add boiling water, then heat and stir very gently until gelatin is melted. Remove from heat and stir in remaining can of undiluted defrosted concentrate.

Pour into 8-inch nonstick square cake pan and chill until firm. Cut into 1-inch squares. Store in refrigerator, covered. *Makes 64 squares, 15 calories each with apple- or orange-juice concentrate.*

# GRANNY'S BRANNIES

Good for what ails you!

**2 six-ounce cans undiluted apple-juice or cider concentrate**
**7 envelopes plain gelatin**
**¾ cup boiling water**
**½ cup seedless raisins or finely chopped pitted prunes or dried apricots**
**¼ teaspoon cinnamon (optional)**
**1 teaspoon vanilla extract**
**½ cup all-bran cereal**

Allow juice concentrate to defrost and reach room temperature. Combine gelatin with 1 can undiluted juice in saucepan. Wait 1 minute, then add boiling water. Heat gently until gelatin melts. Stir in remaining juice, raisins, cinnamon if used, and vanilla.

Pour into an 8-inch square nonstick cake pan and sprinkle the top evenly with bran. Chill until firm; slice into 1-inch cubes. Store in refrigerator. *Makes 64 squares, 20 calories each.*

# PINENIBBLES

**20-ounce can juice-packed crushed pineapple, undrained**
**4 envelopes plain gelatin**
**1 tablespoon honey or equivalent sweetener (optional)**
**1 teaspoon lemon juice (optional)**

Drain pineapple juice into a saucepan and add half the pineapple. Stir in gelatin. Wait 1 minute, until gelatin is softened. Heat and stir over low heat until gelatin is melted. Stir in honey and lemon juice, if desired, and remaining pineapple; mix well. Spread in an 8-inch square nonstick cake pan; chill until firm. Cut into 1-inch squares. Store in refrigerator. *Makes 64 squares, 10 calories each.*

# LOW-CALORIE CHOCOLATE PUDDING

Chocolate pudding isn't simply kid stuff. We could-be fatties love it too! Rich, sweet, chocolaty, a dish of creamy pudding really hits the spot when you long for something fattening.

Now we tell you how to make it the low-cal way, with a minimum of fat and sugar: with skim milk—half the calories of whole milk, plus extra protein

—and protein-rich egg in place of part of the cornstarch. We cut sugar calories in half by replacing part of the sweetener with no-calorie substitute.

Try this when you want to whip up something rich, without blowing your calorie budget.

**1 quart skim milk, divided**
**¼ cup cornstarch**
**½ teaspoon salt or butter-flavored salt**
**4 tablespoons plain unsweetened cocoa**
**3 tablespoons sugar**
**2 eggs**
**Sugar substitute to equal ¼ cup sugar**
**1 tablespoon vanilla**

Set aside ½ cup cold skim milk. Scald remaining milk in a nonstick pan; heat it only until bubbles appear around the edge. Combine the ½ cup cold milk with cornstarch, salt, and cocoa. Stir into hot milk. Add sugar. Cook, stirring over very low flame, until mixture thickens. Beat eggs in a mixing bowl. Gradually beat some of the hot mixture from the saucepan into the eggs. Then return the egg mixture to the saucepan; continue to cook and stir over very low heat until pudding is smooth and thick. Don't allow it to boil. When thick, remove from heat; stir in sugar substitute and vanilla. Pour into a bowl or 8 dessert dishes: chill thoroughly. *Eight servings, 105 calories each.*

**Rum or Brandy Chocolate Pudding:** Omit vanilla; use 2 teaspoons rum or brandy flavoring instead. *105 calories.*

**Mocha Pudding:** Decrease cocoa to 3 tablespoons. Add 2 teaspoons instant coffee powder. *105 calories.*

**Sugar-Free Pudding:** Omit sugar. Increase sugar substitute to an amount equal to ½ cup—check label for equivalents. *90 calories per serving.*

**With Canned Milk:** Use 2 cups canned evaporated skim milk and 2 cups water in place of fresh skim milk. Evaporated milk does not have to be scalded. *5 calories more per serving.*

**With Reconstituted Milk:** Use either instant or noninstant dry milk—the noninstant has fresher flavor. Follow package directions to reconstitute 1 quart milk. Use in place of fresh milk. *Instant milk, about 105 calories each; with noninstant, add about 5 calories per serving.*

**Frozen Chocolate Pudding:** Prepare pudding according to recipe. Cool in refrigerator. When cool, beat 2 egg whites with a pinch each of salt and cream of tartar. Then gently but thoroughly fold into the pudding. Chill in freezer until firm. Allow to soften slightly at room temperature before spooning out. *Ten servings, 90 calories each.*

# CHOCOLATE SPICE PUDDING

This is a pudding for sophisticates; it combines the zesty flavor of chocolate spice cake, the rich and creamy texture of pudding . . . but without all those calories. It's exceedingly low in fat, but rich in dairy protein. In fact, the secret ingredient in the yummy mélange is low-fat cottage cheese.

Cottage cheese? Trust me! Cottage cheese supplies the tang and texture, but there's nothing cottage cheesy about the taste. The flavor is reminiscent of fattening chocolate desserts made with sour cream. So give it a whirl. In your blender, of course. This recipe can also be used for pie filling.

**1 envelope plain gelatin**
**2 tablespoons cold water**
**1 cup boiling water**
   **Sugar substitute to equal ¼ cup sugar**
**1 teaspoon pumpkin-pie spice**
**¼ teaspoon cinnamon (optional)**
   **Pinch of bottled orange rind (optional)**
**1 cup low-fat cottage cheese**
**1 cup cold skim milk**
   **4-serving package instant chocolate pudding mix**
**7 tablespoons raisins (optional)**

Sprinkle gelatin on cold water in blender container. Wait 1 minute, then add the boiling water. Cover and blend on high speed until all gelatin granules are dissolved; scrape down the sides of the blender.

Add sugar substitute and spices: blend until dissolved. Add remaining ingredients, one at a time, in order given. Cover and blend smooth after each addition. Stir in raisins last, if desired. Spoon into 8 dessert cups and chill. Pudding will set quickly. *Eight servings, 90 calories each (raisins add 25 calories per serving).*

**Sugar-Free Version:** This recipe can also be made with sugar-free dietetic chocolate pudding mix. However, dietetic pudding requires cooking. Follow these directions:

Combine the gelatin and cold water and set aside to soften. Combine the pudding mix with 1½ cups skim milk in a nonstick saucepan and cook according to package directions. Remove from heat and stir in softened gelatin, sugar substitute, and spices.

Combine the cottage cheese with boiling water in a covered blender and beat until smooth. Then add the chocolate pudding to the blender container, cover, and blend smooth. Stir in raisins and spoon into dessert cups. Chill. *Eight servings, 80 calories each, including raisins.*

# WORLD'S EASIEST CHOCOLATE MOUSSE

If they can't let you loose near the chocolate mousse, you know how devilishly appealing this creamy concoction can be. And devastatingly fattening, too! The ingredients read like the off-limits list at a cardiac rehabilitation center: eggs, chocolate, sugar, heavy cream, even rum or a liqueur!

A final reason why chocolate mousse doesn't appear on your dinner-party menus is that it's somewhat of a fuss to make. Classic recipes call for melting chocolate in a double boiler, separating eggs, turning the yolks into a custard, whipping the egg whites, whipping heavy cream, and whisking all these separate projects into one creamy indulgence that must be chilled several hours before serving.

This new version shortcuts work as well as calories—calls for no eggs, no melted chocolate, and no cooking. It costs you only five minutes' time and under 170 calories a serving. The secret is sweet-tasting low-fat ricotta cheese, made creamy in the blender or food processor with a little bit of sugar and low-fat cocoa, then lightened with the aid of light whipped cream (the ready-to-spritz kind you buy in the supermarket. Be sure to use "light" whipped cream, not regular, and definitely not "nondairy whipped topping"!). While this mousse is still sufficiently caloric to rate as a special-occasion treat, it contains only a fraction of the calories, fat, and cholesterol of the conventional kind. And its nutrition is boosted by the lean protein and calcium found in part-skim ricotta cheese.

**1 cup part-skim ricotta cheese**
**2 teaspoons vanilla extract**
**2 tablespoons plain cocoa**
**3 to 4 tablespoons sugar (or equivalent sugar substitute)**
  **Pinch of salt**
**1 cup pressurized light whipped cream**

Combine ingredients, except light whipped cream, in food processor or blender and blend completely smooth. Spray light whipped cream into a 1-cup measure, then transfer to a bowl. Add the ricotta mixture and fold both together with a wire whisk or fork. Chill until serving time. Spoon into small stemmed glasses and garnish with fresh fruit, if desired, or a few chocolate curls. *Four servings, without garnish, 170 calories each with sugar; 135 calories each with sugar substitute.*

**Even Easier:** Don't fold whipped cream and chocolate mixture together. Instead, layer them in 4 parfait glasses, adding light whipped cream last.

**Black Forest Parfaits:** Layer chocolate mixture, thinly sliced pitted sweet cherries (about ¼ cup per serving) and light whipped cream in 6 parfait glasses. *Each serving, 130 calories with sugar; 110 calories with sugar substitute.*

*(continued)*

**Sugar-Free:** Use sugar substitute in place of sugar. Use dietetic sugar-free whipped topping mix, prepared according to package directions, in place of the whipped cream. *Each serving, 125 calories.*

**Chomocha Mousse:** Use 4 teaspoons plain cocoa and 2 teaspoons instant coffee powder instead of 2 tablespoons cocoa. *Each serving, 165 calories with sugar; 130 calories with sugar substitute.*

**Jamocha Rum Mousse:** Use 4 teaspoons plain cocoa and 2 teaspoons instant coffee in place of 2 tablespoons cocoa; substitute rum flavoring for the vanilla. *Each serving, 170 calories with sugar; 135 calories with sugar substitute.*

**Chocolate Orange Mousse:** Omit sugar and vanilla. Substitute 4 tablespoons undiluted defrosted orange-juice concentrate. Add a pinch of mixed pumpkin-pie spice, if desired. Garnish with fresh orange slices. *Each serving, approximately 160 calories.*

**Chocolate Pineapple Mousse:** Omit sugar and vanilla; substitute 4 table-spoons undiluted defrosted pineapple-juice concentrate. Garnish with diced fresh or canned unsweetened pineapple, if desired. *Each serving, 160 calories.*

**Chocolate Mousse Filling or Frosting:** Prepare any of the preceding variations and chill thoroughly before spreading on plain cake (angel cake and spon-gecake are the least fattening: *approximately 80 and 100 calories per slice, respectively*). Garnish with fresh fruit.

**Healthier Sandwich Cookies:** Spread chilled mousse mixture on graham crackers or cinnamon grahams. Better yet, add thin slices of unpeeled apple or other bits of fresh fruit. Let the kids make their own. *1 small (square) graham cracker, 30 calories; 1 tablespoon mousse, under 25 calories.*

## EASY CHOCOLATE-ORANGE MOUSSE

2 cups orange juice, divided
1 envelope plain gelatin
1 cup boiling water
1 cup low-fat cottage cheese
   4-serving package instant chocolate pudding mix

Put ½ cup cold orange juice in blender or food processor. Sprinkle on gelatin. Wait 1 minute for gelatin to soften, then add boiling water. Blend until gelatin dissolves (scrape container with a rubber spatula). Add remaining orange juice and cottage cheese; process until completely smooth. Add choco-late pudding mix; process until blended. Pour into a bowl or individual serving dishes and chill until set. (Garnish with fresh orange slices before serving, if desired.) *Eight servings, 105 calories each (garnish additional).*

## SPICY CHOCOLATE MOUSSE

Frozen yogurt can be a handy ingredient in less-fattening desserts, particularly puddings, mousses, and fillings made with gelatin. In these easy blender sweets, the frozen yogurt helps to quick-chill the mixture and speed up the setting time.

1 envelope plain gelatin
1 cup cold water, divided
1 cup boiling water
½ teaspoon cinnamon
3 tablespoons honey, fructose syrup, or sugar substitute to equal 9 teaspoons sugar
1 cup frozen low-fat vanilla yogurt
4-serving envelope instant chocolate pudding mix
1 teaspoon instant coffee

Sprinkle gelatin on 2 tablespoons of the cold water in blender container. Wait 1 minute; then add boiling water. Cover and blend until gelatin dissolves. Add cinnamon and sweetener; cover and blend again.

Add remaining cold water and frozen yogurt; cover and blend smooth. Add chocolate pudding mix and coffee; cover and blend smooth. Refrigerate until set. *Six servings, 120 calories each; with sugar substitute, 95 calories per serving.*

## CREAMY ORANGE MOUSSE

Simply delicious, yet simple to make . . . that's our Slim Gourmet blender-easy Orange Mousse. It looks and tastes like a creamy concoction from a fancy French restaurant, yet it's made with no cream whatsoever, no sugar, butter, or eggs either! This magic mousse is made with lean, nutrition-rich foods like low-fat cottage and ricotta cheese and orange-juice concentrate. Because the orange-juice concentrate is so sweet—naturally—only a small amount of additional sweetener is needed. We use fructose syrup (available at health-food stores), but you could use honey or no-calorie sugar substitute. We've also tried this recipe using tangerine-juice concentrate, with equally delectable results. You might like to try it in other variations (except frozen pineapple juice; the enzyme in pineapple will interfere with the thickening).

The mousse is a lovely dessert by itself, even better (and healthier) when combined with fresh fruits, and makes a fancy filling for our mini-caloried cream puffs.

6-ounce can undiluted orange-juice (or tangerine-juice) concentrate
1 tablespoon plain gelatin
2 tablespoons cold water
2 tablespoons orange liqueur or cold water
1 cup boiling water
1 cup low-fat creamed cottage cheese
¼ cup part-skim ricotta cheese
2 teaspoons vanilla extract
Pinch of grated or bottled orange or lemon peel (optional)
4 tablespoons liquid fructose syrup, or 5 tablespoons honey, or equivalent
    sugar substitute
Cinnamon (optional)
Orange or tangerine sections for garnish (optional)

Allow juice concentrate to defrost slightly.

Sprinkle gelatin on cold water and orange liqueur, if desired, in the blender container. Allow it to soften while you heat 1 cup water to boiling. When gelatin is soft, add the boiling water. Cover blender and process at high speed, scraping often with a rubber spatula, until gelatin granules are completely dissolved. Add cottage cheese and ricotta. Cover and blend until completely smooth. Add vanilla, citrus peel, if desired, sweetener and partly thawed fruit juice. Cover and blend until fruit juice is completely melted and mixture is thoroughly blended.

Pour into a bowl and sprinkle with cinnamon, if desired. Cover and chill 6 to 8 hours, until mousse is the texture of pudding. Garnish with fresh orange or tangerine sections, or other fruit, if desired. Spoon into wine glasses or dessert cups to serve. *Eight servings, 145 calories each; 105 calories less per serving if using no-calorie sweetener.*

## ORANGE CREAM PUFFS

Creamy Orange Mousse (preceding recipe)
¼ cup butter (or margarine)
¾ cup water
½ teaspoon salt
1 cup sifted all-purpose flour
4 eggs

Prepare Orange Mousse filling ahead and chill 6 or 8 hours in refrigerator.

Combine butter and water in a nonstick saucepan over moderate heat, until butter melts and water boils. Lower heat and stir in salt and flour. Cook and stir until the flour mixture leaves the sides of the pan and forms a ball. Remove the pan from the heat and stir in the eggs, one at a time, beating well after each egg is added, until the mixture is smooth and glossy.

Spray a nonstick cooking tin well with cooking spray. Drop the batter by the spoonful into 16 mounds 3 inches apart. Bake, uncovered, in a preheated 400-degree oven for 45 to 50 minutes, until puffed, golden, and crisp. Remove to a wire rack until cool, then chill.

To fill: Slice off the top of each puff and fill with chilled Orange Mousse mixture. Store in refrigerator. *Sixteen filled cream puffs, 145 calories each; 125 calories each with sugar substitute.*

## STRAWBERRY-ORANGE CHARLOTTE RUSSE

**Creamy Orange Mousse (see page 116)**
**Small store-bought spongecake shells**
**Fresh strawberries**
**Cinnamon**

For each serving: spoon ¼ cup chilled mousse into a small spongecake shell. Top with ¼ cup sliced fresh strawberries. Sprinkle with cinnamon. *Each serving: under 200 calories; 170 calories with sugar substitute.*

## POTS DE CRÈME DE CACAO

**3 tablespoons crème de cacao (chocolate liqueur)**
**1 envelope plain gelatin**
   **Sugar substitute to equal 1 tablespoon sugar (optional)**
**¾ cup hot black coffee**
**1 cup 98 or 99 percent fat-free chocolate ice milk**

Combine liqueur and gelatin in blender container. Wait 1 minute, then add sweetener, if desired, and hot coffee. Cover and blend until gelatin granules are dissolved. Add ice milk, cover, and blend smooth. Pour into 4 custard cups and chill until set. If desired, unmold and garnish with a squirt of whipped cream and some chocolate curls. *Four servings, under 90 calories each (without topping).*

## QUICK CAPUCCINO MOUSSE

Have some coffee for dessert! You won't feel as if you're missing a sweet if the coffee treat is capuccino. What's capuccino? Dark, sweet espresso, spiked with cinnamon and lightened half-and-half with warm milk. To make our capuccino calorie-safe, we sweeten it with sugar substitute and lighten it with low-fat milk. Calorically speaking, coffee and cinnamon simply don't count.

To make capuccino you'll need espresso coffee, the dark continental blend.

*(continued)*

But you don't need an espresso maker, or any other special equipment. Brew the espresso in whatever pot or percolator you normally use, but add 2 heaping tablespoons coffee per cupful of water instead of 1.

Also add ⅛ teaspoon ground cinnamon per cupful of water. At serving time, fill the coffee cups only half full and sweeten to taste. Then lighten the coffee by filling the cups with gently warmed low-fat milk. Delicious!

Spiced espresso coffee is such a dynamite taste you might like to try the combination in a diet-wise dessert.

¼ **cup cold water**
1 **tablespoon plain gelatin**
1¼ **cups hot espresso coffee**
½ **teaspoon cinnamon**
1 **pint low-fat vanilla ice milk, regular or sugar-free**

Put cold water in blender container, then sprinkle on gelatin. Wait 1 minute, until gelatin is soft, then add hot coffee and cinnamon. Cover and blend until all gelatin granules are dissolved. Add the ice milk a little at a time. Blend, covered, after each addition. Spoon into 6 dessert cups and chill until set. Serve with whipped low-calorie topping, if desired, and sprinkle with additional cinnamon. *Six servings, 65 calories each.*

## LAYERED FRUIT MOUSSE

Here's another light dessert that's delicious, made with orange-juice concentrate and frozen strawberries, or any other combination of fruit-juice concentrate and frozen fruit, except fresh or frozen pineapple. (Pineapple enzyme interferes with the jelling action of gelatin.) You'll have 3 ounces of juice concentrate left over, which can be refrigerated and used as a "sauce" over other fruits, or combined with 9 ounces water to reconstitute as juice.

½ **of a 6-ounce can frozen orange-juice concentrate**
1 **envelope unflavored gelatin**
1 **cup boiling water**
1½ **cups frozen whole unsweetened strawberries**

Allow frozen orange-juice concentrate to defrost. (Use any juice concentrate except pineapple.) Do not dilute. Combine half of the undiluted concentrate with the gelatin in a blender container. Wait 1 minute, until the gelatin softens, then add the boiling water. Cover and blend on high speed, scraping once or twice, until all gelatin granules are dissolved. With blender running, add frozen whole berries through the small opening, a few at a time, until blended.

Pour into a glass bowl or 4 glass dessert cups, and refrigerate until set.

Dessert will set in less than an hour, and form its own foamy "whipped" topping. Garnish with fresh fruit, if desired. *Four servings, 70 calories each (using orange concentrate).*

## APPLE-WINE REFRIGERATOR MOUSSE

1 envelope plain gelatin
2 tablespoons sweet red wine
2 tablespoons orange juice
¾ cup boiling water
½ cup applesauce
½ cup low-fat plain or vanilla yogurt
1 tablespoon honey or sugar substitute to equal 4 teaspoons sugar

Put gelatin in blender container with wine and juice. Let soften 2 minutes. Add boiling water. Blend, scraping sides of container, until gelatin granules are dissolved. Add applesauce, yogurt, and honey. Blend thoroughly. (May be blended by hand.) Pour into serving dish, 4 individual dessert glasses, or mold. Chill several hours, until set. *Four servings, 65 calories each with honey, 50 calories each with sugar substitute (vanilla yogurt adds less than 10 calories per serving).*

Additional orange juice may be substituted for wine. *60 calories per serving.*

An additional ½ cup of applesauce may be substituted for yogurt. *60 calories per serving.*

## JAMOCHA SWIRL

Coffee, chocolate, and rum combined create Jamocha, a flavor favorite even in light desserts. Here's my favorite, made with gelatin and low-fat ricotta cheese. It tastes like a richly marbled mousse.

2 tablespoons plain gelatin
¼ cup cold water
1 cup hot strong coffee
⅓ cup dark or golden rum
1 cup part-skim ricotta cheese
2 tablespoons free-pouring brown sugar or molasses or honey
1 cup skim milk
 4-serving envelope vanilla instant pudding mix
1 cup low-fat ice milk (coffee, chocolate, or vanilla)
1 tablespoon plain cocoa powder
8 teaspoons cookie crumbs, from 3 chocolate wafers, crushed (optional)

Sprinkle gelatin on cold water in blender. Wait 1 minute. Meanwhile, simmer coffee and rum 1 minute. Pour coffee and rum into blender container with gelatin mixture; cover and blend until gelatin granules dissolve. Add ricotta; blend until smooth. Add brown sugar and milk; blend smooth. Add pudding mix; blend smooth. Add ice milk; blend smooth.

Pour out ⅔ cup of the mixture and combine it with cocoa, stirring until smooth. Set cocoa mixture aside at room temperature. Chill the remaining coffee mixture in the refrigerator until it begins to set and thicken. Spoon half the coffee mixture into a bowl. Add the cocoa mixture, then the remaining coffee mixture.

Swirl lightly with a knife or rubber scraper, creating a marble pattern. Return to refrigerator until set. Sprinkle with crushed chocolate-cookie crumbs, if desired. *Eight servings, 165 calories each (cookie crumbs add 10 calories per serving; replacing brown sugar with honey adds approximately 5 calories per serving).*

## EASY BLUEBERRY MOUSSE

When the fresh fruit counter at your supermarket suffers from off-season shrinkage, that's the time to check the freezer case for unsugared frozen fruits, an ideal ingredient for calorie-safe sweets.

**16-ounce bag unsweetened frozen blueberries**
**4-serving envelope grape or raspberry gelatin (regular or sugar-free)**
**1 cup boiling water**
**2 tablespoons cold water**
**1 cup defrosted whipped topping**

Thaw berries only until loose. Stir gelatin mix in boiling water until dissolved. Stir in berries and cold water. Mixture should be syrupy-thick. If not, refrigerate until slightly thickened, then gently fold in whipped topping. Chill until firm. *Six servings, 140 calories each with regular gelatin; 95 calories each with sugar-free gelatin.*

**Blueberry Mousse Pie:** Spoon filling into prepared graham-cracker pie shell and chill until set. Other berry and gelatin combinations may be substituted. *Eight servings, 190 calories each, regular gelatin; 155 calories, sugar-free.*

## BLUEBERRY FLUMMERY

1 pint defrosted unsweetened blueberries
½ cup port wine or grape juice
2½ tablespoons cornstarch
  Pinch of salt (optional)
½ cup cold water
  Sugar substitute to equal 2 tablespoons sugar (optional)
  Vanilla low-fat yogurt (optional)
  Cinnamon (optional)

Combine blueberries and wine in a heavy saucepan; heat to boiling, then lower heat and simmer 5 minutes. Stir cornstarch and salt, if desired, into cold water until dissolved; then stir the cornstarch mixture into the simmering blueberries until thickened. Remove from heat and sweeten to taste, if desired. Spoon into a bowl or individual dessert cups and chill. Top with a dollop of vanilla yogurt and a sprinkle of cinnamon, if desired. *Four servings, 105 calories each (vanilla yogurt is 12 calories per tablespoon).*

## YOGURT PEACH MOUSSE

1½ cups boiling water
  2 four-serving envelopes lemon gelatin dessert mix, regular or low-calorie
  1 cup ice cubes and water
  1 cup plain low-fat yogurt
1½ cups peeled, diced fresh peaches (about 3 peaches)
  2 tablespoons sliced almonds

Stir or blend boiling water into gelatin until dissolved. Fill a 1-cup measure with ice cubes, then add cold water to the top. Pour ice and water into gelatin mixture. Blend or stir until ice melts. Blend or stir in yogurt until thoroughly mixed. Chill mixture until syrupy, then fold in diced peaches. Sprinkle with almonds. Chill several hours, until set. *Eight servings, 130 calories each with regular gelatin; 55 calories each with low-calorie gelatin.*

## CRANBERRY YOGURT MOUSSE

  2 cups (8 ounces) raw cranberries
¾ cup water
  4-serving envelope cherry gelatin mix
1½ cups low-fat vanilla yogurt

Combine cranberries and water in a saucepan. Cover and simmer 10 minutes. Remove from heat and stir in cherry gelatin until dissolved. Cool, then refrigerate until syrupy and slightly set. Fold in vanilla yogurt and chill until firm. *Six servings, 115 calories each with regular gelatin; 70 calories each with sugar-free gelatin.*

## EASY PUMPKIN PUDDING

    2 **envelopes plain gelatin**
  ¼ **cup cold water**
 1½ **cups boiling water**
      **6-ounce can undiluted partly thawed orange-juice concentrate**
    2 **cups cooked or canned unsweetened pumpkin**
    4 **tablespoons brown sugar or equivalent granulated substitute**
    2 **teaspoons pumpkin-pie spice (or to taste)**
      **4-serving package instant vanilla pudding mix**

Combine gelatin and cold water in mixing bowl. Wait 1 minute, until gelatin softens, then stir in boiling water until completely dissolved. Stir in juice concentrate until completely melted. Beat in pumpkin, brown sugar, and pumpkin-pie spice until blended. Beat in vanilla pudding mix until completely smooth. Spoon into a bowl or individual dessert cups and refrigerate several hours. *Makes ten servings, 115 calories each; 95 calories each with sugar substitute.*

**Easy No-Bake Pumpkin Pies:** Prepare the preceding mixture. When partially set, spoon into two 8-inch prepared graham-cracker pie shells. Refrigerate until set. *Two pies, 16 servings, 155 calories each; 145 calories each with sugar substitute.*

## PUMPKIN CUSTARD

    2 **cups cooked or canned unsweetened pumpkin**
    4 **eggs**
  ¾ **cup skim milk**
  ¾ **cup honey**
    4 **tablespoons all-purpose flour**
  ¼ **teaspoon salt**
    2 **teaspoons vanilla extract**
 1½ **teaspoons pumpkin-pie spice**

Beat ingredients together in electric mixer bowl or blender. Pour into baking dish. Place the dish in a larger baking dish containing 1 inch boiling water. Place in preheated 400-degree oven and bake 1 hour, or until a knife inserted in the center comes out clean. Chill before serving. *Eight servings, 180 calories each.*

## PUMPKIN-GINGERSNAP LAYERED MOUSSE

Here's a no-bake refrigerator pumpkin mousse that's layered with ginger-snaps. It looks and tastes like a rich, moist layer cake, with the creaminess and flavor of traditional pumpkin pie. It's easy to whip up in your blender.

¼ **cup cold water**
1 **envelope plain gelatin**
1 **cup boiling water**
1 **egg**
1 **cup part-skim ricotta cheese or uncreamed pot cheese**
1¼ **cups cooked or canned plain pumpkin**
4 **tablespoons easy-pouring brown sugar**
3 **tablespoons sugar**
1 **teaspoon vanilla extract**
½ **teaspoon apple-pie spice or cinnamon**
¼ **teaspoon salt**
4 **ounces thin ginger snaps**

Put cold water in blender container and sprinkle on gelatin. Wait 1 minute, until gelatin is soft, then add boiling water. Cover and blend until gelatin granules dissolve. While blender runs, add the egg through the small opening.

Uncover blender and add ricotta. Cover and blend until all graininess disappears. Add remaining ingredients, except ginger wafers, and blend smooth.

To assemble dessert: Put a layer of the mousse mixture in the bottom of a loaf pan. Top with a single layer of ginger wafers, broken up to fit. Add another layer of mousse, then more broken wafers. Continue adding layers of mousse and broken wafers; the top layer should be mousse. Cover and chill several hours until set. Cut into thin slices to serve. *Ten servings, 130 calories each with ricotta (110 calories each with pot cheese).*

**With Graham Crackers:** Substitute broken-to-fit cinnamon graham crackers for the gingersnaps. Omit apple-pie spice; substitute ¾ teaspoon pumpkin-pie spice, or ¼ teaspoon each ground ginger, cloves, and nutmeg.

**Sugar Reduced:** For all or part of the sugar substitute granulated low-calorie sweetener, the kind you use spoon for spoon in place of sugar. *Approximately 25 calories less per serving.*

## PUMPKIN-YOGURT MARBLED MOUSSE

    1 quart low-fat frozen vanilla yogurt
 1½ cups cooked or canned unsweetened pumpkin (not pie filling)
  ¼ cup skim milk
 1½ teaspoons pumpkin-pie spice
    3 tablespoons brown sugar, honey, or equivalent no-calorie sweetener (op-
       tional)
    8 gingersnaps or cinnamon graham crackers, crushed into crumbs

Transfer frozen yogurt from freezer to refrigerator until it's softened slightly (like soft-serve frozen custard or yogurt). Combine pumpkin, milk, spice, and sweetener in a large bowl. Add soft frozen yogurt and gently fold together until marbled.

Spoon into 10 parfait glasses and sprinkle with crumbs. Cover and freeze solid. Soften briefly at room temperature before serving. Or pile into a solid pie pan (no holes in the bottom). Sprinkle the top with crumbs; cover and freeze. Soften before cutting into wedges. *Ten servings, 110 calories each (brown sugar or honey adds about 15 calories per serving).*

## NONDAIRY LIGHT CARROT KUGEL
## (NOODLE PUDDING)

Rosh Hashanah is one of the sweet lover's favorite Jewish holidays. It's traditional to start off the new year with dishes sweetened with fruit, honey, and other good-tasting things. Unfortunately, a heavy hand with calories can bring a new meaning to the "Day of Atonement."

If you're a Slim Gourmet cook, you can celebrate without caloric excess, and still keep the taste of tradition. One sweet-but-healthy ingredient that's a traditional part of Rosh Hashanah goodies is good old carrots.

This nondairy version of kugel is made with shredded carrots and fine noodles. It's particularly appealing to the eye.

    1 cup cooked and drained fine noodles
  ½ cup shredded carrot
       8-ounce can juice-packed crushed pineapple, drained
    4 tablespoons golden raisins
    2 eggs, lightly beaten, or equivalent egg substitute
    2 tablespoons brown sugar or 1 tablespoon honey (optional)
  ½ teaspoon ground cinnamon

Mix all ingredients lightly but thoroughly. Place mixture in a nonstick 8-inch baking dish which has been sprayed with cooking spray. Bake 30 minutes in a preheated 350-degree oven, or until set. Let stand 5 minutes before cutting into serving portions. *Six servings, 105 calories each; with sugar or honey, approximately 15 calories more per serving; with egg substitute, 15 calories less per serving.*

# EGGNOG MOUSSE

I hate to be a party pooper, but the cheerless news about eggnog is that this calamitous concoction contains everything you've been told to avoid. I mean everything: booze, butterfat, sugar, eggs, cholesterol . . . and calories! At nearly 500 calories or more a cupful, eggnog (with booze) is one of the most anti-diet devastations ever dreamed up. Caloric-wise, it's the holiday equivalent of the piña colada (another calorie- and cholesterol-laden drink that dieters should avoid).

Now that I've delivered such Scrooge-like news, let's restore some holiday spirit with calorie-sparing desserts based on the flavor of eggnog. These cool and creamy desserts capture the taste . . . without all the fat and calories!

1 envelope plain gelatin
1 cup water, divided
¼ cup brandy
1 egg
4 ice cubes
  Pinch of salt
5 tablespoons sugar
1 teaspoon vanilla
1½ cups part-skim ricotta cheese
  Pinch of ground nutmeg
  Diced oranges or other fresh fruit garnish (optional)

Sprinkle gelatin in blender; add ¼ cup cold water. Set aside. Meanwhile, combine brandy with remaining ¾ cup cold water and heat to a rolling boil (to evaporate alcohol calories). Pour into blender. Cover and blend until gelatin is dissolved. With blender running, add raw egg through small opening and blend until mixed. Add ice cubes and blend until melted. Add salt, sugar, vanilla, and ricotta; cover and blend until all graininess disappears and mixture is liquid.

Pour into a glass bowl and sprinkle with nutmeg. Chill until set. Spoon into dessert dishes (or eggnog cups). Garnish with oranges, seedless grapes, fresh strawberries, or other fruit, if desired. Eat with a spoon. *Six servings, 120 calories each (mousse only).*

**Eggless:** Substitute equivalent liquid no-cholesterol egg substitute for egg; or omit egg and add 3 additional tablespoons ricotta. *Approximately 5 calories less per serving.*

*(continued)*

**With Rum:** Substitute dark rum for the brandy; use brown sugar or granulated brown-sugar substitute for the sugar.

**Sugar-Free:** Substitute granulated sugar substitute for the sugar. *40 calories less per serving.*

**Nesselrode Pudding:** Follow the basic recipe using rum instead of brandy, if desired. When mixture begins to set, stir in 1 cup mixed diced dried fruit (you may cut fruit into tiny pieces with a sharp knife or scissors). Spoon into individual dessert cups, if desired; chill until set. *Eight servings, 160 calories each.*

## BANANA-RUM TRIFLE WITH GRAHAM CRACKERS

Eggnog Mousse (preceding recipe)
6 large rectangular cinnamon graham crackers
1 very ripe banana
  Orange or pineapple garnish (optional)

Prepare the preceding basic recipe using rum; chill just until mixture begins to thicken. Spoon some of the mixture into a loaf pan; add a layer of graham crackers (broken to fit, if necessary); add a layer of mousse mixture and a layer of sliced bananas. Add another layer of mousse, graham crackers, and a final layer of mousse. Chill until set. Garnish if desired. *Ten servings, 120 calories each (without garnish).*

## AMBROSIA FLAN

6 tablespoons well-drained juice-packed crushed pineapple
1 cup skim milk
8 tablespoons flaked coconut
3 eggs
4 very ripe bananas, mashed
2 teaspoons vanilla extract
  Dash of salt
  Nutmeg and cinnamon

Put the drained pineapple in the bottom of a casserole. Combine the milk and coconut in a small nonstick saucepan. Cook and stir over very low heat until mixture simmers. Simmer 2 minutes. Meanwhile, beat eggs in a large bowl. Gradually beat in hot milk mixture. Beat in bananas, vanilla, and salt.

Turn the mixture into the casserole and sprinkle the top with cinnamon and nutmeg. Place the casserole in a shallow pan partly filled with hot water. Place the pan in a preheated 350-degree oven; bake about 30 minutes, or until the custard is set. Serve warm or chilled. *Six servings, 165 calories each.*

## Rice Pudding

Rice pudding is an old-fashioned sweet that has a lot to offer nutrition-conscious moderns when it's made the low-calorie way. These recipes are protein-rich, with the good dairy nutrition of eggs and fat-free milk. The sweetness comes from raisins and calorie-free sugar substitutes.

# HIGH-PROTEIN SUGAR-FREE RICE PUDDING

3 cups skim milk
4 tablespoons raw rice
¼ teaspoon salt or butter-flavored salt (optional)
6 tablespoons raisins
1 egg, beaten
1 teaspoon vanilla extract
  Sugar substitute to equal ½ cup sugar
  Pinch of bottled orange or lemon peel
¼ teaspoon cinnamon

Combine milk, rice, and salt, if desired, in a heavy nonstick saucepan (or in the top of a double boiler). Cover and cook over very low heat (or over boiling water) for 1 hour. Stir in raisins in the last 10 minutes of cooking. Remove from heat and stir in egg. Cook and stir over low heat 1 to 2 minutes. Remove from heat and stir in vanilla, sugar substitute, and peel. Sprinkle with cinnamon and chill. *Eight servings, 90 calories each.*

# QUICK LO-CAL RICE PUDDING

2½ cups skim milk
1 cup dry quick (instant) rice
¼ teaspoon cinnamon
6 tablespoons raisins
¼ teaspoon salt or butter-flavored salt (optional)
2 whole eggs, lightly beaten
1 teaspoon vanilla extract
  Sugar substitute to equal 6 tablespoons sugar
  Nutmeg

Combine first 5 ingredients in a heavy nonstick saucepan over very high heat. Cook and stir until boiling. Lower heat to a gentle simmer and continue cooking for 15 minutes, stirring occasionally. Slowly pour the hot mixture into the beaten eggs, beating continuously. Stir in vanilla and sugar substitute. Sprinkle with nutmeg and chill. *Six servings, 210 calories each.*

# WINTER PEACH RICE PUDDING

2 eggs or 4 egg whites
2½ cups skim milk
  1 tablespoon arrowroot or cornstarch
    Dash of salt
  1 teaspoon vanilla extract or almond flavoring
  3 tablespoons honey or fructose (optional)
1½ cups leftover cold cooked rice (unseasoned)
 12 dried peach halves, sliced in thin julienne strips
    Cinnamon, nutmeg, or apple-pie spice

Beat together eggs, milk, arrowroot, salt, vanilla, and sweetener, if desired. Stir in rice and peaches. Spoon into baking dish. Sprinkle with spice. Bake uncovered at 325 degrees for 50 to 60 minutes, or until set. *Eight servings, about 135 calories each without sweetener; about 155 calories with sweetener; 15 calories less per serving with egg whites.*

**With sugar substitute:** Follow preceding recipe, omitting honey. After pudding is baked, stir sugar substitute equivalent to 4 tablespoons sugar into the pudding, just until blended. *135 calories per serving.*

# SPICED CHOCOLATE RICE PUDDING

If your store carries sugar-free chocolate-drink mix, here's a zesty rice pudding you can make!

2½ cups water
  3 single-serving envelopes sugar-free chocolate milk, milkshake, or hot
      cocoa mix
  1 cup dry quick (instant) rice
  6 tablespoons raisins
  ½ teaspoon brandy or rum flavoring or vanilla extract
  ½ teaspoon butter-flavored salt (optional)
  ½ teaspoon pumpkin-pie spice
  2 eggs, lightly beaten

In a heavy nonstick saucepan, heat water to boiling. Stir in chocolate mix until dissolved. Stir in all remaining ingredients, except eggs. Simmer over very low heat, stirring occasionally, for 12 to 15 minutes. Slowly pour hot mixture over eggs, beating continuously. Chill. *Six servings, 200 calories each.*

# SUGAR-FREE REFRIGERATOR RICE PUDDING

**1 envelope plain gelatin**
**2 cups skim milk, divided**
**½ cup dry quick (instant) rice**
   **Sugar substitute to equal 3 tablespoons, or to taste**
**½ cup raisins**
   **Pinch of salt**
   **Nutmeg or cinnamon**

Sprinkle gelatin on ¼ cup skim milk to soften. Meanwhile, combine remaining milk with rice. Gently heat to a simmer. Remove from heat and stir in softened gelatin until dissolved. Stir in sugar substitute, raisins, and salt. Spoon into a small loaf or cake pan and sprinkle with nutmeg or cinnamon. Chill in refrigerator until set. *Six servings, 100 calories each.*

**Fruit-Juice Rice Pudding (milk-free):** Follow preceding recipe, substituting apple, orange, or canned pineapple juice (not fresh or frozen pineapple juice) for the milk. Omit sugar substitute, if desired. *Approximately 110 calories per serving.*

# 7

# CHEESECAKES AND OTHER EASY CHEESY TREATS

## Cottage-Cheese Desserts

Cottage cheese is healthful. Natural and nutritious. Low in fat and calories. High in protein. And just plain boring. A victim of its own virtue!

If you can't stand the sight of cottage cheese it's because something as saintly as cottage cheese wasn't meant to be seen naked. Yet that's the way most people see it: piled up in a penitent mound next to a hamburger—where the french fries are supposed to go!

Cottage cheese shouldn't be taken plain, like medicine. Its real virtue is in its versatility, the welcome it affords flavors, the way it adds low-calorie nourishment and appetite satisfaction to dishes that might otherwise be off limits to waistline-watchers.

Sweet ideas you never thought of for using cottage cheese:

• Use equal parts cottage cheese and skim milk in place of cream in your favorite quiche filling. Blender-beat the cheese and milk smooth before adding other ingredients.

• Stir smooth and creamy cottage cheese into your favorite rice-pudding mixture before baking . . . and stir in extra protein.

• Blender-beat cottage cheese with gelatin dessert mix to make a pretty mold or mousse, layered with fresh or canned fruit. Combine a 4-serving envelope of gelatin mix (any flavor) with 1 cup boiling water. Blend smooth. Then add 8 ounces cottage cheese. Cover and blend smooth again. When slightly set, layer with fruit, then chill till firm.

• Mix cottage cheese with canned crushed pineapple and spread between layers of store-bought spongecake. Top with fresh or defrosted berries for an easy protein-enriched sweet.

• Keep a supply of cottage cheese for cooking stored in your freezer. (Yes, cottage cheese can be frozen—right in its own container–if you plan to cook with it!)

• Use low-fat cott<sub>age</sub> cheese as a nutritious filling for omelets and crêpes. Top with sweetened berries.

• Use cottage cheese as a topping for bread, toast, rolls, or bagels, instead of cream cheese.

• Use low-fat, protein-rich cottage cheese in place of high-calorie cream cheese to make a "cream cheese" frosting for gingerbread or spicecake. But first beat the cottage cheese smooth in the blender.

• Use low-fat cottage cheese in place of cream cheese in cheesecake recipes. (Reduce the amount of other liquids called for by 25 percent.)

• Use blender-beaten cottage cheese instead of sour cream on top of blintzes, fresh fruits, in dips, dunks, and spreads. Add a little skim milk and blender-beat smooth. Add more milk if needed.

## PEACH-FILLED CHEESECAKE

Picture a luscious dairy-rich cheesecake filled with fresh, ripe, sweet peach slices, drizzled with glistening fruit glaze.

"Please," you say. "Don't tempt me! I'm on a diet!"

Well, the delight we've just described is off the forbidden list—a grand finale dessert for only 135 calories!

CAKE
   4 egg whites
     Pinch of cream of tartar
1½ cups (12 ounces) low-fat cottage cheese
   ¼ cup vanilla yogurt
   3 egg yolks
   ¼ teaspoon salt or butter-flavored salt
   3 tablespoons sugar or 2 tablespoons fructose
     Sugar substitute to equal ½ cup sugar

FILLING
   1 cup unsweetened apple juice or white grape juice, divided
1½ teaspoons plain gelatin (½ envelope)
     Sugar substitute to equal 2 tablespoons sugar (or to taste)
   4 very ripe peaches, peeled and sliced

To prepare cake: Put the egg whites and cream of tartar in a nonplastic bowl and set aside. Combine all remaining cheesecake ingredients in a blender.

*(continued)*

Cover and blend smooth. Beat the egg whites until stiff peaks form. Pour the cheese mixture into the egg whites. Gently but thoroughly fold together; don't overmix. Spoon the mixture into a nonstick 9-inch cake pan.

Bake in a preheated 350-degree oven about 45 minutes, or until thoroughly set. Remove from oven. Cool. Chill in the refrigerator. As the cake cools it will sink down in the middle and form a depression for the filling.

To Prepare Filling: While the cheesecake bakes, put ½ cup of the unsweetened fruit juice in a small saucepan and sprinkle the gelatin onto it. Wait 1 minute, then heat gently over low heat until gelatin dissolves. Remove from heat and stir in sweetener. Then stir in remaining fruit juice. Chill in the refrigerator until syrupy.

Meanwhile, peel and slice the peaches very thin. When the cake is cold and the gelatin mixture is syrupy but not set, assemble the cake this way: Layer the sliced peaches in the depression of the cake. Then spoon on the glaze, until peaches are covered. Chill in the refrigerator until serving time. *Eight servings, 135 calories each.*

## FRESH NECTARINE-FILLED CHEESECAKE

The delicious taste of fresh nectarines deserves to be savored without cooking, so if you're keen on nectarines, you won't want to waste them by baking a pie. (If you're a waistline watcher, you certainly won't want to waste the calories, either!)

CAKE
   **12-ounce container low-fat cottage cheese**
⅓ **cup vanilla low-fat yogurt**
 2 **tablespoons honey or fructose or equivalent sugar substitute**
 3 **egg yolks**
 4 **egg whites**
   **Pinch of salt**

FILLING
 1 **cup peach or apricot nectar or unsweetened pineapple juice**
 2 **tablespoons honey or fructose or equivalent sugar substitute (optional)**
 4 **unpeeled, pitted, very ripe, sweet nectarines, thinly sliced**

To prepare cake: Combine cheese, yogurt, sweetener, and egg yolks in covered blender and blend smooth. Combine egg whites and salt in an electric mixing bowl and beat stiff. Pour the cheese mixture into egg whites and gently but thoroughly fold together. Spoon mixture into a 9-inch round cake pan or springform pan.

Bake in a preheated 350-degree oven 45 minutes. Remove from oven and cool, then chill. Cake sinks in the middle to form a depression for fruit filling. Remove cake from pan before filling.

To Prepare Filling: Simmer nectar in an uncovered saucepan until reduced by half. Remove from heat and allow to cool. Stir in sweetener, if desired.

Arrange nectarine slices in the center of the cheesecake, overlapping. Coat with fruit nectar glaze. Return to refrigerator and chill thoroughly. *Nine servings, about 145 calories each with honey or fructose; 120 calories each without.*

# PINEAPPLE-TOPPED STRAWBERRY CHEESECAKE

Strawberry cheesecake? Or pineapple? If you can't make up your mind, this dessert relieves you of decisions. It's both! Also low-calorie and cholesterol-wise. No eggs, a minimum of fat, and very little sugar. You can even make it totally sugar-free by choosing a diet gelatin dessert mix instead of the regular mix called for in the ingredient list.

If you like this diet dessert, you might like to experiment with other combinations: pineapple gelatin in the filling and canned pitted cherries in the topping, for example. Or lemon gelatin and peach topping.

CRUST
**⅔ cup graham-cracker crumbs**
**2 tablespoons diet margarine**

STRAWBERRY CHEESE FILLING
**1 cup boiling water**
**4-serving envelope strawberry gelatin dessert mix (regular or low-calorie)**
**3 cups low-fat cottage cheese**
**Sugar substitute to equal 4 tablespoons sugar**
**½ teaspoon butter-flavored salt**

PINEAPPLE TOPPING
**8-ounce can juice-packed pineapple, undrained**
**2 teaspoons lemon juice**
**2 teaspoons arrowroot or cornstarch**
**Sugar substitute to equal 2 tablespoons sugar**

To prepare crust: Lightly combine graham-cracker crumbs and diet margarine and press firmly onto the bottom of an 8-inch springform pan. Chill in refrigerator.

To prepare filling: Stir boiling water into gelatin mix until dissolved. Cool in refrigerator until lukewarm.

Put the cheese, sugar substitute, and salt in blender; cover and beat smooth. Add gelatin mixture a little at a time, blending smooth.

Spoon into chilled crust and refrigerate until firm. Meanwhile, prepare topping.

To prepare topping: Combine topping ingredients, except sugar substitute, in a saucepan. Cook and stir until thickened. Remove from heat and stir in sugar substitute. Cool in refrigerator 15 minutes. When topping is cool and cake is firm, spread the topping on the cheesecake and refrigerate 1 hour or more, until serving. *Eight servings, 165 calories each, with regular dessert mix, 130 each with low-calorie gelatin.*

## FRENCH APPLE-CHEESE TART

     8-inch frozen pie shell
 3 apples, peeled, cored, thinly sliced
 5 tablespoons golden raisins
 1 teaspoon cinnamon
 ½ teaspoon nutmeg
     Granulated sugar substitute to equal 4 tablespoons sugar or equivalent
        fructose
 ½ cup skim milk
 ½ cup uncreamed cottage cheese
 2 eggs
 2 tablespoons honey
 2 teaspoons vanilla extract
 1 teaspoon lemon juice
     Pinch of grated lemon peel

Allow pie shell to defrost at room temperature. Remove it from its foil pan by carefully folding in quarters. Unfold it in a round nonstick 9-inch straight-sided cake pan. Center the pastry, then press it to fit with your fingertips, starting in the center. Use gentle pressure to stretch the pie shell up the sides of the cake pan.

Combine the sliced apples, raisins, cinnamon, and nutmeg; mix lightly. Spoon into the pie shell. Sprinkle with sugar substitute. Combine remaining ingredients in blender or food processor and blend smooth. Pour over apple filling. Bake uncovered on the bottom rack of a preheated 425-degree oven for 15 minutes. Lower heat to 325 degrees and bake an additional 25 to 30 minutes, or until cheese topping is set. *Ten servings, 150 calories each; 165 calories each with fructose.*

## APPLE-CHEESE DANISH "PIE"

Danish pastry is what you really want, but cottage cheese is what you should be eating, according to your bathroom scale.

Cottage cheese for breakfast? What an awful way to wake up!

Take heart, would-be skinnies. We've got a pair of breakfast treats that taste like Danish pastry, but nourish like cottage cheese. They're made with cottage cheese and other protein-powered dairy goodies like milk and eggs, touched with the sweet taste of fruit.

They're filling but nonfattening, and extra-easy to whip up in your blender. And, like Danish pastry, these breakfast treats can double as a dessert or snack —but a filling snack that will keep you safe from hunger for several hours.

> 7 **round milk lunch crackers**
> **20-ounce can unsweetened presliced apples, undrained**
> 4 **tablespoons sugar**
> **Sugar substitute to equal 1 cup sugar**
> 1 **teaspoon cinnamon**
> 3 **tablespoons raisins**
> 1 **cup low-fat cottage cheese**
> 1 **whole egg**
> ½ **cup skim milk**

Arrange crackers in an 8-inch nonstick cake pan, 6 in a circle and 1 in the center (crackers need not be touching). Stir apples, sugar, sugar substitute, cinnamon and raisins together and spoon over crackers.

In covered blender, beat cottage cheese, egg, and milk smooth. Pour over apples. Bake in a preheated 350-degree oven 1 hour. Serve warm or chilled. *Eight servings, 155 calories each.*

## TANGY PINEAPPLE "CREAM" PIE

> 1 **cup drained canned unsweetened pineapple tidbits**
> **8-inch ready-to-fill commercial graham-cracker pie shell**
> **Pineapple juice (from the canned pineapple)**
> **Cold water**
> 1 **tablespoon plain gelatin (1 envelope)**
> 1 **cup boiling water**
> 1 **cup low-fat cottage cheese (uncreamed or pot-style)**
> **4-serving package instant vanilla pudding mix**
> ¼ **teaspoon cinnamon**

Drain a 15- or 16-ounce can of juice-packed pineapple tidbits and reserve the juice. Measure 1 cup of the drained tidbits; then arrange the tidbits in a single layer in the bottom of the pie shell. Pour the reserved pineapple juice into a measure and add cold water to make 1¾ cups. Set aside. (Refrigerate remaining tidbits for other uses.)

Put ¼ cup cold water in the blender container and sprinkle on gelatin. Wait 1 minute, until softened, then add boiling water. Cover and blend on high speed until gelatin granules are dissolved (scrape blender jar). Add the reserved pineapple juice–water mixture; cover and blend. Add the cottage cheese; cover and blend smooth. Add the instant pudding mix; cover and blend smooth. Mound mixture over pineapple in pie shell and sprinkle with cinnamon. Chill several hours, until set. *Ten servings, 135 calories each.*

## FRESH ORANGE-PINEAPPLE-COCONUT "CREAM" PIE

1 large eating orange
  8- or 9-inch ready-to-fill graham-cracker pie shell (commercial or home-made)
1 cup cold water, divided
1 envelope plain gelatin
1 cup boiling water
1 cup canned unsweetened pineapple juice (not fresh or frozen)
1 cup low-fat uncreamed cottage cheese
¼ teaspoon coconut flavoring (optional)
1 tablespoon grated orange peel (from orange)
  4-serving package vanilla instant pudding mix
2 tablespoons shredded unsweetened dried coconut

Peel the orange and cut into chunks. Pick out seeds, if any, with the top of a sharp knife as you slice the orange. Arrange the orange chunks in a single layer in the bottom of the pie shell. Set aside.

Meanwhile, put ¼ cup cold water in the blender container and sprinkle on the gelatin. Wait 1 minute, until softened. Then add boiling water; cover and blend on high speed until gelatin dissolves (scrape blender jar). Add remaining ¾ cup cold water, the pineapple juice, and cottage cheese; cover and blend smooth. Add coconut flavoring, if desired, grated orange peel, and pudding mix; cover and blend smooth. Mound mixture over orange chunks in pie shell. Sprinkle the top lightly with shredded coconut. Chill several hours until set. *Ten servings, 150 calories each.*

## HONEY-APPLE QUICHE

As a sweetener, honey has more calories than sugar, but it's so much sweeter that you need fewer calories' worth of honey to do the same job sugar would do.

Honey has a distinctive flavor that combines well with sugar substitute. Blend and you have the basis of some tasty, calorie-saving sweets!

1 frozen 8-inch pie crust
3 cups peeled, sliced apples or 20-ounce can unsweetened apples (*not* pie
    filling)
¼ cup honey
1 tablespoon lemon juice
4 tablespoons raisins or currants
1 teaspoon apple-pie spice
    Sugar substitute to equal 4 tablespoons sugar
1 cup low-fat cottage cheese
1 egg
½ cup skim milk
1 teaspoon salt or butter-flavored salt
1 teaspoon vanilla extract

Remove the pie crust, still frozen, to a straight-sided 9-inch cake pan and allow it to defrost. With your fingertips, stretch the pastry as thin as possible to cover the inside of the cake pan. Trim off and discard the excess.

Stir apples, honey, lemon juice, raisins, and spice together; spoon into the cake pan. Sprinkle with sugar substitute.

Beat smooth in a blender: cottage cheese, egg, milk, salt, and vanilla. Pour over apples. Bake in a 350-degree oven 1 hour. Cool. *Eight servings, 195 calories each.*


## EASY BLENDER PUMPKIN-CHEESE PIE

    8-inch ready-to-fill graham-cracker pie shell
1 cup cooked or canned plain pumpkin
1½ cups low-fat creamed large-curd cottage cheese
3 eggs
1 tablespoon rum flavoring or vanilla extract
1½ teaspoons pumpkin-pie spice
    Pinch of salt
5 tablespoons brown sugar
    Brown or white sugar substitute equal to 4 tablespoons sugar (optional)

Unwrap pie shell. Combine remaining ingredients in blender; cover and blend on high speed until very smooth. Pour into pie shell. Bake in a preheated 275-degree oven 1 hour or more, until filling is set. Chill several hours before serving. *Eight servings, 195 calories each.*

# CINNAMON CHOCOLATE CHEESE PIE

Once the crust is ready, everything else goes into the blender, in the order given. For an even easier treat—and less fattening—skip the crust, spoon into 6 custard cups and chill several hours.

CRUST

¾ cup plain or cinnamon graham-cracker crumbs
2 tablespoons melted butter or margarine

FILLING

1 cup skim milk, divided
1 envelope plain gelatin
1 cup boiling water
  Sugar substitute to equal ¼ cup sugar
1 cup low-fat cottage cheese
  4-serving package instant chocolate pudding mix
½ teaspoon vanilla extract
½ teaspoon salt or butter-flavored salt
½ teaspoon cinnamon

To make crust: Mix together crumbs and butter. Spray a 9-inch nonstick pie pan with cooking spray for no-fat cooking, then press the crumb mixture into the sides and bottom, coating evenly.

Bake in a preheated 350-degree oven 6 to 8 minutes, watching carefully so that crust doesn't burn. Remove from oven; cool thoroughly before filling.

To prepare filling: Put ¼ cup cold milk in the blender jar. Sprinkle on gelatin to soften. Add boiling water, then cover and blend, scraping sides often, until all gelatin granules are dissolved. Add sugar substitute and blend until dissolved.

Add remaining milk and cottage cheese. Cover and blend smooth.

Add chocolate pudding mix, vanilla, salt, and cinnamon. Cover and blend smooth. Pour into cooled pie shell and chill several hours until firm and set. Serve from pie pan. *Nine servings, 130 calories each. In custard cups, without crust, six servings, 120 calories each.*

For a nice garnish, just before serving, top each cup with a tablespoon of whipped cream *(25 calories)*; whipped evaporated skim milk, prepared according to label directions *(5 calories)*; pressurized whipped cream *(10 calories)*; or sugar-free low-cal whipped topping mix made according to package directions *(5 calories)*.

## CHOCOLATE ORANGE PIE

If you've ever snitched a chocolate candy filled with orange fondant, you know that the bitterness of chocolate and the sweet tang of orange make a devilishly delightful combination. Unfortunately, candy is fattening! However, you can steal the flavor from the candy box—without all those unwanted calories—by combining chocolate and orange to flavor lower-caloried desserts.

    6-ounce can orange-juice concentrate
 1  cup low-fat cottage cheese
 ¼  cup skim milk
 1  tablespoon vanilla extract
 3  tablespoons plain cocoa
 1  teaspoon cornstarch
 5  tablespoons granulated fructose or honey
 2  eggs
    Graham-cracker or chocolate-cookie ready-to-fill pie shell
    Diced fresh orange for garnish (optional)

Defrost orange concentrate, but do not dilute. Pour it into a blender or food processor (using the steel blade). Add the cottage cheese, milk, and vanilla. Process until cottage cheese is completely smooth. Add cocoa, cornstarch, and fructose; blend smooth. Add eggs and blend with on-off motions just until smooth; pour into pie shell.

Place in a cold oven. Set temperature at 300 degrees. Bake undisturbed for 1 hour 10 minutes. Turn off oven. Leave pie in the oven, with the door slightly ajar, for 1 additional hour, or until cool. Transfer pie to the refrigerator and chill thoroughly. To serve: cut pie in 10 wedges. (Garnish with diced fresh orange, if desired). *Ten servings, 165 calories each; 10 calories more per serving with honey.*

## CHOCOLATE COOKIE PUDDING PIE

Here's a kid-pleasing treat you can put together quicker than you can say, "Clean your room."

Our Chocolate Cookie Pudding Pie is actually an icebox layer cake of skinny chocolate wafers and creamy chocolate filling. We've stretched the pudding filling with nutritious low-calorie ingredients like skim milk, cottage cheese, and gelatin. Not only do the cottage cheese and gelatin add some protein, they help provide the rich, creamy texture without cream calories. The nutritious additions double the volume with no increase in sugar, so you've created a healthier dessert with less of that bad white stuff.

We've pitched this decalorized dessert toward small fry because kids really love it. But, frankly, so do grownups—especially because it's not icky-sweet.

Why not spike it with a little brandy or rum (or flavoring) for X-rated sophistication?

> **1 envelope plain gelatin**
> **1¼ cups cold skim milk, divided**
> **1 cup boiling water**
> **Approximately 2 cups ice cubes**
> **¾ cup (½ of 12-ounce container) low-fat pot-style cottage cheese**
> **4-serving envelope instant chocolate pudding mix**
> **Approximately 16 thin round chocolate wafers**

Sprinkle the gelatin granules in the blender container. Add ¼ cup skim milk. Wait 1 minute for gelatin to soften, then add boiling water. Blend on high speed, scraping down container often, until all gelatin is dissolved.

Fill a 2-cup measure with remaining 1 cup skim milk, then ice cubes. Add to blender; cover and blend on high speed until ice cubes are melted.

Add cottage cheese; cover and blend smooth.

Add pudding mix; cover and blend smooth. (Mixture will be thick.)

Pour a little of the mixture in the bottom of a round 8- or 9-inch pie or cake pan with a nonstick finish. Arrange about 8 cookies in a single layer on top of the pudding, edges touching, with 1 cookie in the middle. Add another layer of pudding and a second layer of cookies. Cover with remaining pudding mixture. Chill several hours in the refrigerator, until set. Cut into 9 wedges to serve. *120 calories per serving.*

**Some Variations:** Any combination of cookie and pudding flavors can be used. Be sure to use thin, crisp, wafer-type cookies that aren't rich or too sweet (not too much sugar or fat means fewer calories; read the label and choose a cookie in which the main ingredient is flour, not sugar). Try vanilla wafers with chocolate pudding; lemon wafers with vanilla pudding; or double lemon: lemon wafers, lemon pudding.

**Broken Cookie Pie:** If you've got a boxful of broken cookies—the victim of a careless supermarket bagger—you can arrange the pieces between layers of the filling.

**X-Rated Cookie Pie:** For a more sophisticated grownup dessert, spike the filling with 2 tablespoons brandy or rum, or any fruit-flavored liqueur, or 2 teaspoons flavoring.

## SLIMMED-DOWN PHILLY CREAM-CHEESE CAKE

For the taste of cream cheese without all those cream calories, discover the versatility of low-calorie ("light") cream cheese. It has the taste and texture of cream cheese, but it's called "imitation" because it's made with more milk protein and less butterfat than the federal standards for cream cheese allow. Actually, it's more nutritious than the so-called "real thing."

2 tablespoons diet margarine
7 tablespoons graham-cracker crumbs
1½ packages (12 ounces) low-calorie ("light") cream cheese or Neufchâtel cheese
9 tablespoons fructose, or sugar substitute to equal ⅔ cup sugar
1½ tablespoons flour
3 teaspoons grated orange or lemon rind or a pinch of bottled rind
2 teaspoons vanilla extract
3 whole eggs
1 egg yolk
2 tablespoons skim milk

Spread the bottom and sides of an eight-inch springform pan with 2 tablespoons diet margarine. Sprinkle with crumbs and press into place. Chill in the refrigerator.

Combine remaining ingredients in a blender, cover, and beat smooth. Pour into chilled pan. Bake in a preheated 250-degree oven 1 hour. Turn off heat, open door partly, and allow cake to remain in the oven for 1 more hour.

Refrigerate. *Makes 12 servings, 140 calories each; Neufchâtel adds 20 calories per serving; sugar substitute subtracts 30 calories per serving.*

**Cherry Topping (optional):** Drain 1 pound can unsweetened pitted red cherries and reserve ½ cup juice. Combine juice, cherries, and ½ teaspoon arrowroot in a saucepan. Cook and stir until glaze thickens and clears. Remove from heat and stir in sugar substitute to taste and a few drops red food coloring, if desired. Allow to cool.

After the cheesecake is baked and cooled, spoon the cherry topping on the cheesecake and chill well. *Add 20 calories per serving.*

## SPEEDY PINEAPPLE CHEESECAKE

1 cup canned unsweetened crushed pineapple (*not* fresh)
  Pineapple juice (from the canned pineapple)
  Ready-to-fill graham-cracker pie shell
1 envelope plain gelatin
  Water
8 ounces low-calorie ("light") cream cheese or Neufchâtel cheese
1 cup frozen low-fat vanilla yogurt
  Cinnamon or apple-pie spice

Empty the crushed pineapple into a strainer over a cup to catch the juice. Press to eliminate as much moisture as possible. Spread the well-drained pineapple in the bottom of the pie shell. Reserve the juice.

Sprinkle the gelatin on 2 tablespoons cold water in the blender container. Wait 1 minute until gelatin softens. Measure pineapple juice and add water to make 1 cup; heat to boiling.

Add boiling juice mixture to the gelatin; cover and blend on high speed until gelatin dissolves. Cut cream cheese into chunks and add to blender; cover and blend smooth. Add vanilla yogurt; cover and blend smooth. Spoon into the pie shell and sprinkle with spice. Chill until set. *Eight servings, 180 calories each.*

# APPLE-CHEDDAR CHEESECAKE

Nothing goes with apple pie like Cheddar cheese. Unfortunately, a 2-ounce chunk of cheese is 230 calories, almost as fattening as the pie itself. That's because cheese is half fat. Together they add up to more calories than most dieters can afford for a whole dinner.

You can still enjoy the luscious pairing of tart apples and sharp Cheddar with this low-calorie, protein-rich apple cheesecake spiked with Cheddar.

Since namby-pampy mild Cheddar, sharp Cheddar, and super-zippy extra-sharp Cheddar all have the same high calorie count, it makes sense to choose the sharpest, meanest, nastiest Cheddar you can find! That way you get more cheese flavor for fewer fat calories.

**8 thin wafer cookies (lemon or vanilla)**
**3 apples, peeled and thinly sliced**
**¼ teaspoon apple-pie spice**
**½ cup vanilla low-fat yogurt**
**2 eight-ounce packages low-calorie ("light") cream cheese or Neufchâtel cheese**
**3 eggs**
**6 tablespoons shredded extra-sharp Cheddar**
**3 tablespoons sugar**
**Sugar substitute to equal 5 tablespoons sugar**

Arrange the cookies in the bottom of a nonstick 9-inch cake pan in a single layer, edges touching. Arrange the apples on top, and sprinkle with pie spice. Combine remaining ingredients in a blender, cover, and blend smooth. Spoon over apples.

Bake in a 350-degree oven for 45 minutes, until set. Serve warm or chilled, straight from the pan. *Ten servings, 190 calories each with low-fat cream cheese; 225 calories each with Neufchâtel.*

**Completely Sugar-Free Version:** Replace wafers with sugar-free dietetic cookies—available in health-food stores or the diet shelf of your supermarket. Replace vanilla yogurt with plain low-fat yogurt. Omit sugar; increase sugar substitute to equal 12 tablespoons or ¾ cup. Add 2 teaspoons vanilla extract to the blender. Follow assembly and baking directions in the preceding recipe.

## NO-BAKE CREAM-CHEESE PIE

Ready-to-fill graham-cracker pie shell
1 envelope plain gelatin
¼ cup cold water
2 cups skim milk
Granulated sugar substitute to equal 4 tablespoons sugar
8-ounce package low-calorie ("light") cream cheese or Neufchâtel cheese
4-serving envelope instant vanilla pudding mix
1 tablespoon lemon juice
2 tablespoons grated lemon or orange rind
¼ teaspoon salt
Strawberry Romanoff Sauce (see page 158; optional)

Unwrap pie shell and set aside. Sprinkle gelatin on cold water in a small saucepan, and set aside to soften. Combine milk, sugar substitute, and cream cheese in blender; cover and blend smooth. Add vanilla pudding mix, lemon juice, rind, and salt; cover and blend smooth. Spoon into pie shell and chill until set.

To serve: Top each slice of pie with Strawberry Romanoff Sauce (see page 158), if desired. *Ten servings, 170 calories each; 215 calories each with sauce; Neufchâtel adds 10 calories per serving.*

## PRONTO PINEAPPLE-CREAM-CHEESE PIE

This quick-setting pie filling owes some of its speed—and creamy texture—to the judicious combination of commercial ice milk and plain gelatin.

Be sure to use ice milk instead of ice cream; the calorie difference is substantial, especially in the most fat-reduced brands. Ice cream contains 10 to 25 percent fat, and 250 to 350 calories a cupful. Many ice milks, by way of comparison, are less than 185 calories. Look for calorie data and fat content on the label. In some states, there are ice milks available with less than 1 percent fat ("99 percent fat-free"—food manufacturers prefer to make positive statements!)

1 cup canned unsweetened crushed pineapple, drained
Ready-to-fill crumb crust
3 tablespoons pineapple juice (from the canned pineapple)
1 envelope plain gelatin
1 cup boiling water
Sugar substitute to equal 4 tablespoons sugar
8-ounce package low-calorie ("light") cream cheese or Neufchâtel cheese
1 cup low-fat vanilla ice milk, packed
Cinnamon

Spread the well-drained pineapple in the bottom of the pie crust. Put the 3 tablespoons juice in your blender container; sprinkle on the gelatin and wait

1 minute, until gelatin softens. Then add boiling water and sugar substitute. Cover and blend until gelatin granules are completely dissolved. Add cheese; cover and blend smooth. Add ice milk; cover and blend smooth. Refrigerate the container 15 minutes. Then pour the filling into the pie crust. Sprinkle with cinnamon. Chill until set. *Eight servings, 185 calories each.*

## EASY REFRIGERATOR CHEESE PIE

With low-fat ice milk as a shortcut ingredient, this cheese-pie filling is extra easy. With ice milk you add several basic ingredients in one step: milk, thickener, vanilla, sugar, and salt. But, most important, the ice milk chills the mixture and speeds the setting. (Most gelatin-based no-cook pie fillings take all day in the refrigerator, but this one is ready in an hour or two.)

In buying ice milk, look for the fat content; the less, the better. In some areas, 98 or 99 percent fat-free ice milk is available (by contrast, ice cream may contain 16 percent fat, or more).

Low-sugar dieters can make this dessert with dietetic ice cream. And, for an even slimmer dessert, omit the packaged piecrust, spoon the prepared filling into custard cups or parfait glasses, and chill until set.

2 tablespoons cold water
1 envelope plain gelatin
1 cup boiling water
8 ounces low-calorie ("light") cream cheese or Neufchâtel cheese
  Sugar substitute to equal 5 tablespoons sugar
  Pinch of butter-flavored salt (optional)
  Pinch of bottled lemon peel (optional)
1 cup (packed) low-fat vanilla ice milk (or diet ice cream)
  8- or 9-inch packaged graham-cracker crust
  Winter Peach Topping (optional)

Put the cold water and gelatin in your blender jar. Wait 1 minute. Add the boiling water. Cover and blend on high speed, until all the gelatin is dissolved. Add the cream cheese, sugar substitute, salt, and lemon peel, if desired. Cover and blend smooth.

Add the ice milk. Cover and blend smooth. Put the blender jar in your refrigerator for 15 or 20 minutes, until the filling begins to thicken and set.

Spoon into a prepared graham-cracker crust and chill until firm enough to slice, about 1½ hours. *Eight servings, 165 calories each with low-calorie cream cheese; 185 calories each with Neufchâtel.*

**Winter Peach Topping:** After the cheese filling is firmly set, you may like to prepare this topping:

**16-ounce can sliced sugar-free peaches (reserve juice)**
**1 cup of the juice from can of peaches**
**Water**
**1½ teaspoons (½ envelope) plain gelatin**
**2 tablespoons sugar or equivalent sugar substitute, or to taste**

Drain peach juice into a measuring cup. Add water to make 1 cup. Put 2 tablespoons of the juice into a small saucepan with the gelatin. Wait 1 minute, then heat gently over low flame, until the gelatin is melted. Stir in sugar or substitute and remaining juice. Chill until syrupy.

Arrange the peach slices on top of the chilled pie. Spoon the thickened juice over the peaches, using only as much as needed. Return to the refrigerator and chill firm. *Adds 40 calories to each of eight servings. (30 calories with sugar substitute).*

# WINTER PEACHES 'N' CREAM CHEESE PIE

Fresh peaches are among my favorite summer fruits, so it's only natural that dried peaches are among our winter favorites. A dried peach half tastes like candy, yet it's low-calorie—about 35 calories per half.

When peaches are to be cooked in winter recipes, I prefer dried to canned. They have more natural sweetness and better flavor. Peaches are picked ripe for drying but not-quite-ripe for canning (that's why commercially canned peaches look better than they taste).

If you can't find dried peaches in your supermarket, try a health-food shop or specialty food store. Dried apricots could be used in place of peaches in this recipe.

**8 dried peach halves (or 16 apricot halves)**
**½ cup peach or apricot liqueur (fruit juice may be substituted)**
**Ready-to-fill graham-cracker pie shell**
**8-ounce container low-calorie ("light") cream cheese or Neufchâtel cheese**
**½ cup skim milk**
**3 eggs**
**3 tablespoons honey or fructose or 4 tablespoons sugar**
**2 teaspoons vanilla extract**
**Pinch of salt**

Slice dried peach halves in ½-inch strips; soak in the liqueur for 30 minutes or more. Drain all the liqueur into blender container. Arrange peach slices in the bottom of the pie shell.

Add remaining ingredients to the liqueur. Cover and blend on high speed until completely smooth. Pour over peaches. Bake in a preheated 300-degree oven about 50 minutes, until filling is set. Turn off heat; open oven door and allow pie to cool slowly. Chill thoroughly before serving. *Eight servings, about 250 calories each; 15 calories less per serving with fruit juice in place of liqueur; 15 calories more per serving with Neufchâtel.*

## ITALIAN CHOCOLATE-CHIP CANNOLI PIE I

These two pie fillings are sophisticated chocolate-cheese blends based on cannoli, the rich Italian pastry filled with creamy ricotta cheese spiked with liqueur. We use white crème de cacao for these fillings. The liqueur adds chocolate flavor and sweetness but no brown color or alcohol calories. Because the filling is baked, the alcohol calories cook off, leaving only the sweetness and flavor.

In our first version we use pot cheese (dry cottage cheese) instead of the higher-caloried ricotta.

**12-ounce container low-fat pot cheese (dry cottage cheese)**
**2 eggs**
**½ cup white crème de cacao liqueur**
**Sugar substitute to equal ¼ cup sugar**
**¼ teaspoon bottled orange peel (optional)**
**2 egg whites**
**⅛ teaspoon salt**
**3 tablespoons miniature chocolate chips**
**Ready-to-fill graham-cracker pie shell**

Combine first 5 ingredients in blender; cover and beat smooth. Meanwhile, combine egg whites and salt in a nonplastic mixer bowl; beat stiff with an electric mixer. Gently but thoroughly fold in the cheese mixture; then gently fold in chocolate chips. Spoon into pie shell and bake in a preheated 325-degree oven 1 hour. Chill before serving. *Eight servings, 180 calories each.*

## CANNOLI PIE II

This version is somewhat higher in calories, because of the more fattening ricotta cheese. Be sure to choose a part-skim brand.

**15-ounce container part-skim ricotta cheese**
**2 eggs**
**½ cup crème de cacao liqueur**
**Sugar substitute to equal ¼ cup sugar**
**⅛ teaspoon salt**
**3 tablespoons miniature chocolate chips**
**Ready-to-fill packaged graham-cracker crust**

Combine first 5 ingredients in covered blender and beat smooth. Mix in chocolate chips. Pour into pie shell and bake in a preheated 300-degree oven 1 hour. Cool at room temperature, then chill. *Eight servings, 195 calories each.*

# ITALIAN CHOCOLATE-BANANA STRATA

Picture layers of chocolate and ripe banana separated by a creamy liqueur-spiked filling. That's our Italian Chocolate-Banana Strata, a cross between a mousse and an old-fashioned icebox cake.

 1 envelope plain gelatin
 ¼ cup white crème de cacao liqueur
 3 cups ice-cold skim milk
 ¾ cup part-skim ricotta cheese
 ⅛ teaspoon salt or butter-flavored salt
 3 or 4 ice cubes
   4-serving box vanilla instant pudding mix
12 chocolate icebox cookies
 1 large ripe banana, sliced

Sprinkle gelatin on liqueur and set aside to soften. Combine milk, ricotta, and salt in blender; cover and blend completely smooth.

Gently heat gelatin in liqueur until it melts. Add to blender and blend smooth. Add ice cubes and blend until ice is melted. Add pudding mix and blend smooth. (Mixture should be thick. If not, chill in refrigerator a few minutes and it will thicken.)

Arrange 6 cookies in the bottom of a loaf pan. Add a layer of the pudding mixture, a layer of bananas, more pudding mixture, a layer of the remaining cookies and then the remaining pudding mixture. Chill 12 hours, until set and the flavors are blended. *Ten servings, 150 calories each.*

**Sugar-Free Version:** Use a 4-serving envelope of dietetic sugar-free vanilla pudding mix and dietetic chocolate cookies. Substitute 2 teaspoons brandy or rum flavoring mixed in ¼ cup cold water in place of chocolate liqueur. Because dietetic pudding mix is not "instant" and needs cooking, follow this procedure:

1. Soften gelatin in cold water mixed with brandy (or rum) flavoring; set aside.

2. Prepare pudding mix with 2 cups skim milk, according to package directions.

3. Remove from heat and combine hot pudding, ricotta cheese, and soft gelatin in covered blender and blend smooth.

4. Chill in refrigerator until slightly thick.

5. Layer with bananas and cookies in a loaf pan.

6. Chill until set.

*Ten servings, 110 calories each.*

# ONE-EGG CREAM-CHEESE CUSTARD

Here's a bake-and-chill "custard" that's made with low-calorie cream cheese and only one egg, so it has less cholesterol than the real thing. Our "custard" is also less fattening.

3 cups skim milk
1 envelope plain gelatin
2 tablespoons cornstarch
1 egg
  8-ounce package low-calorie ("light") cream cheese or Neufchâtel cheese, cut in chunks
½ cup honey
2 teaspoons vanilla extract
1 teaspoon grated orange rind
¼ teaspoon salt
  Nutmeg

Combine ingredients, except nutmeg, in blender. Cover and blend smooth. Pour into a glass ovenproof casserole or nonstick loaf pan. Sprinkle top with nutmeg. Bake in a preheated 325-degree oven 1 hour. Cool, then refrigerate several hours. Serve chilled, topped with chopped fresh fruit or Strawberry Romanoff Sauce, if desired. *Ten servings, 135 calories each; 15 calories more per serving with Neufchâtel.*

# HEARTLESS COEUR À LA CRÈME

Quick, what goes with strawberries? Shortcake? If you were French you'd say "fromage blanc." American translation: cottage cheese. So why not be fashionably French—and figure conscious—and combine strawberries with lean, low-calorie fromage blanc? Perhaps you're familiar with the fancy French dessert Coeur à la Crème, a stylized version of cottage cheese and berries. The cottage cheese is blended with heavy cream and packed into a special perforated heart-shaped mold. After it's allowed to drain, the heart-shaped cottage cheese is unmolded and garnished with fresh berries. You can get the same flavor without the fuss (and heavy cream calories) in our "heart-less" version, no special mold needed.

1 cup low-fat cottage cheese
½ cup part-skim ricotta cheese
  Pinch of salt
2 pints fresh strawberries or 1 pint fresh strawberries and 10 ounces frozen unsweetened strawberries

¼ cup honey or fructose or equivalent sugar substitute
1 cup pressurized whipped cream (or light whipped cream in aerosol can, if available)
½ cup low-fat vanilla yogurt

Beat together cottage cheese, ricotta, and salt with an electric mixer. Spoon into a glass bowl or individual dessert cups or parfait glasses.

Wash and hull 1 pint fresh berries (leave whole if small, or cut in halves). Wash and hull remaining berries (or defrost, if frozen) and puree in the blender. Combine whole and pureed berries and sweeten to taste. Spoon berry mixture over cheese mixture.

Spray chilled cream into a 1-cup measure. Empty into a larger bowl and gently fold together with the yogurt. Top dessert with yogurt mixture. (Garnish with a few whole berries, if desired.) Chill until serving time. *Ten servings, 110 calories each (approximately 30 calories less per serving with alternative ingredients).*

## PEACH-CHEESE DESSERT FONDUE

2 cups ice-cold skim milk
1 cup low-fat cottage cheese
  4-serving envelope instant vanilla pudding mix
1 teaspoon cinnamon (or to taste)
8 peeled ripe, sweet peaches or unpeeled nectarines, sliced
  Juice of 1 lemon

Combine cold milk and cottage cheese in blender, cover, and beat completely smooth. Add pudding mix and beat smooth. Pour into a bowl and sprinkle with cinnamon. Surround with fresh fruit slices, which have been lightly tossed with lemon juice. Spear the fruit with party toothpicks or use fondue forks. Dip the fruit slices in the cold sauce to eat. *Eight servings, 140 calories each with peaches, 180 with nectarines.*

**Peach-Cheese Strata:** Prepare the dipping sauce and chill. Layer in parfait glasses with sliced fresh peaches, nectarines, or other fruit.

**Winter Peaches and Creamed Cottage Cheese:** Slice dried peach halves into bite-size chunks and mix into low-fat cottage cheese (use 4 halves per cup of cottage cheese). Allow the mixture to chill several hours before serving (peaches will absorb moisture and will flavor the cheese). Season to taste with a few drops of vanilla or almond flavoring, a dash of cinnamon or pie spice, a shake of honey or sugar substitute. *Total calories: 305 (without honey).*

## SPEEDY STRAWBERRY CRÈME PARFAIT

½ cup low-fat cottage cheese
½ cup thinly sliced fresh strawberries, sweetened with 2 teaspoons honey or fructose syrup or equivalent sugar substitute
¼ cup plain or vanilla low-fat yogurt
2 tablespoons pressurized whipped cream (or pressurized light whipped cream)

Spoon ingredients into 2 parfait glasses or dessert cups, in the order given. Refrigerate until serving time. *Two servings, approximately 105 calories each (20 calories less per serving with sugar substitute).*

## "CHEESECAKE" PARFAITS

1¼ cups cold skim milk
1 cup low-fat cottage cheese
4-serving envelope instant vanilla pudding mix
4 unpeeled pitted ripe nectarines, thinly sliced

Combine milk and cottage cheese in covered blender; blend smooth. Add pudding mix; blend smooth. Chill in refrigerator until thickened.
Layer cheese-pudding mixture with sliced nectarines in 8 stemmed parfait glasses and chill until serving time. *Eight servings, 125 calories each.*

## BRANDY-APRICOT CHEESE SQUARES

1 tablespoon butter or margarine
½ cup graham-cracker crumbs
1 pound low-fat pot cheese (dry cottage cheese)
⅓ cup apricot brandy or liqueur
3 eggs
3 tablespoons honey or 4 tablespoons sugar
Pinch of salt
1½ ounces golden raisins
½ cup dried apricot halves, cut in strips
Sugar substitute to equal 2 tablespoons sugar (optional)
Pinch of ground cinnamon or pumpkin-pie spice (optional)

Spread 1 tablespoon butter on the bottom of a nonstick 8-inch square or round cake pan. Sprinkle on the graham-cracker crumbs and press firmly onto the bottom.

In a blender container, combine the cheese, brandy, eggs, honey, and salt. Cover and blend smooth, scraping down sides well.

Pour half the mixture into the pie shell. Cover with the raisins, apricot strips, and sugar substitute, if desired, sprinkling evenly over the filling. Pour on remaining filling, covering all the fruit. Sprinkle the surface with spice, if desired.

Bake in a preheated 325-degree oven 45 to 55 minutes, until set. Cool. Cut into squares or wedges to serve. *Eight servings, 190 calories each.*

## PINEAPPLE-CHEESE BREAKFAST SQUARES

**8 or 9 plain or cinnamon graham crackers**
**1 cup unsweetened crushed pineapple**
**1 cup evaporated skim milk**
**4 eggs**
**1 teaspoon salt**
**2 teaspoons vanilla**
**5 tablespoons sugar**
**Sugar substitute to equal 1 cup sugar**
**2 tablespoons cornstarch**
**2 cups low-fat cottage cheese**
**Cinnamon**

Break up graham crackers and arrange to cover the bottom of a nonstick 8-inch square cake pan. It's not necessary that the bottom be completely covered. Cover the crackers with a thin layer of well-drained pineapple. Combine remaining ingredients, except cinnamon, in a blender. Cover blender and beat smooth. Pour mixture over pineapple and sprinkle with cinnamon.

Bake in a preheated 250-degree oven for 1 hour, then turn off the heat and let it cool in the oven. Refrigerate. *Eight squares, 190 calories each.*

## BLUEBERRY-TOPPED "CREAM CHEESE" TARTS

One of the fun things to do with farmer whipped "cream cheese" and blueberries is to make it into berry-topped tarts or fresh-fruit sandwich cookies. You can make those up ahead of time, or just serve the makings and let the kids help themselves. (Actually, you don't have to be a kid to enjoy this sweet and creamy blueberry treat. I like to serve crackers, a crock of whipped farmer cheese, and fresh berries as a light dessert, and let my guests make their own "grownup Oreos.")

FOR EACH TART
**1 milk lunch cracker or other large nonsweet cracker, or graham cracker**
**1 tablespoon low-calorie ("light") cream cheese or farmer whipped "cream cheese" (see page 236)**
**2 tablespoons fresh raw blueberries**

Spread each cracker with "cream cheese." Arrange blueberries (as many as will fit) in concentric circles on the cheese. Serve immediately, or refrigerate until serving time. Or simply serve crackers, a crock of farmer whipped "cream cheese" and a bowl of chilled fresh blueberries, and let the snackers create their own fresh fruit tarts. *Each tart, approximately 85 calories.*

## BLUEBERRY-FILLED SANDWICH COOKIES

If there's anything that can lure kids away from junk jelly, it's the berries! Especially blueberries. Instead of spreading cream cheese (or peanut butter) sandwiches with sweet purple goo, substitute a layer of fresh, sweet berries instead. The kids will love it!

**Arrowroot biscuits, or thin vanilla or lemon wafers**
**Low-calorie ("light") cream cheese or farmer whipped "cream cheese" (see page 236)**
**Fresh blueberries**

Spread each cookie with 2 teaspoons "cream cheese." Arrange the raw blueberries in a single layer on a plate. Press one of the cookies into the blueberries, cheese-side down, to pick up the berries. Top with another cookie, cheese side down, to make a fruit-filled "sandwich cookie." *Approximately 40 calories per "sandwich."*

**Kid-Pleasing "Cream Cheese" and Blueberry Sandwiches:** Spread 2 slices of whole-wheat bread or toast with farmer whipped "cream cheese." Press ¼ cup fresh blueberries in a single layer onto 1 slice. Top with second slice of bread or toast. *Each sandwich, 185 calories.*

# 8

# FROSTINGS, FILLINGS, SAUCES, GLAZES, JAMS, JELLIES, AND OTHER TOPPINGS

### Nonfattening "Frosting"

Nutritious icing? Nonfattening frosting? Whoever heard of such a thing! The very idea is a paradox, a contradiction in terms. Frosting, after all, is mostly sugar—pure calories. And whatever else you add is even worse: butter, margarine, shortening . . . chocolate!

Here's a rich and creamy-tasting low-calorie "frosting base" that old country Italian cooks have known about for generations: ricotta.

Ricotta is the same thick and creamy, sweet-tasting fresh "pot cheese" that's used in making lasagne or ravioli. Its flavor is dairy-sweet and creamlike—not at all sour like yogurt or cheesy like some other fresh cheeses. Ricotta is available in supermarket dairy cases in both whole-milk and low-fat part-skim versions. Naturally, it's the latter, lower-caloried version you want to choose.

Because it's made from milk, part-skim ricotta is rich in dairy nutrition, high in both protein and calcium. A 15-ounce container of part-skim ricotta, enough to frost two layers (16 servings), is only 320 calories. Yet it contains 48 grams of protein and 1,156 milligrams of calcium (the equivalent of roughly 4 cups of milk). A can of vanilla icing, on the other hand, contains 1,992 calories, and precious little else!

How do you turn a container of ricotta into frosting? You simply empty it into a mixer bowl, blender container, or food processor and whip it fluffy, thinning with a little flavoring liquid. That's the creative part: the liquid can be defrosted fruit-juice concentrate, cider, applesauce, any favorite liqueur, or rum or brandy. Or any combination of liquids and flavorings—and sweeteners, if desired. For example: honey, maple syrup, fructose syrup, combined with lemon or lime juice, or even no-calorie sugar substitute. You can add such flavorings and extracts as vanilla, almond, walnut, coconut, or chocolate. Or you could make a milk-chocolate icing by adding cocoa powder and skim milk, or a mocha topping with cocoa and cold coffee.

Defrosted fruit-juice concentrates are sweet enough so that no added sugar or sweetener is needed. Remember that the cake your frosting goes on is sweet, and you may choose one of the less-fattening types of cake: angel food or spongecake, for example.

## WHIPPED RICOTTA

Ricotta cheese is one of the best calorie-wise cooking substitutes for heavy cream. Fresh part-skim ricotta—whipped to a creamy smoothness in your blender or food processor—adds the same dairy-fresh flavor and texture as cream, with only a fraction of the fat and calories.

Because ricotta is much denser than cream you need only half as much in cooking. Therefore, a half cup of whipped ricotta at 171 calories can replace a cupful of heavy cream at 821 calories. More good news: a cupful of heavy cream has 88 grams of fat and 326 milligrams of cholesterol, while a half cupful of part-skim ricotta has only 10 grams of fat and 38 milligrams of cholesterol —a healthier choice by far!

Empty a 15-ounce container of fresh part-skim ricotta cheese into a blender or food processor (using the steel blade) and process on high speed until smooth and creamy. Return it to the container and store in the refrigerator. Use it as a topping for fresh fruits (or vegetables), as a base for low-calorie dips, or as a creamy protein-rich spread for bread or graham crackers. *21 calories per tablespoon.*

More ricotta ideas:

## CRÈME FRAÎCHE I

**1 cup part-skim ricotta cheese**
**3 tablespoons commercial sour cream or sour half-and-half**
   **Salt or butter-flavored salt to taste (optional)**

Combine ingredients in blender or food processor. Process until completely smooth and creamy. Store in the refrigerator in a covered container. *Sixteen servings, approximately 25 calories each.*

## CRÈME FRAÎCHE II

**15-ounce container part-skim ricotta cheese**
**1 envelope butter-flavored granules**
**4 to 5 tablespoons plain low-fat yogurt**

Combine ingredients in blender or food processor. Process until completely smooth. Store in a covered refrigerator container. *Thirty-six servings, 10 calories each.*

## CRÈME FRAÎCHE III

**8-ounce package low-calorie ("light") cream cheese or Neufchâtel cheese**
**3 tablespoons fresh skim milk**
**2 to 3 tablespoons plain low-fat yogurt or buttermilk**

Cut cream cheese into cubes. Combine with remaining ingredients in blender or food processor. Process until completely smooth. Store in a covered container in the refrigerator. *Twenty servings, 25 calories each.*

## WHIPPED APPLE-CREAM TOPPING
## FOR FRUIT DESSERTS

Combine ½ cup each whipped ricotta and smooth unsweetened applesauce; stir smooth. Spray pressurized light whipped cream into ½-cup measure; add to the ricotta mixture and gently fold in with the tines of a fork (don't overmix and deflate it). Use as a topping for diced apples, sliced oranges, other fresh fruits. Makes approximately 1½ cups. *Topping: 12 calories per tablespoon.*

## DIETER'S APPLE-CREAM "HARD SAUCE"

**1 envelope (½ package) low-calorie whipped topping mix**
**½ cup cold apple juice**
**Pinch of pumpkin-pie spice**

Combine ingredients in a deep bowl and beat with electric mixer until thick as whipped cream. Chill. Approximately two cups. *Each tablespoon, 7 calories.*

## TANGY WHIPPED TOPPING FOR FRUIT I

**1 cup plain low-fat vanilla yogurt (or plain yogurt plus ½ teaspoon vanilla**
**extract and sugar substitute to equal 5 teaspoons sugar)**
**1 envelope (½ package) low-calorie whipped topping mix**

Beat together at high speed until the consistency of a thick custard sauce. Chill—mixture thickens in the refrigerator. *Makes about 1⅔ cups, 15 calories per tablespoon.*

*(continued)*

**Tangy Topping II:** Spray pressurized half-and-half or "light" whipped cream into a bowl; add an equal amount of yogurt (not sweetened yogurt or frozen yogurt); lightly fold together. Use as a dessert topping, sprinkled with cinnamon. Approximately 9 calories per tablespoon.

## BITTERSWEET CHOCOLATE SAUCE

Not only is chocolate sinfully fattening; it's almost always found in the company of other nutritionally-naughty companions: sugar, butter, cream, cake, cookies, and other foods of calorically similar ilk.

What can a figure-conscious health-minded cook do to raise the "morals" of chocolate? One way to enjoy chocolate, while giving it redeeming nutritional value, is to couple it with healthful, low-calorie ingredients like fruit and lean protein-rich dairy foods. Our favorite way to enjoy chocolate is Italian-style: in a rich and creamy sauce that's delicious with crisp cubes of fresh apple or pear or chunks of sweet orange.

You can pair this deliciously rich-tasting sauce with any combination of fruit in parfait glasses—or use it as a dipping sauce for berries or other fruit, fondue style. The nice thing about these dessert ideas is that they work on two totally different levels: as a ved-d-dy sophisticated grand finale to an elegant dinner party on the one hand, or a healthy fun treat that kids really enjoy. Either way, it's a dessert you can feel very virtuous about serving.

## BITTERSWEET CHOCOLATE CREAM SAUCE
## FOR FRESH FRUIT

> **2 squares (1 ounce each) unsweetened baking chocolate or 6 tablespoons plain cocoa**
> **¼ to ⅓ cup strong black coffee**
> **15-ounce container part-skim ricotta cheese**
> **4 tablespoons sugar or equivalent sugar substitute**
> **2 teaspoons vanilla extract**
> **Pinch of salt**
> **Butter flavoring or butter-flavored salt (optional)**

If baking chocolate is used, combine it with the coffee in a small saucepan over very low heat until melted.

Combine remaining ingredients in blender or food processor, using the steel blade. Blend until smooth. Add chocolate and coffee and blend smooth. (Thin sauce with more coffee if cocoa is used.) Cover and chill in refrigerator. Spoon over fresh fruit or use as a dipping sauce for chunks of fresh fruit. *Eight servings, 100 calories each with baking chocolate; 55 calories each with cocoa and sugar substitute.*

**Black Forest Coupe:** For each serving: Put ½ cup pitted ripe sweet cherries in a glass dish and spoon on ¼ cup Bittersweet Chocolate Sauce. (There's a handy, inexpensive gadget in kitchenware shops that neatly punches the pits out of cherries—and olives.) When fresh cherries aren't available, use frozen unsweetened (*not* canned) cherries. *Each serving, 140 calories; 95 calories with cocoa and sugar substitute.*

**Pears Helène:** Put ½ cup cubed unpeeled ripe pears into a glass dish and top with Bittersweet Chocolate Sauce (and a few chocolate curls, if desired). *150 calories per serving; 105 calories with cocoa and sugar substitute.*

**Orange Mephistopheles:** Peel and dice seedless eating oranges, catching any juice. Top each ½ cup with ¼ cup Bittersweet Chocolate Sauce. *150 calories each serving; 105 calories with cocoa and sugar substitute.*

## CHOCOLATE FRESH FRUIT FONDUE

**Bittersweet Chocolate Sauce**
**Shaved chocolate (optional)**
**4 cups fresh fruit for dipping**

Prepare sauce as directed. Pour into a bowl and garnish with shaved chocolate, if desired. Chill until serving time.

At serving time, arrange sliced or cubed fruit around the bowl. Provide long fondue forks for spearing the fruit. Suggestions: seedless eating-orange sections, large unpeeled chunks of eating apples or pears, banana chunks, seedless grapes, large whole strawberries. *Eight servings, approximately 65 calories each (depending on fruit); 10 calories less with lower-calorie Bittersweet Chocolate Sauce.*

## BEST EVER STRAWBERRY SAUCE

"That is the *best ever* strawberry sauce," exclaimed a friend, finishing her mini-sundae. "What's in it?"

"Strawberries," I replied.

"What else?"

"Nothing else."

Proving again that often the simplest things are the best. Our strawberriest of strawberry sauces was simply strawberries, whirred until chunky in the blender, then spooned over vanilla ice cream (or, in this case, low-fat ice milk). The sauce was "thickened" only by berry pulp—no flour, cornstarch, or boiled sugar syrup. The ripeness of the berries provided the bright red hue. The tangy tart sweetness and fresh flavor came from the berries themselves—and the fact that nothing else had been added to dilute the taste. Nor had anything been taken away by cooking. Not only delicious but nutritious. (Raw fruit sauces keep all their natural vitamin C, otherwise lost through cooking.)

**1 pint ripe strawberries**

Berries should be ripe and sweet. Wash and hull them. Put in a blender, and cover. Turn on and off repeatedly until berries are crushed but chunky. (Don't overblend or you'll have a smooth puree.) Use as a topping for low-fat ice milk, cottage cheese, unsweetened yogurt, spongecake, sugar-free puddings, home-made low-calorie cheesecake, pancakes or French toast, orange ice, crêpes stuffed with cottage cheese, dessert omelets, or other fresh fruit. *Four servings, 30 calories each.*

**Other "Best Ever" Fruit Sauces:** Use 2 cups pitted Bing cherries, ripe peeled peaches or apricots, fresh blueberries, blackberries or raspberries, cubed ripe mango or papaya, when available.

**For Sweeter Fruit Sauce:** Sweeten to taste with sugar substitute. Or add 1 teaspoon honey *(20 calories)* or fructose *(15 calories).*

**With Frozen Fruit:** Frozen whole berries or other loose-packed fruits without sugar may be substituted. Defrost first; retain juice.

**To Keep in the Freezer:** Add 1 tablespoon lemon juice per cupful. Defrost before using.

**Fourth of July Parfaits:** Thinly slice 2 ripe sweet bananas. Alternate layers of Best Ever Strawberry Sauce, bananas, and blueberries (about 1 cup total) in tall parfait glasses. *Four servings, 100 calories each.*

## ORANGE-PINEAPPLE SAUCE

**1 sweet eating orange**
**¼ of the orange peel**
**2 cups canned juice-packed unsweetened crushed pineapple**
  **Few drops honey, fructose, or sugar substitute to taste**

Peel and dice orange; pick out seeds. Retain about ¼ of the peel and slice it fine. Combine all ingredients in blender. Cover and blend until chunky. Use as a topping for cake, ice milk, yogurt or cottage cheese. *Six servings, 55 calories each.*

## STRAWBERRY ROMANOFF SAUCE

**6-ounce can frozen orange-juice concentrate**
**1 pint ripe fresh strawberries**
  **Pinch of grated orange or lemon peel (optional)**

Allow orange concentrate to defrost. Wash and hull berries; slice very thin lengthwise. Stir undiluted concentrate (and grated peel, if desired) into sliced berries. Chill in the refrigerator.

Use as a topping for thin slices of sponge or chiffon cake, or over frozen low-fat yogurt or ice milk. *Six servings, 80 calories each (sauce only).*

## SMASHED BERRY SAUCE

**1 pint strawberries or 10 ounces frozen unsweetened strawberries or raspberries**
**¼ cup undiluted unsweetened red or purple grape juice**

Wash and hull berries (or defrost, if frozen). Combine with grape juice in blender container or food processor, using the steel blade. Cover and process with short on-off motions just until berries are coarsely chopped, not pureed.

Use as a topping for thin slices of chiffon cake or on low-fat ice milk or frozen yogurt. *Six servings, 25 calories each with strawberries, 40 calories each with raspberries (sauce only).*

**Smashed Blueberries:** Mix 2 cups defrosted frozen berries (or other unsweetened fruit) with 2 tablespoons brandy. Store in refrigerator and use as a topping for low-fat ice milk. *Topping under 10 calories per tablespoon; ice milk about 45 calories per ¼ cup.*

**Blueberry Toddler Treat:** Baby food without sugar! Puree defrosted frozen blueberries (or a combination of fruits) in blender.

## FRESH (OR FROZEN) PEACHSAUCE

What do you do with overripe peaches? Most likely you'll avoid them—particularly if you're shopping for fruit to freeze or can. For that reason, overripe peaches (and nectarines) are usually bargain priced. Nobody wants them. However, past-prime fruit is the perfect ingredient for "peachsauce" for the freezer. "Peachsauce" is really nothing more than peach puree, which you can enjoy all year as a low-calorie topping for sundaes, a sauce for cottage cheese or yogurt, a natural fruit "syrup" for pancakes or French toast, or the flavorful base for fruit drinks, barbecue sauce . . . or anything else that could profit from real peach flavor.

Overripe peaches are even better than perfect fruit because their flavor is even sweeter and "peachier." That's because very soft peaches have developed their maximum natural sugar and flavor. The only time of year to make peachsauce is during the peach season. Off-season peaches that have become soft were never ripe to begin with. So, in looking for peaches for peachsauce, be sure to buy those that have ripened naturally and are now merely soft with just a few bruised spots (which you can cut away and discard). Avoid peaches that have become rotten or moldy. Expect to pay only half the going price, and if you're buying a quantity of the merchant's leftovers, you can usually negotiate an even lower price.

**Overripe freestone peaches or nectarines**
**Lemon juice**
**Fructose, honey, or sugar substitute (optional)**

Halve peaches and remove skin and pits. The peel of overripe peaches or nectarines should slip off easily. If not, you can simplify peeling by dropping the whole fruit in a pot of boiling water for a few seconds. Remove each peach with a fork and slip off the skin. Put the peeled, pitted peaches in the blender or food processor, using the steel blade, and puree smooth. Add 1 tablespoon fresh lemon juice for each cupful of peachsauce; this will prevent it from overdarkening. Transfer to 1-cup glass jelly jars; label and refrigerate or freeze.

Peachsauce used as a topping for ice milk or frozen yogurt needs no sweetening. Add 1 tablespoon fructose or honey or equivalent sugar substitute per cup for a sweeter peachsauce to use with cottage cheese, plain yogurt, or as a topping for tart fruit, toast, or pancakes. *Three average peaches make 1 cup peachsauce, 10 calories per tablespoon; with fructose or honey under 15 calories per tablespoon (7 calories more per tablespoon with nectarines).*

**Orange Peachsauce I:** Peel and pit 6 medium peaches. Remove skin and seeds from 2 juice oranges. Combine the fruits in a blender or food processor, using the steel blade, and blend smooth. The citrus fruit will retard darkening of the peach puree. *Makes approximately 2½ cups, 11 calories per tablespoon.*

**Orange Peachsauce II:** Puree peeled, pitted peaches. Combine each 2 cupfuls of the puree with the contents of 6-ounce can orange-juice concentrate, defrosted but undiluted. Add no sweetener. *Makes 2¾ cups, 15 calories per tablespoon.*

**Pineapple Peachsauce (Mock Mango Sauce):** Substitute 6-ounce can defrosted undiluted pineapple-juice concentrate for the orange-juice concentrate. Add no sweetener. *Makes 2¾ cups, 16 calories per tablespoon.*

**Ginger Peachy Sundaes:** Crush, pulverize, or process gingersnaps (1 for each serving) into crumbs. To assemble sundaes: Put a scoop of low-fat vanilla ice milk or frozen yogurt into a stemmed glass. Top with ¼ cup Peachsauce and gingersnap crumbs. *Each serving, 135 calories.*

**Cottage-Cheese Peachy Banana-Split Lunch:** Split a banana lengthwise and arrange 2 scoops (¾ cup) low-fat cottage cheese on the halves; top with ⅓ cup Peachsauce. *275 calories.*

**Peachy Keen Spritzer:** Combine ½ cup Peachsauce (or Orange Peachsauce) with ice cubes and seltzer in a tall glass. (Add a few whole berries or mint leaves for garnish, if desired.) *80 calories with Peachsauce; 120 calories with Orange-Peachsauce.*

**Peach Wine Kir:** Combine ¼ cup dry white wine with ¼ cup Peachsauce over ice in a tall glass. Add seltzer (and fruit garnish, if desired). *90 calories (garnish additional).*

**Oriental Basting Sauce:** For each serving of meat or poultry to be baked, barbecued, or broiled, combine ¼ cup Peachsauce with 1 tablespoon soy sauce and 2 teaspoons catsup. Mix well and spread on lean steak, chops, or cut-up chicken. Add a pinch of ground ginger, if desired. *Sauce: 11 calories per tablespoon.*

**Peach Topping or Spread:** Use plain or sweetened Peachsauce as a low-sugar (or sugarless) substitute for jam or syrup. Spread on toast, or add it to bagels or English muffins which have been topped with low-fat cream cheese. Gently heat Peachsauce and serve it with pancakes or French toast (no butter needed)

**Peach Jel-low:** Soften 1 envelope plain gelatin in 1 cup cold water, or apple or orange juice. Heat until melted. Stir in 1 cup Peachsauce. Add diced fruit, if desired. Chill until set. *Four servings, 45 calories each with water; 75 calories with juice (diced fruit additional).*

## BRANDIED APRICOT SUNDAE SAUCE

½ **cup dried apricots**
1 **cup water**
¼ **cup apricot brandy**

Simmer ingredients until fruit is thick and soft. Spoon over vanilla low-fat frozen yogurt or ice milk. Try adding a tablespoon of raisins, or cinnamon or pumpkin-pie spice to taste. *Six servings topping, about 60 calories each.*

## NO-SUGAR-ADDED CHOCOLATE-ORANGE SYRUP OR SAUCE

This sophisticated sugarless syrup makes a dandy topping for low-fat ice milk or frozen yogurt, or for crêpes or sliced fresh fruit:

6-**ounce can unsweetened orange-juice concentrate**
1 **tablespoon plain unsweetened cocoa**
1½ **teaspoons cornstarch**
¼ **cup cold water**
1 **teaspoon vanilla extract**
   **Pinch of salt (optional)**

Blend ingredients together, or combine in tightly covered jar and shake up until well blended. Pour into a small nonstick saucepan. Cook and stir over moderate heat until mixture simmers and thickens. Serve hot or chilled (thicker when chilled). *One cup, 25 calories per tablespoon.*

**Chocolate Flaming Fruit Sauce:** Prepare preceding recipe. After sauce simmers and thickens, add 2 tablespoons fruit brandy. Ignite the vapors. Spoon sauce, still flaming, over crêpes, fresh fruit, or other dessert. *25 calories per tablespoon.*

## HOT BLUEBERRY WINE SAUCE

1 **pint blueberries, fresh or unsweetened frozen**
¼ **cup Concord or other sweet red wine, or bottled grape juice, diluted with an equal amount of water**
  **Dash of cinnamon**

If berries are frozen, allow them to defrost in a saucepan, to retain juices. Add wine and cinnamon and heat to boiling. Spoon hot sauce over thin slices of chiffon cake, spongecake, or low-fat ice milk or frozen yogurt. *Six servings, 50 calories each (sauce only).*

## HOT PINEAPPLE SAUCE

  **16-ounce can unsweetened crushed pineapple, undrained**
1 **teaspoon vanilla extract**
2 **teaspoons cornstarch**
  **Dash of cinnamon or mixed apple-pie spice**
2 **teaspoons lemon juice (optional)**
  **Sugar substitute equal to 3 tablespoons sugar, or to taste (optional)**

Combine ingredients (except sugar substitute) and heat and stir until simmering. Remove from heat and sweeten to taste, if desired. Spoon over thin slices of chiffon cake or low-fat ice milk or frozen yogurt. Store extra in refrigerator and reheat as needed. *Six servings, 50 calories each (sauce only).*

## CHERRIES JUBILEE SAUCE

Cherries Jubilee is the best known of the flaming fruit desserts. Despite its flash and glamour, it's really just a hot cherry sundae. But, at the last minute, some high-proof booze is poured over the simmering cherry sauce. The rising vapor is ignited with a match and burns away in a blaze of glory. If your timing is right, you can even manage to spoon the sauce, still flaming, onto the dessert —a feast for the eye.

No reason why waistline watchers can't put on their own pyrotechnic display, using low-fat, low-calorie ice milk instead of ice cream and natural fruits and juices with no sugar added. What about the booze? The alcohol— and alcohol calories—burn away, remember? Now that really is spectacular.

16-ounce can unsweetened, pitted red cherries, undrained
1 tablespoon cornstarch
⅓ cup brandy (vodka may be substituted)

Heat and stir cherries and cornstarch together in a saucepan or chafing dish until liquid thickens and clears.

To serve: Have cherry sauce simmering in a chafing dish. Add liquor; then ignite the vapors by holding a burning long match or straw over the simmering sauce. Spoon, while flaming, over low-fat ice milk or frozen yogurt, using a long-handled ladle. *Eight servings, 45 calories each, sauce only. 1 scoop (⅓ cup) 98 percent fat-free vanilla ice milk adds 60 calories: 1 scoop frozen vanilla yogurt, approximately 65 calories.*

NOTE: To simplify serving, scoop ice milk into serving dishes ahead of time and store in freezer until ready to serve. Use caution; avoid long floppy sleeves and trailing scarves while preparing flaming dishes.

**Bananas Jubilee:** Peel 4 ripe, sweet bananas and slice into 8 glass serving dishes, and top with flaming cherries. Serve immediately. *Eight servings, 95 calories each.*

## PYROMANIAC'S PLUMS

4 large ripe, sweet unpeeled purple plums, thinly sliced
¼ cup plum wine or Sauterne
¼ cup water
¼ cup gin

Combine plums, wine, and water in a small saucepan or chafing dish and simmer until soft, about 7 to 10 minutes.

To serve: Pour gin on simmering plum sauce and ignite the vapors with a long match. Spoon flaming sauce over ice milk with a long-handled ladle. *Eight servings, 20 calories each (sauce only).*

## BRANDIED PEACH SAUCE FOR
## WARM GINGERBREAD

1 cup canned peach nectar
2 tablespoons plain brandy or 1 teaspoon brandy flavoring
1 tablespoon cornstarch

Cook and stir ingredients over low heat until thick and bubbling. Spoon over slices of gingerbread. *Sauce: Eight servings, about 25 calories each.*

# WHOLE CRANBERRY SAUCE

Fresh raw cranberries have seven times the natural food fiber of commercial jellied cranberry sauce. Why buy calorie-laden cranberry sauce that's mostly sugar when you can have the real thing?

**6-ounce can undiluted cider concentrate, thawed**
**2½ cups raw cranberries**
   **Fructose, honey or ½ cup white raisins (optional)**

Combine cider with cranberries in a heavy saucepan. Simmer uncovered over low heat until all the berries have popped open. Cool, then refrigerate. Add fructose to taste (46 calories per tablespoon), honey (64 calories per tablespoon), or sugar substitute, if a sweeter sauce is desired. Or add ½ cup white raisins (208 calories) to the cranberries before cooking. *Makes 2½ cups, 12 calories per tablespoon (without sugar or raisins).*

# WHOLE-BERRY CRANBERRY SAUCE

**1 envelope plain gelatin**
**2 cups bottled unsweetened red grape juice, divided**
**4 cups fresh cranberries**
   **Sugar substitute to equal ½ cup sugar**

Soften the gelatin in 3 tablespoons grape juice and set aside. Combine remaining grape juice with cranberries in a saucepan and simmer, covered, until cranberries have popped open and are tender. Remove from heat and stir in gelatin mixture and sugar substitute until dissolved. Chill. *Sixteen servings, 35 calories each. (Regular cranberry sauce: 100 calories!)*

**Cherry-Cranberry Sauce:** Combine 4 cups fresh cranberries and 2 cups water in a saucepan. Cover and simmer over very low heat until cranberries have popped open. Remove from heat and stir in 4-serving package fruit-flavored gelatin until completely dissolved. cover and chill in refrigerator until set. *Ten servings, 50 calories each with regular gelatin; 20 calories, sugar-free.*

# SUGAR-FREE ORANGE-CRANBERRY SAUCE

Here's a delicious and colorful variation on the cranberry-sauce theme, a bright orange relish with confetti flecks of cranberry red.

**1 thin-skinned orange**
**½ of the orange's peel**
**1 packet liquid pectin**
   **6-ounce can undiluted orange-juice concentrate**
**1 cup raw cranberries**
   **Sugar substitute to equal 3 tablespoons sugar (optional)**

Quarter the orange and remove the peel. Discard half the peel. Cut the other half into fine strips. Combine orange, peel, pectin, and undiluted juice in blender or food processor (using the steel blade), and process until peel is finely minced. Add raw cranberries and process until finely chopped. Sweeten to taste, if desired.

Pour into 2 8-ounce jelly jars; cover and refrigerate undisturbed for 24 hours, until thick. Serve with poultry, meat, or game. Keep refrigerated. (Extra jar may be frozen.) *Approximately 15 calories per tablespoon.*

**Honey Orange-Cranberry Marmalade:** Follow preceding recipe; sweeten to taste with honey. Serve with crackers or bread. *(Recipe sweetened with ¼ cup honey makes a spread with 23 calories per tablespoon.)*

**With Gelatin Instead of Pectin:** Follow recipe, but omit liquid pectin. Sprinkle 1 envelope plain gelatin on ⅓ cup water in a small saucepan. Wait 1 minute, until gelatin softens. Then heat gently over very low flame, just until gelatin dissolves. Add gelatin to mixture in place of pectin.

**Uncooked Cranberry-Orange Relish:** Make this in your blender, grinder, or food processor. Chop 3 cups raw cranberries. Peel and cut up 1 eating orange, removing any seeds. Chop up the orange and half the peel. Stir in 1 cup raisins and sugar substitute, if desired. Chill before serving. *Ten servings, 60 calories each.*

## BAKED CRANBERRY SAUCE

You can slow-bake this in the oven along with your turkey.

**4 cups (1 quart) fresh cranberries**
**4 tablespoons water or sweet red wine**

Combine cranberries with water or wine in a casserole. Cover and slow-bake until berries pop open, about 45 minutes at 300 degrees, about 30 minutes at 325 degrees. Serve warm or chilled. The sauce is tart and tangy with no sweetener added, or sweeten with a few drops honey or sugar substitute to taste. *Eight servings, 25 calories each.*

## PINEAPPLE-CRANBERRY SAUCE

**16-ounce can crushed unsweetened juice-packed pineapple**
**4 cups fresh cranberries**
**Sugar substitute to equal ½ cup sugar (optional)**

Combine pineapple and cranberries, and simmer until cranberries pop open. Sweeten to taste, if desired. Chill. *Sixteen servings, 30 calories each.*

# EASY APPLESAUCE

One of the easiest and best sweets to serve is homemade applesauce. If peeling, coring, and cutting up apples for applesauce isn't your idea of easy, try our lazy Slim Gourmet way . . . no peeling needed! Healthier, too, because you get more of the natural high-fiber pectin when the apples are cooked with the peel. Much of the vitamin value and pectin are found in, and close to, the peels. By cooking the peels along with the apples you get a nutritional bonus. (Pectin is considered one of the most important sources of food fiber, with cholesterol-lowering benefits.)

Your applesauce will take on a rosy glow from the peels, a pretty pinkish hue *without* artificial coloring. The flavor is superior to commercial applesauce and the chunky texture is much more appetizing than the soupy kind. Most important, it's less fattening, because there's no sugar added. Our applesauce is only 50 calories a half-cup serving, instead of 115 for the sugar-saturated stuff from a jar.

Homemade applesauce has lots of uses: as a topping for low-fat ice milk (applesauce sundaes); warmed up as a sauce for breakfast pancakes or French toast (instead of calorie-laden syrup); as a fruited sweetener for plain low-fat yogurt (instead of sugary preserves).

Here's how:

**Unpeeled apples**
**Water**

Cut each apple into quarters, off center, missing the core. Then, simply slice off the core. Now, put the unpeeled apple quarters in a heavy saucepan and add 2 tablespoons water for each apple. Cover tightly and simmer until apples are soft, about 10 minutes. Allow to cool. Lift out the peels and discard them. Beat applesauce smooth or leave chunky; sweeten to taste, if desired, with no-calorie sweetener, fructose, or a few drops honey. *Each ½-cup serving is 50 calories without honey; honey adds 20 calories per teaspoon; fructose adds 15 calories per teaspoon.*

**Pineapplesauce:** Prepare a 3-pound bag of apples for cooking, as directed above. Substitute an undiluted 6-ounce can defrosted pineapple-juice concentrate for the cooking water. *Twelve servings, under 100 calories each.*

**Pineapplesauce II:** Prepare 3 pounds apples for cooking. Add an undrained 16-ounce can crushed unsweetened pineapple to the pot, and cook as directed above. Add no other liquid. *Sixteen servings, 55 calories each.*

**Double Applesauce:** To 3 pounds prepared apples add a 6-ounce can undiluted defrosted apple-juice concentrate. *Twelve servings, 95 calories per serving.*

**Cider-Spiced Applesauce:** Add 6-ounce can undiluted defrosted cider concentrate and 1 teaspoon apple-pie spice (or more, to taste). *95 calories per serving.*

**Sherry-Spiked Applesauce:** To 3 pounds prepared apples, add ¾ cup sherry (or any other white cocktail wine—how about dry vermouth?). *70 calories per serving.*

**Golden-Raisin Applesauce:** To 3 pounds prepared apples, add 1 cup golden raisins and 1 cup water. Spice to taste with cinnamon or pumpkin-pie spice. *85 calories per serving.*

**Other Variations:** Use frozen orange-juice concentrate or other fruit juice in place of the water, *95 calories per serving.* Try ¾ cup bottled red grape juice for rosier applesauce, *60 calories per serving.* Use other dried fruits instead of raisins (how about chopped-up dried apricots? *80 calories per serving*). For grownup X-rated applesauce, use brandy, rum, or red wine for the cooking liquid (the alcohol calories evaporate).

## Refrigerator Jams with Little or No Sugar

If you're a Slim Gourmet, it's easy to make jams and jellies. Any time of year. Without canning supplies. And with hardly any sugar . . . or none at all!

That's because we make our jams a few jars at a time and store them in the refrigerator. From fruit that's fresh, canned or frozen—even fruit juice.

Conventional jams and jellies are mainly empty-caloried sugar, but our spreads are mostly fruit. They're not as sweet as commercial jams, but you can always augment the sweetness with low-calorie sugar substitute, if you wish.

Use these directions as a base for experimenting with your own favorite fruits or combinations: berries, cherries, peaches, nectarines, apricots, apple, orange, or grape juice. Add the amount of sugar called for in the recipe, but no more. After the prepared spread is removed from the heat, taste-test for sweetness, then augment with sugar substitute if necessary.

Those on sugar-free diets can eliminate the sugar altogether and replace it to taste with sugar-free sweeteners; sugar isn't necessary in these mixtures. The jelling comes from natural thickeners: gelatin, arrowroot, cornstarch, or pectin.

Because these jams aren't "canned"—and lack the preserving qualities of enormous quantities of sugar—they *must* be stored in the refrigerator.

## LOW-CAL FRESH PEACH JAM

2 cups sliced peeled fresh peaches, pitted
1 envelope plain gelatin
1½ teaspoons cornstarch (or arrowroot)
3 tablespoons cold water
2 tablespoons lemon juice
6 tablespoons fructose or 9 tablespoons sugar or equivalent substitute, or
   to taste

Wash and prepare fruit. Combine gelatin, cornstarch, water, and lemon juice in a saucepan. Wait 1 minute for gelatin to soften, then heat gently and stir constantly until gelatin dissolves. Add peaches and fructose or sugar (if used); heat to boiling. Simmer, stirring constantly, for 3 minutes.

Remove from heat and stir in sugar substitute, if used, until dissolved. Use more or less to taste, according to the sweetness of the fruit. Refrigerate in covered jars. *Approximately 2 cups, 15 calories per tablespoon with fructose; 20 calories per tablespoon with sugar; 10 calories per tablespoon with sugar substitute.*

## LOW-CAL JAM WITH FROZEN FRUITS

Follow the preceding recipe, but substitute 2½ cups of frozen peaches, strawberries, blueberries, pitted cherries, or other unsweetened fruit.

## LOW-CAL ORANGE JELLY

**6-ounce can frozen orange-juice concentrate, unsweetened (apple- or grape-juice concentrate may be substituted)**
**1 envelope plain gelatin**
**1½ cups cold water**
**1 packet liquid pectin**
**4 to 6 tablespoons sugar or equivalent substitute**

Allow juice concentrate to defrost. Combine in a saucepan with remaining ingredients (except sugar substitute). Cook and stir until boiling; boil 1 minute, stirring constantly. Remove from heat; skim. Stir in sugar substitute, if used. Refrigerate in covered jars. *Approximately 2½ cups, 15 calories per tablespoon (5 calories less per tablespoon with sugar substitute).*

## BLENDER FRUIT "BUTTER"

**2 cups sliced or crushed unsweetened fruit (fresh, defrosted, or canned)**
**1 envelope plain gelatin**
**2 tablespoons cold water or fruit juice**
**½ cup boiling water or fruit juice**
**4 tablespoons fructose or 6 tablespoons sugar or equivalent substitute, or to taste**

Prepare fruit. Sprinkle gelatin on cold water or juice in blender. Wait 1 minute and add boiling liquid. Cover and blend until all gelatin dissolves. Add fruit, cover and blend smooth. Sweeten to taste. Refrigerate in covered jars. *Approximately 2¼ cups, 10 calories per tablespoon (5 calories more per tablespoon with fruit juice; 5 calories less per tablespoon with sugar substitute).*

# RAW BLUEBERRY JAM WITH LITTLE OR NO SUGAR

Must be refrigerated or frozen.

1 pint fresh blueberries
1 packet liquid pectin
2 tablespoons fresh lemon juice
4 tablespoons fructose or 6 tablespoons sugar or equivalent sugar substitute,
    or to taste

Combine ingredients in blender or food processor; cover and process until berries are pureed. Pour into 2 covered 1-cup jelly jars; refrigerate 24 hours, or until set. (Transfer one of the jars to the freezer, for later.) Jam will keep in the refrigerator 1 or 2 weeks. *Two cups, 10 calories per tablespoon without sugar (15 calories per tablespoon made with fructose or sugar).*

## EASY BLUEBERRY BREADSPREAD

Wash and drain 1 pint blueberries. Puree smooth in the blender or food processor. Sweeten to taste, if desired, with sugar substitute. Pour into a covered jar. Refrigerate several hours before using; the puree will thicken slightly and "set" into a soft-spread consistency. Store in the refrigerator. *One and a half cups, 10 calories per tablespoon.*

## SLIM SUGARLESS STRAWBERRY PRESERVES

1 envelope plain gelatin
½ cup bottled unsweetened red or purple grape juice, divided
1 quart (2 pints) fresh strawberries
1 tablespoon lemon juice

Sprinkle the gelatin over ¼ cup of the grape juice; set aside. In a saucepan, combine remaining grape juice with strawberries and lemon juice. Cook and stir uncovered, about 5 minutes. Crush the berries with a fork while they cook. Add softened gelatin mixture to the strawberries and stir until dissolved. Allow to cool, then ladle into two 8-ounce jars. Store in refrigerator or freezer. *10 calories per tablespoon.*

## RASPBERRY-ORANGE PRESERVES

2 cups fresh raspberries
2 tablespoons cold water
3 ounces (½ can) undiluted defrosted orange-juice concentrate
1 envelope plain gelatin

Cover and cook the raspberries and water 3 minutes. Uncover and break up fruit with a fork.

*(continued)*

Meanwhile, combine defrosted orange juice and gelatin. Let stand 1 minute until gelatin granules are soft. Stir the orange-gelatin mixture into the hot raspberry mixture. Cook and stir over low heat only until gelatin granules are completely dissolved. Cool and spoon into jars. Refrigerate or freeze. *Approximately 2 cups, 10 calories per tablespoon.*

## BLUEBERRY JAM WITH GELATIN

1 envelope plain gelatin
⅓ cup bottled unsweetened purple grape juice, divided
1 tablespoon lemon juice
2 pints fresh blueberries

Soften gelatin in 2 tablespoons grape juice. Meanwhile, cook and stir remaining grape juice, lemon juice, and blueberries together in an uncovered saucepan, about 5 minutes, until berries are thick and crushed. Stir in softened gelatin mixture over low heat until dissolved. Cool, then spoon into covered jars and freeze or refrigerate. *Approximately 4 cups, 10 calories per tablespoon.*

## PINEAPPLE JAM

16-ounce can unsweetened crushed pineapple
1 envelope plain gelatin

Pour juice from crushed pineapple into a small saucepan. Sprinkle on gelatin and set aside. Meanwhile puree crushed pineapple smooth in a covered blender.

Heat gelatin-juice mixture over low heat, only until gelatin dissolves, then pour into pureed pineapple. Cover and blend again. Spoon into jars and refrigerate or freeze. *Two cups, 10 calories per tablespoon.*

## BLENDER-EASY PINEAPPLE PRESERVES

1 envelope plain gelatin
2 tablespoons cold water
½ cup boiling water
20-ounce can juice-packed crushed pineapple, undrained
5 tablespoons sugar or 3 tablespoons fructose or equivalent substitute, to
   taste

Sprinkle the gelatin in blender container. Add the cold water and allow to soften 1 minute. Add the boiling water, then cover the container and whir on high speed until all the gelatin granules are dissolved.

Add the canned pineapple (including the juice) and sugar or fructose or substitute. Blend on low speed just long enough to combine; don't overblend. Pour into three small jars, one for the refrigerator and two for the freezer. Keep refrigerated. *15 calories per tablespoon with sugar or fructose; 10 calories per tablespoon with substitute.*

## GROWNUP CIDER JELLY

   **12-ounce can (or two 6-ounce cans) frozen unsweetened cider or apple-juice concentrate**
2 **envelopes plain gelatin**
2½ **cups water**
9 **tablespoons sugar**
1 **bottle liquid pectin (6 ounces)**
   **Sugar substitute to equal ½ cup, or to taste (optional)**

Defrost frozen concentrate. Combine with gelatin in saucepan. Wait 1 minute, then heat gently until gelatin melts. Add water, sugar, and pectin. Heat to boiling. Cook and stir at a rolling boil for 1 minute. Remove from heat and stir in sugar substitute, if desired. Pour into jars. Cover, label, date, and refrigerate. Or store in freezer. *Four cups, 20 calories per tablespoon.*

**For No-Sugar Jelly:** Omit sugar and increase sugar substitute accordingly, or to taste. *Approximately 15 calories per tablespoon.*

**For Not-Too-Sweet Jelly:** Omit sugar substitute.

**Grownup Grape Jelly:** Substitute two 6-ounce cans undiluted grape-juice concentrate for the apple. *20 calories per tablespoon.*

## SLIM GOURMET SUGARLESS MARMALADE SPREAD

1 **thin-skinned juice orange, unpeeled**
   **6-ounce can orange-juice concentrate, defrosted, undiluted**
½ **of a 6-ounce bottle liquid pectin**

Quarter unpeeled orange, or cut into chunks. Remove seeds. Chop coarsely in blender or food processor, using steel blade. Add remaining ingredients and blend on high speed or process until peel is finely chopped. (Add 1 to 4 tablespoons honey or granulated sugar substitute, if a sweeter spread is desired.) Pour into a jar and refrigerate, undisturbed, until mixture thickens and sets (all day or overnight). Keep stored in refrigerator. *About two cups, 15 calories per tablespoon (with ¼ cup honey added, 20 calories per tablespoon).*

# 9

# A YEAR-ROUND HARVEST OF FRUIT-BASED FAVORITES

**Mother Nature's Fruits Make the Perfect Sweet**

The ideal dessert.

If you could design it yourself, you'd probably make it sweet and delicious but quick-and-easy . . . a "convenience food" with little or no preparation needed. Inexpensive and eye-appealing. In a variety of flavors. And, since we're dreaming, why not make it guilt-free and nutritious? Something you can eat all you want of . . . without getting fat!

Good news. Mother Nature has already designed a whole line of luscious low-calorie sweets and treats. They're known as "fresh fruit." In all the most appealing flavors: peach, strawberry, blueberry, pineapple, apricot, melon, and more! Mother Nature sweetens her treats with natural fruit sugar that won't rot your teeth. She packs them with just the right balance of natural vitamins. Even includes moisture and "bulking agents" like natural food fiber to fill you up and prevent overeating.

### Fruit Lover's Calorie Guide

| Fruit | Amount | Fresh | Unsweetened Canned, or Frozen With Sugar* |
|---|---|---|---|
| Apple | 1 fruit | 80 | |
| | 1 cup, sliced | 64 | applesauce—100 |
| Apricot | 1 fruit | 20 | 20 |
| Blackberry | 1 cup | 84 | 98 |
| Blueberry | 1 cup | 90 | 242* |
| Grapefruit | ½ fruit (184 gr.) | 40 | 55 (¾ cup, 183 gr.) |
| Grapes | 1 cup | 70–107 | 231 |
| Peach | 1 fruit | 38–58 | 48–56 |
| Pear | 3½ oz. | 61 | 32 (with a little liquid) |
| Pineapple | 1 slice | 44 (84 gr.) | 33 (with a little liquid) |
| Plum | 1 cup, sliced | 87 (with pits) | 114 (with a little liquid) |
| Raspberries (red) | 1 cup | 70 | 245* |
| Strawberries | 1 cup | 55 | 235* (whole) |
| Melon: | | | |
|   Cantaloupe | 1 cup | 48 | |
|   Honeydew | 1 cup | 56 | 143* (combined) |
| Cherry: | | | |
|   Sweet, pitted | 1 cup | 102 | 119 |
|   Sour, pitted | 4 oz. | 66 | 127* |

## MELON MÉLANGE

**Cantaloupe balls**
**Honeydew balls**
**Watermelon balls**
**Fresh blueberries**
**Fresh lime juice**
**Fresh mint**

Mix equal quantities of melon balls (or any preferred proportion). Garnish with a few fresh blueberries for color, a squeeze of lime and a sprig of mint for added dash. *Each half-cup serving, approximately 35 calories.*

## LOWER-CALORIED FRUIT-FLAVORED YOGURT

**1 cup plain low-fat yogurt**
**2 tablespoons (or more) defrosted orange- or pineapple-juice concentrate (to taste)**
**Dash of salt (optional)**
**Few drops vanilla extract (optional)**
**Few drops honey or sugar substitute to taste (optional)**

Combine to taste. *About one cup, Approximately 210 calories.*

# FRESH FRUIT YOGURT

**1 cup plain low-fat yogurt**
**¼ cup mashed fresh ripe strawberries, peaches, drained crushed unsweetened**
   **pineapple (or any fresh fruit puree)**
   **Few drops vanilla extract (optional)**
   **Pinch of salt (optional)**
   **Sugar substitute or fructose to taste (optional)**

Combine to taste. *About 1¼ cups, approximately 175 calories.*

# EASY RUM-RAISIN YOGURT

Stir 2 tablespoons raisins and 1 teaspoon rum or brandy flavoring into 1 cup plain low-fat yogurt. If raisins are hard, refrigerate several hours for them to soften. If desired, sprinkle lightly with 1 teaspoon free-pouring brown sugar or granulated low-calorie sugar substitute. *215 calories.*

# LOW-CALORIE STRAWBERRY SWISS-STYLE YOGURT

**5 or 6 very ripe berries**
   **Granulated sugar substitute to equal 2 teaspoons sugar**
**1 cup plain low-fat yogurt**
   **Few drops of vanilla (optional)**

With a fork, crush berries and sugar substitute together; then stir into chilled yogurt, along with a little vanilla if desired. *165 calories, instead of 225 for sugar-sweetened "fruit" yogurt.*

# NO-BAKE RAW BERRY CRISP

The taste and texture of fresh fruit in season are too precious to kill with cooking. Baking and cooking change the flavor of fruit as well as its texture. Heat robs fruit of its natural sweetness and flavor; that's why a peach or an apple that's perfectly sweet as is seems to require sugar and spice when baked in a pie. Even though cooking negates the perception of sweetness, heat does nothing to lower the calorie count. So, if cooking requires the addition of sugar, the fruit when cooked becomes more fattening than it would be if served fresh and raw.

This is a quick and easy way to save the sweetness, freshness, and flavor of raw fruit.

2 **pints fresh berries (blueberries, blackberries, etc.)**
2 **to 4 tablespoons maple syrup or sugar substitute to taste (optional)**
2 **large shredded-wheat biscuits**
  **Cinnamon**
  **Light whipped cream or Yogurt Crème Chantilly (recipe below) (optional)**

Wash and pick over berries; separate the softer ones. Put half the berries (including all the soft ones) in blender or food processor; puree smooth. (Sweeten to taste, if desired.) Mix the whole berries with the puree and refrigerate until serving time.

To serve: Spoon berry mixture into 6 dessert cups and top each with some crumbled shredded wheat. Sprinkle with cinnamon. (If desired, top with light whipped cream, under 10 calories per tablespoon; or Yogurt Crème Chantilly.) *Six servings, 140 calories each with maple syrup; 115 calories without (cream topping additional).*

**Yogurt Crème Chantilly:** Spray light whipped cream into a 1-cup measure. Gently fold it into 1 cup plain low-fat yogurt. Use as a topping for any fresh fruit. *Two cups, under 10 calories per tablespoon.*

**Gingersnappy Peach or Nectarine Crisp:** Follow the basic recipe, but substitute ripe peaches or nectarines (peeled and sliced) for the berries, and crushed gingersnap crumbs for the shredded wheat. *Each serving (made with 2 peaches and 2 cookies), 145 calories (without maple syrup).*

Other ideas for berries:

**Berry Favorite Breakfast:** 1½ cups Special K or other high-protein unsweetened cereal, ½ cup sliced fresh strawberries, ¾ cup skim milk, sweetener to taste. *Only 225 calories.*

**Berry Favorite Lunch:** 1 cup low-fat cottage cheese, 4 tablespoons crushed juice-packed pineapple, ½ cup sliced fresh strawberries, few drops vanilla, sweetener to taste. *225 calories.*

For the kids:

**Berry Fondue:** Shake a pint of hulled fresh strawberries in 4 tablespoons brown sugar. Impale each berry on a party toothpick. Fill a small bowl with vanilla yogurt and surround it with berries on picks. The kids will know what to do. *Four servings, 75 calories each.*

**Pink Milk:** No chemical colors, no fake flavors! Fill 1-cup measure with ice cubes, then fill to the top with cold water. Put in blender container. Add ⅓ cup dry skim milk. Add 5 or 6 very ripe hulled strawberries and blend smooth. (May be sweetened with a little honey, if desired.) *Approximately 95 calories.*

# POLYNESIAN CROCKED FRUIT

Here's an idea that's as colorful as a Hawaiian sunset and just as appealing: a crockful of chilled fresh fruit, marinated in pineapple juice and the juices of the fruit itself . . . spiked with rum, if you like. You can keep it in the refrigerator and use it as appetizer or dessert, on salads, cottage cheese, yogurt, ice milk, or spongecake. Calorie-wise and convenient!

I like to use a big two-quart clear glass apothecary jar (because the mélange is so pretty to see!). But a crock or covered cookie jar—or a big glass pickle bottle—will do as well. Simply fill the container with bite-size chunks of ripe raw fruit, then pour on undiluted pineapple-juice concentrate. The juices blend deliciously. Rum or rum flavoring is a spirited addition for adult audiences.

You can vary the fruits to suit your whim and what's available. (Bananas, if used, should be added at serving time, not to the refrigerator jar.)

  **2 eating oranges, peeled, seeded, cut into chunks**
  **5 cups mixed fresh fruit, for example:**
  **1 cup fresh or canned unsweetened pineapple chunks**
  **1 medium mango, peeled and diced, or 2 fresh peaches, or 3 nectarines**
  **1 papaya or small cantaloupe, diced**
  **½ cup dark sweet cherries, pitted**
  **½ cup seedless green grapes or unpeeled apple or pear, diced**
  **1 cup blueberries**
    **6-ounce can undiluted unsweetened pineapple- (or pineapple-orange-) juice concentrate, defrosted**
  **⅔ cup white rum or 1 tablespoon rum flavoring (optional)**

Peel the rind from oranges. On a plate (to catch the juice), cut the oranges into slices, then into bite-size chunks. Remove any seeds with a sharp knife. Put the orange chunks and any reserved juice into a crock or large glass jar.

Next, prepare any fruit that tends to darken or turn brown (peaches, nectarines, apples, pears, for example). Add these to the jar and stir well with the orange chunks. (The ascorbic acid in the orange juice will penetrate the fruit and keep it fresh-looking.) Prepare and add remaining fruit. Combine defrosted pineapple juice with rum or rum flavoring, if using, and pour into the jar. Cover and chill in refrigerator.

Stir before serving. Use as desired; will keep several days when refrigerated. *About 18 ½-cup servings, approximately 60 calories each (just fruit or with rum flavoring); 80 calories each with rum.*

**South Seas Sundae:** Top a scoop of low-fat vanilla ice milk with ½ cup fruit, including juice. Sprinkle with 1 teaspoon toasted coconut flakes, if desired. *About 115 calories with coconut, 105 calories without.*

**Hawaiian Yogurt Sundae:** Substitute a scoop of low-fat vanilla or fruit-flavored yogurt, frozen. *115 calories.*

**Polynesian Sangría:** Combine ¼ cup ice-cold dry red wine with ¼ cup mixed fruit (including juice) in a tall glass. Fill with chilled club soda. *80 calories.*

**Surfside Salad Lunch:** Put 2 scoops chilled low-fat cottage cheese in a bowl. Top with ½ cup mixed fruits. *140 calories.*

**Yogurt Shake:** In a covered blender combine ¾ cup mixed fruit (including juice) with ½ cup plain low-fat yogurt and 5 or 6 ice cubes. Blend on high speed until ice is melted. Serve immediately. *160 calories.*

**Banana Compote:** Slice a ripe banana into 2 dessert dishes. Top each with ½ cup mixed fruit, including juice. Sprinkle with cinnamon or apple-pie spice and serve immediately. *Two servings, 80 calories each.*

**Yogurt Strata Parfait:** Into each tall parfait glass layer ½ cup plain, vanilla, or fruit-flavored low-fat yogurt with ½ cup mixed fruit. *130 calories with plain yogurt; 155 calories with vanilla yogurt; 175 calories with fruit-flavored yogurt.*

**Trader's Shortcake:** Top a small single-serving spongecake dessert shell (or thin slice of spongecake) with ½ cup mixed fruit, including juice. *145 calories per serving. Top with yogurt Crème Chantilly (see page 175).*

## ALL-SEASON FRUIT MEDLEY

Here's a dessert idea that makes the most of our convenience technology, bringing together fresh, frozen, canned, and dried fruits from a variety of seasons and climates. The citrus fruits keep the apples and pears from browning, and the combined juices soften the dried apricots. (Vary the recipe to suit your whim and what's available.)

    **10-ounce package frozen unsweetened melon balls, partly thawed**
**2 unpeeled red apples, cored and diced**
**2 eating oranges, peeled, seeded, cut into chunks**
**1 ripe pear, cored and diced**
    **16-ounce can pineapple tidbits, packed in juice, undrained**
**½ cup dried apricots**
**1 tablespoon shredded orange peel (optional)**

Combine all ingredients in large covered jar and store in the refrigerator for at least 12 hours before serving. *Sixteen servings, under 60 calories each.*

Spoon into champagne glasses, along with a little of the juice, and top each serving with 1 tablespoon vanilla yogurt and 1 teaspoon shredded coconut, if desired. *Under 80 calories each serving.*

Or: Spoon over ½ cup low-fat cottage cheese for a delicious quick lunch or high-protein snack. *140 calories each serving.* Or: Serve over a scoop of low-fat vanilla ice milk or frozen yogurt for an any-season sundae. *About 105 calories each serving.* (Heat fruit to bubbling in a saucepan or microwave oven for a Hot Fruit Sundae.)

# WINTER ORCHARD COMPOTE

**4 ripe fresh pears**
**2 red McIntosh apples**
**½ cup sliced seedless green grapes**
**6-ounce can undiluted orange-juice concentrate, defrosted**
**Pinch of cinnamon**

Dice unpeeled pears and apples; discard the cores and seeds. Combine diced fruit with remaining ingredients in a jar, cover, and store in the refrigerator. Serve at breakfast, brunch, or dessert (or spoon over cottage cheese or ice milk). *About six cups compote, approximately 80 calories per ½-cup serving.*

## Peaches: They're Deliciously Low-Cal

Ripe peaches can add a measure of pleasure to even the strictest diets. Stirred into unsweetened yogurt, sliced peaches make a calorically acceptable dessert. Sliced into unsweetened breakfast cereal or arranged on a lunchtime cottage-cheese plate, fresh ripe peaches add natural sweetness and flavor to calorie-limited meals.

# FRESH PEACH MELBA

**8 ripe, sweet peaches**
**10-ounce package sweetened raspberries, defrosted**

Peel peaches and slice into 6 dessert dishes. Put raspberries in covered blender and blend chunky. Spoon over peaches. (Add a dollop of yogurt, if desired.) *Six servings, 115 calories each (1 tablespoon plain low-fat yogurt is 10 calories).*

# NECTARINES WITH RASPBERRY SAUCE

**3 large, ripe, sweet nectarines, pitted and sliced**
**1 tablespoon brandy or rum (optional)**
**10-ounce package frozen sweetened raspberries, partly thawed, or 2 cups whole unsweetened partly-thawed raspberries**

Stir sliced nectarines with brandy or rum, if desired, and divide among 6 stemmed glasses. Puree raspberries in blender; spoon on top of nectarines. Serve immediately. *Six servings, 95 calories each with brandy and sweetened berries; 70 calories each without sugar or brandy.*

## NO-SUGAR-ADDED RAW PEACH PIE

1½ teaspoons (½ envelope) plain gelatin
1 cup chilled unsweetened white grape juice, divided
  Sugar substitute to equal 3 tablespoons sugar (optional)
  Prepared 8- or 9-inch commercial graham-cracker crust
4 or more fresh ripe peaches, peeled, pitted, sliced

Combine gelatin with ¼ cup of the chilled grape juice in a small saucepan. Wait 1 minute, then heat gently until melted. Stir in remaining chilled grape juice and sugar substitute, if desired. Chill in freezer or refrigerate until syrupy but not set.

Fill ready-to-use crust with sliced peaches. Pour the chilled thickened grape "syrup" over the fruit and chill several hours, until set. *Eight servings, approximately 130 calories each.*

**Lemon Gelatin-Glaze for Raw Fruit Pie:**   Measure contents of a 4-serving envelope peach or lemon gelatin, either regular or sugar-free, and use half. (Save the other half for a future fresh fruit pie.) Dissolve in 1 cup boiling water and mix well. Chill until syrupy.

Meanwhile, fill a pie shell with peach slices or other fresh fruit. Spoon partially-set gelatin over peaches until they are encased in a thick glaze. Chill until set. *With peaches: Eight servings, 155 calories each; 120 calories each with sugar-free gelatin.*

## RAW FRUIT PIE OR TART
## WITH APPLE-JUICE GLAZE

  6-ounce can undiluted apple-juice concentrate
1 envelope plain gelatin
¾ cup cold water
2 to 3 cups raw fruit (bananas, berries, plums, any fruit *except* raw papaya or pineapple)
  Ready-to-fill graham-cracker pie crust, or spongecake tart, or 8 small ready-to-fill spongecake cups

Defrost apple juice just enough to remove it from the can. Sprinkle gelatin on cold water. Wait 1 minute, then heat gently; just until gelatin dissolves. Remove from heat and stir in undiluted apple juice until melted. Refrigerate just until syrupy.

Meanwhile, arrange fruit attractively in pie crust or tart or spongecake cups. When apple gelatin is slightly thick, spoon it gently over fruit, using only as much as you need to entrap fruit in a see-through glaze (about ½ to ⅔ the amount). Chill until set. Store in the refrigerator. *Eight servings, approximately 160 calories each (depending on ingredients chosen).*

# BRANDIED FRESH PEACHES
# WITH "ITALIAN CREAM"

Here's an elegant but simple low-calorie dessert.

**4 ripe sweet peaches or nectarines**
**2 teaspoons lemon juice**
**1 cup part-skim ricotta cheese**
**1 tablespoon undiluted defrosted orange-juice concentrate**
**2 tablespoons peach or apricot brandy**
**1 teaspoon honey or fructose or sugar substitute to taste (optional)**
**½ teaspoon grated lemon peel**

Choose only ripe fruit. To peel easily, impale a peach on the end of a fork and submerge for 30 seconds in a saucepan of very hot water. Skin will easily slip off. (If nectarines are used, don't peel.) Slice the fruit into a bowl; sprinkle with lemon juice. Divide the fruit into 4 brandy glasses.

In a covered blender or electric mixing bowl, combine the ricotta, orange-juice concentrate, and brandy; beat until the consistency of thick cream. Add sweetener to taste, if desired. Spoon over peaches and sprinkle with peel. *Four servings, 170 calories each; with peaches; 205 calories each with nectarines; honey or fructose adds 5 calories per serving.*

# AFTER-SCHOOL FRUIT CUPS

Speedy sweets needn't be sugar-packed and fattening. Needn't be a lot of work, either. In fact, they needn't be kid stuff. If you're looking for a nutrition-rich pick-me-up for the four-o'clock slump, you might like to try these easy recipes. Make blender-quick fruit and juice combinations in the morning and pour them into paper cups. Store them in the refrigerator until ready.

**1¼ cups water, divided**
**1 tablespoon plain gelatin**
**6-ounce can frozen juice concentrate (except pineapple)**
**2 cups fruit (except fresh pineapple)**

**With Blender:** Put ¼ cup cold water in the blender jar; sprinkle on gelatin. Wait 1 minute. Heat remaining 1 cup water to boiling. Pour into blender jar; cover and blend, scraping often, until gelatin granules dissolve. Add undiluted frozen concentrate; cover and blend until melted.

Meanwhile, slice or dice fruit. Divide fruit among 4 paper cups. Pour gelatin mixture over fruit. Chill several hours, until set.

**Without Blender:** Combine gelatin and water in a small saucepan. Wait 1 minute, then heat gently, stirring occasionally, until gelatin melts. Remove from heat and add frozen juice concentrate. Stir constantly until dissolved. Pour over sliced or diced fruit in paper cups. Chill until set. *Makes four servings.*

Some combinations to try:

Unpeeled diced red apple and orange juice *125 calories*
Unpeeled sliced nectarines and apple juice *145 calories*
Peeled, cubed eating oranges and apple juice *130 calories*
Canned juice-packed pineapple tidbits and orange juice *155 calories*
Sliced fresh strawberries and orange juice *120 calories*
Fresh or frozen unsweetened blueberries and grape juice *145 calories*
Sliced bananas and orange juice *155 calories*

## Instant Sweet Lover's Treat . . . Peel a Banana!

Can you name a wonderful food that tastes rich, sweet, starchy, and fattening, yet is low in calories . . . an instant food that's ready-to-eat as soon as it's unwrapped . . . a food that needs no refrigeration or cooking, that can be tucked in lunchboxes, handbags, luggage, and attaché cases . . . a food that can be used as a fruit or a vegetable, a snack, salad, breakfast, drink, or dessert . . . or an ingredient in breads, cakes, pies, pastries, ice creams, custards, puddings, or in main courses or side dishes . . . a food that's also a "sugar substitute," potassium supplement, and a good source of fiber and pectin . . . a sweet that's good for everybody including special dieters, athletes, joggers, people with heart disease or high blood pressure . . . a food that everybody loves: babies, kids, grownups, even people without teeth!

What wonderful food is this?

The banana.

Some things you may not know about the banana:

• Despite its rich, sweet taste and starchy texture, the banana is *not* fattening. The average banana is only 100 calories, about the same as a large apple or pear. A banana tastes like a candy bar but it supplies appetite-appeasing fiber and pectin, plus vitamins and minerals, especially iron and potassium. No fat . . . and no sugar added!

• For out-of-hand eating, bananas should be allowed to ripen to the point where their yellow skins have developed some brown flecks.

• Bananas must be picked green to develop flavor. Even in the tropics bananas are harvested green and ripened off the plant. If ripened on the plant they lose their characteristic flavor.

• The banana is one fruit that has a use at any stage of ripeness. New bananas —green-tipped, firm, and not yet sweet—can be baked, broiled, or lightly sautéed as a vegetable. All-yellow, just-ripe bananas are slightly sweet, and firm enough to toss with salad ingredients. Yellow bananas with brown flecks have the sweetness and texture desired for finger snacks. As the brown flecks increase, the banana becomes sweeter and softer. Bananas too ripe for out-of-hand eating are a sweet ingredient in recipes.

• For a fruit of tropical origin, bananas actually like a cool, dry climate. The best spot to store bananas is a dry place, with a temperature between 60 and 65 degrees. Much higher or lower temperatures will interfere with the ripening process.

• Bananas emit their own natural ethylene ripening gas. The best way to speed up ripening is to store them in a sealed bag or other container that keeps their ripening gas trapped.

• Conversely, the best way to slow down ripening is to expose bananas to air, thereby allowing the ripening gas to dissipate.

• Or you can prevent ripe bananas from overripening by storing in the refrigerator. The old "Chiquita Banana" song notwithstanding, you *can* store bananas in the refrigerator if it suits your purpose. The peels will darken, but the fruit itself will remain unchanged for five to seven days.

• You can even freeze them! Pop unpeeled bananas in a plastic bag and store them in the freezer. Allow the unpeeled banana to thaw just enough so you can peel it. Then, mash the fruit and use it in any recipe that calls for mashed ripe banana.

• Overripe or frozen bananas may be too mushy for out-of-hand eating, but the fruit will be at its absolute sweetest. Mashed overripe bananas are a delicious way to sweeten and flavor sugarless skim-milkshakes, frozen desserts, puddings, and custards. Or use them in a low-calorie banana loaf.

## TROPICAL BANANA POPS

Cut large very ripe bananas into 4 chunks each. Roll each chunk in defrosted undiluted pineapple- or orange-juice concentrate, then in toasted coconut, crushed plain granola cereal, high-protein cereal, or all-bran. Insert popsicle sticks or small wooden skewers. Arrange the pops on wax paper or a nonstick pan in the freezer. (Wrap after pops are frozen firm.) Remove from freezer several minutes before serving. *Each pop: approximately 85 calories with high-protein cereals or all-bran; 100 calories with granola or coconut.*

## TROPICAL BANANA FREEZE

Put very ripe unpeeled bananas in a plastic bag in the freezer. Remove as needed to make this easy blender drink or dessert:

Remove 1 banana from the freezer and allow it to defrost just enough to remove the peel. Cut the partly-thawed, peeled banana into chunks and put it in the blender or food processor with a few drops of vanilla extract and coconut flavoring. Add skim milk or low-fat yogurt and blend smooth. A small amount of milk or yogurt will create a "frozen custard." Add more milk or yogurt for a milkshake. Add a whole egg for a high-protein instant breakfast or lunch. (Top with a dash of cinnamon or nutmeg, if desired.) *Skim milk has approximately 45 calories per ½ cup; plain low-fat yogurt, 70 calories per ½ cup; a large egg, 80 calories; the banana, 100 calories.*

## YOGURT BANAMBROSIA

1 banana, peeled and sliced
1 red apple, cored and diced
1 eating orange, peeled, seeded, in chunks
1 cup canned unsweetened crushed pineapple, well drained
1 cup seedless green grapes, sliced in half
1 cup low-fat vanilla yogurt or low-fat plain yogurt sweetened to taste with
    vanilla extract and sugar substitute

Combine banana and apple in a bowl. Cut the orange over the bowl to catch any juice. Add orange chunks; stir well (the juice will delay browning of the apple and banana). Stir in pineapple, grapes, and yogurt.

Chill at least 1 hour before serving. *Six servings, 115 calories each; 105 calories each with plain yogurt.*

## BANANAS ROSANNA

1 pint fresh strawberries
6-ounce can orange-juice concentrate, thawed, undiluted
4 small or 3 large ripe bananas

Wash, hull, and cut up strawberries. Mash with undiluted orange-juice concentrate; or combine them in the blender or food processor and blend smooth. Set out 6 stemmed dessert glasses. Slice the bananas and alternate with the strawberry-orange sauce. *Six servings, 130 calories each.*

**Sundae Sauce:** Puree strawberries and undiluted orange-juice concentrate; store in a covered jar in the refrigerator. Use as a topping for low-calorie ice milk or frozen yogurt. *Two cups, 15 calories per tablespoon.*

# OVEN-FRIED BANANAS

4 ripe bananas, peeled, halved
2 teaspoons butter (or margarine)

Choose yellow (firm-ripe) bananas. Cut them in half crosswise. Spray a small square nonstick cake pan with cooking spray. Preheat oven to 450 degrees. Put the butter in the pan; place in the hot oven just long enough for butter to melt. Place the bananas in the pan and tilt the pan so the bananas roll and become lightly coated with butter. Place the pan on the bottom oven shelf and bake only 5 minutes, turning the bananas once, until just browned. Serve with salt and pepper as a starchy side dish, or sprinkled with cinnamon and sugar substitute as a dessert. *Eight servings, 60 calories each.*

# COCONUT-BAKED BANANAS

3 large bananas, peeled
2 tablespoons diet margarine
1 tablespoon lemon juice
4 tablespoons shredded coconut

Cut peeled bananas in half, then split lengthwise. Place split side down in a shallow baking dish. Spread the surface of each banana lightly with diet margarine. Sprinkle with lemon juice and coconut. Bake in a preheated 375-degree oven for 15 minutes. Serve warm. *Six servings, 85 calories each.*

### Orange Plus Strawberry, They're Terrific Together

What's better than strawberries or oranges? Strawberries *and* oranges! Together these favorite fruits are a wonderful example of food synergy: when combined, they each taste even more delicious. Like a good marriage, each brings out the best qualities of the other.

Both fruits are low-calorie and nutritious. Although oranges and orange juice are most associated with vitamin C, people are surprised to learn that strawberries have about the same amount of C as oranges, and have fewer calories. What's more, strawberries have triple the appetite-appeasing fiber of oranges, and 13 times as much fiber as orange juice. A half cup of diced oranges is about 40 calories, a half-cup of fresh sliced strawberries about 35. Instead of orange juice with breakfast, why not enjoy a dish of sliced oranges and strawberries combined?

Keep this magic flavor combination in mind when thinking up light, less-fattening desserts. Stir sliced strawberries into orange yogurt, or vice versa. Top strawberry ice milk or frozen yogurt with blender-crushed orange or a spoonful of orange-juice concentrate. Sweeten strawberries with low-sugar orange marmalade instead of sugar. Instead of sugary frosting, spoon blender-crushed strawberry purée over orange spongecake. Layer strawberries in orange gelatin molds. Or do it the other way around. At lunchtime remember oranges and strawberries as the perfect pair for a cottage-cheese plate.

## STRAWBERRIES ROMANOFF

The romantic attraction of strawberries for orange flavor has been memorialized in the classic dessert "Strawberries Romanoff." To prepare this easy classic, you simply marinate fresh ripe berries in equal parts fresh-squeezed orange juice and orange liqueur. At serving time, the berries are topped with whipped cream.

You can decalorize this classic by changing the ratio: 2 tablespoons orange liqueur to 1 cup orange juice. Pour this over a pint of hulled berries and refrigerate 6 to 8 hours, stirring occasionally. *Four servings, 80 calories each. That's without the whipped cream, which adds 27 calories a level tablespoon (or, more likely, 105 calories a quarter-cupful!).*

## STRAWBERRIES AND SUNSHINE

Or you can try this liqueurless variation.

**6-ounce can orange-juice concentrate, defrosted**
**1 pint ripe strawberries**
**½ cup pressurized whipped cream**
**½ cup plain low-fat yogurt**

Defrost orange-juice concentrate, but do not dilute.

Wash and hull berries but leave them whole. Stir them with the undiluted orange-juice concentrate. Refrigerate until serving time.

Spoon berries into 4 stemmed glasses.

Spray whipped cream into ½ cup measuring cup to fill. Empty into a small bowl. Add the yogurt and fold together until blended. Spoon this mixture over berries. *Four servings, approximately 190 calories each.*

## FRESH (RAW) PEACH PIE

This peach pie is made in the refrigerator . . . no cooking needed. When peaches taste so sweet and delicious fresh, it's a shame to cook them. Conventional peach-pie recipes can rob fresh peaches of their sweet taste and succulent texture, giving them a cooked, "canned" taste, and requiring lots of pound-provoking sugar and thickeners. Our peach filling is held together with a fruit juice and gelatin.

1 envelope plain gelatin
4 tablespoons cold water
1 cup canned peach nectar (or other fruit juice)
  Granulated sugar substitute to equal 4 tablespoons sugar (optional)
4 large ripe, sweet peaches
  Ready-to-fill graham-cracker pie shell
  Yogurt crème chantilly (see page 00) (optional)

Sprinkle gelatin on cold water in a small saucepan. Wait 1 minute, then heat gently over low heat until gelatin melts. Don't boil. Remove from heat and stir in nectar. Chill in freezer 10 minutes, until syrupy. Sweeten to taste, if desired.

Meanwhile, peel and slice peaches. To peel easily, drop a peach into boiling water for 20 to 30 seconds, then remove with a fork. Skin will slip off easily.

Fill pie shell with sliced peaches. Spoon nectar glaze over peaches. Chill in refrigerator several hours before serving. *Eight servings, 130 calories each, without topping.*

## ORANGE-STRAWBERRY YOGURT SUNDAES

FOR EACH SERVING
1 scoop (⅓ cup) low-fat vanilla frozen yogurt
4 or 5 ripe strawberries, sliced
2 tablespoons undiluted defrosted orange-juice concentrate

Surround the scoop of frozen yogurt with berry slices and drizzle on the undiluted orange-juice concentrate. Serve immediately. *Each serving, 140 calories.*

## ORANGE STRAWBERRIES JUBILEE

1 pint low-fat vanilla ice milk or orange sherbet
2 tablespoons undiluted defrosted orange-juice concentrate
2 tablespoons water
4 tablespoons brandy or rum
1 pint fresh strawberries, hulled

Set out the ice milk or sherbet in 4 dishes. In a chafing dish, warm the juice, water, and brandy. Add the strawberries and stir gently until heated through. With a long match, light the mixture. Spoon the flaming strawberries over the ice milk or sherbet. *Six servings, 205 calories each.*

## EASY BLUEBERRY-PINEAPPLE STRATA

**16-ounce can crushed pineapple, in syrup or juice**
**1 envelope plain gelatin**
**Granulated sugar substitute (optional)**
**1 pint fresh blueberries**

Pour syrup or juice from pineapple into a small saucepan and sprinkle on gelatin. Wait 1 minute, until gelatin softens, then cook and stir over low heat just until gelatin melts. Remove from heat and stir in crushed pineapple. Sweeten to taste with granulated sugar substitute, if desired. Chill until slightly set.

Layer fresh blueberries with pineapple mixture in a clear glass bowl or in individual glass dessert cups; finish with a layer of pineapple. Chill until set. Serve with Yogurt Crème Chantilly, if desired (recipe given). *Eight servings, 90 calories each with syrup-packed pineapple; 60 calories each if juice-packed.*

## SANGRÍA FRUIT CUPS

**Unpeeled diced red apples**
**Unpeeled diced pears**
**3 tablespoons golden raisins**
**Fresh tangerines, peeled and sectioned**
**White sangría**

Combine the fruit in a bowl and cover with wine. The wine adds flavor but very few calories to the fruit. Chill all day or overnight in the refrigerator. At dessert time, use a slotted spoon to apportion the fruit into wine glasses. *Less than 60 calories per ½-cup serving.*

(The wine can be saved for drinking at another meal, if desired. Or use it to "spike" chicken.)

### Freeze Fruit the Low-Calorie Way

Wouldn't it be nice to reach into your freezer in February and "harvest" some blueberries or cherries? Freezing fruit is so easy; why not store some this summer for the fruitless months ahead?

Freezing is the fuss-free way to put up fruit—ideally suited to busy people, singles, couples, and small families. Freezing is simpler than canning; it requires no special equipment (except, of course, freezer space) and there's less that can go wrong. Freezing is the preferred method for preserving no-sugar-added fruits. While it's possible to can fruits without added sugar, the results are nowhere near as successful as freezing.

Fruit can be frozen using a variety of methods. Most cookbooks focus on techniques for freezing fruit in sugar or syrup. Neither method appeals to Slim Gourmet cooks! Here are my favorite ways to freeze fresh fruit with no sugar added.

FRUITS THAT "DARKEN" OR TURN COLOR: Apples, pears, peaches, nectarines, apricots may be frozen raw with the addition of ascorbic acid ("fruit-fresh" preparations, crushed Vitamin C tablets, lemon juice, orange juice, or Vitamin C-enriched fruit juice). However, these sour ingredients make the fruit less palatable without added sugar or sweetener. You can avoid the need for sour preservatives by partially cooking the fruit in a small amount of water or fruit juice, just enough to keep it from scorching, just until the fruit reaches boiling. Then divide into jars or containers; label and freeze.

FRUITS THAT DON'T DARKEN: Berries, cherries, pineapple, melon can be frozen raw with nothing added, or covered with a "syrup" of unsweetened fruit juice.

Here are preparation tips for individual fruits:

APPLES: Peel, core, and slice or dice. Combine in a heavy pot with 2 tablespoons water or apple or other fruit juice. Heat to boiling. Cool, then pack into covered jars. Or make into applesauce or baked apples; then freeze.

APRICOTS: Wash, halve, and remove pits. No need to remove peel. Heat to boiling in a small amount of water, apple or orange juice, or peach or apricot nectar. Cool; pack in jars with juice.

BLUEBERRIES, Blackberries, Raspberries, Elderberries, Huckleberries, etc.: Don't wash; handle as little as possible. Three methods: (1) Simply overwrap the containers as they come from the store with a double layer of plastic wrap and freeze as is. (2) Or spread fruit in a shallow layer on cookie tins and fast-freeze, uncovered. When frozen firm, pack fruit in jars (will be loose-packed, allowing you to remove a little at a time), and cover. (3) Or gently transfer fresh raw fruit to small jars or other vapor-proof containers. Cover, label, and freeze. To serve: don't defrost. Rinse frozen berries in cold water and serve while still partially frozen to retain firmness. Or rinse and defrost completely to use in recipes.

CANTALOUPE, WATERMELON, ETC.: Remove seeds, cut in cubes, or use a melon baller. Spread in a layer on a cookie tin. Fast-freeze, uncovered. When frozen solid, transfer to plastic bags or covered jars and freeze.

CHERRIES: Wash and dry; remove stems and pits. (1) Transfer to jars and freeze with nothing added, or cover with red grape juice. (2) Or heat to boiling in a small amount of water or red grape juice. Transfer to covered jars and freeze.

PEACHES, NECTARINES: Peel peaches (submerge briefly, one at a time, in a pot of boiling water, until skin slips off easily; no need to peel nectarines). Cut in half or in thick slices; discard pits. Heat to boiling in a small amount of water, fruit juice, or peach nectar. Cool, pour into jars, and freeze.

PEARS: Peel, halve or quarter, and remove cores. Heat to boiling in apple juice or pear nectar. Jar and freeze.

PINEAPPLE: Quarter lengthwise. Remove core and peel from each quarter. Slice or dice the fruit. (1) Arrange slices in a single layer on cookie tin. Fast-freeze, uncovered, until frozen solid. Transfer to plastic bags or jars. (2) Or heat to boiling in pineapple juice. Cool, then pour into covered jars.

PLUMS: Wash, don't peel. Cut in half or slice thin; discard pits. Freeze with nothing added, or covered with fruit juice.

STRAWBERRIES: Wash and core; leave whole. (1) Dry berries, then pack whole in plastic bags or covered jars. (2) Or slice berries, pack into jars, cover with red grape juice. Seal and freeze.

CHUNKY FRUIT SAUCES: Delicious fresh fruit toppings (for ice milk, yogurt, cottage cheese, spongecake) are easy to freeze. Combine each cupful of sliced or diced fresh fruit with ¼ cup water or any fruit juice. Cover and heat to boiling. Allow to cool, then pour into small covered jars. Store in freezer. Fruit sauces can be used cold with yogurt or cottage cheese or reheated to boiling and served hot. Hot sauces can be flamed by adding a tablespoon or two of brandy, rum, or liqueur to the simmering sauce and igniting the vapors with a long match.

## Treats with Dried Fruit

The approach of winter doesn't mean the end of naturally sweet fruit treats. Dried fruit is a way of saving some of summer's sweetness to brighten up winter.

If you're wary of dried fruit because you've been told it's fattening, consider this: Two dried apricot halves total 20 calories. One whole fresh apricot is also 20 calories!

The undeserved fattening image comes from weight comparisons with fresh fruit. After the moisture is removed, dried fruit weighs much less. So it takes many more apples or grapes to make a pound of dried fruit than a pound of fresh. A pound of raisins is 1,310 calories, while a pound of grapes is only 207, but grapes are 80 percent water. Of course, dried fruit becomes fattening if you eat raisins as if they were grapes!

In addition to being an easy-to-pack snack, dried fruit is a natural sweetness adder to calorie-light desserts. While sugar adds only sweetness, dried fruit adds flavor, fiber, and nutrition, too.

If you can't find dried fruit in bite-size bits in your supermarket, buy a package of whole mixed dried fruit and dice it up yourself. Here's a tip: dried fruit is easier to cut with kitchen shears.

# FRENCH FRUITED FROMAGE DESSERT

1 cup fruit bits (or diced mixed dried fruits)
1½ cups low-fat pot cheese or low-fat uncreamed cottage cheese
2 tablespoons orange liqueur, or 1 tablespoon fructose or honey or equivalent sugar substitute
2 teaspoons grated lemon or orange peel
¼ teaspoon grated nutmeg

Stir ingredients together until well mixed, then pack into 4 custard cups (or other cups) or a 3-cup mold. Cover and refrigerate several hours. Unmold (and garnish with orange wedges or other fresh fruit, if desired). *Four servings, 170 calories each, dessert only; 150 calories per serving with sugar substitute.*

**Fall Fruited Yogurt or Cottage Cheese:** For each 1-cup serving of plain low-fat yogurt or ¾ cup serving of low-fat cottage cheese, stir in 4 tablespoons mixed diced dried fruit, ½ teaspoon vanilla extract, pinch of cinnamon; mix well. Sweeten, if desired, with sugar substitute to taste. *One serving, 230 calories.*

## Prunes, Good for What Ails You!

This sunny sweet has long evoked giggles and bathroom humor over its reputation as Mother Nature's non-junkfood fruit-flavored version of Ex-Lax. In addition to tasting good, prunes have a well-documented history of usefulness in "promoting regularity," which is a genteel way of saying that prunes have a laxative effect that helps prevent constipation.

Irregularity is such a common problem—particularly among Americans with poor eating habits—that a taste-good food that promises relief should be extremely popular. Unfortunately, this good-for-what-ails-you medicinal image tends to blind potential prune lovers to its other luscious virtues.

Prunes taste terrific and that's reason enough to enjoy them; they have a soft, chewy texture and a rich, sweet, fruity taste that's great alone or as an accent to other ingredients. Better yet, prunes are naturally sweet with no sugar added. They contain no fat, and they're low in calories, only 20 each (average size). A prune, after all, is nothing more than a pitted plum with enough of the moisture removed to prevent it from spoiling. This latter factor makes the prune an ideal snack-food sweet that's convenient to eat anywhere, any time of the year. Prunes are nutrition-rich, particularly in vitamin A, iron, and potassium.

Now, back to that laxative factor. As opposed to drugstore remedies, prunes promote regularity in a gentle, totally natural way—with little likelihood of overdoing. Conveniently packable, prunes are the perfect traveler's snack food:

your passport to preventing restaurant-meal irregularity when you have to choose all your meals from menus that contain little bulk or roughage.

At home, prunes can be part of any dieter's menu: served with breakfast or chopped into cereal, packed with brown-bag lunches, diced into fruit salads, or imaginatively used as a cooking ingredient.

## PRUNE SPONGE SQUARES

  3 **eggs, separated**
    **Dash of salt**
½ **cup sugar**
  2 **teaspoons lemon juice**
  1 **teaspoon grated lemon rind (optional)**
  1 **cup sifted all-purpose flour**
½ **cup chopped prunes (about 12 prunes)**
½ **cup high-protein cereal**
  3 **tablespoons granulated sugar substitute (optional)**

Beat egg whites and salt until stiff. Gradually beat in sugar. Set aside.

Beat egg yolks until light, then beat in lemon juice and rind, if desired. Fold yolk mixture into beaten whites. Gently fold in flour, then prunes and cereal.

Preheat oven to 350 degrees. Spray an 8-inch nonstick square cake pan with cooking spray. Spread batter evenly in pan. Bake 40 minutes, or until cake tests done. While still warm, cut into 16 squares. Sprinkle with sugar substitute, if desired. *Each square, 85 calories.*

### Enjoy Apples!

An apple a day can keep the pounds away . . . if you use crisp, crunchy apples as a doughnut substitute or stand-in for chocolate cake! At less than 100 calories apiece, apples are the ideal diet treat.

Apples can be more than a hand-to-mouth snack. Apples, applesauce, and apple juice can be imaginative seasoning ingredients in your low-calorie kitchen.

There's something so special about the scent of apple desserts that you won't want to pass them up, even if you are calorie-careful. Here are some decalorized treats, proving that there's more to apple than pie.

# APPLE AMBROSIA

**2 red unpeeled apples, cored and diced**
**2 eating oranges, peeled, cut in bite-size chunks**
**1 banana, peeled and sliced**
**3 tablespoons shredded dried coconut**
**2 tablespoons sherry or pineapple juice (optional)**

Arrange fruit in layers in a glass apothecary jar, sprinkling coconut between layers. Add wine or juice, if desired. Cover and chill several hours. Serve chilled in stemmed glasses. *Six servings, 75 calories each (wine or juice adds 20 to 40 calories per serving).*

**Apple Ambrosia Frozen Yogurt Parfaits:** For each serving: Top a scoop of frozen vanilla or pineapple low-fat yogurt with ¼ cup Apple Ambrosia, including a tablespoon of the juice. *Each serving, approximately 80 calories.*

# RUM-RAISIN BAKED APPLES

The alcohol calories evaporate.

**Baking apples**
**Raisins**
**Allspice**
**Dark rum**

Core apples without cutting through the bottom. Stuff each apple with 1 tablespoon raisins. Sprinkle liberally with allspice and add 2 tablespoons rum. Arrange apples in a nonstick pan and bake in a preheated 350-degree oven about 30 to 40 minutes, only until apples are just tender. Baste frequently with the sauce that forms in the pan. *Each apple, about 150 calories.*

**Chunky Rum-Raisin Applesauce:** (Not exactly for kids or invalids!) Peel and dice 4 apples. Combine in a saucepan with ¼ cup rum, ¼ cup water, ¼ cup golden raisins. Cover and simmer just until tender and chunky. Serve warm or chilled. (Spice with cinnamon or mixed pumpkin-pie spice, if desired.) *Four servings, 130 calories each.*

**Rum-Raisin Apple Sundae:** Spoon 2 tablespoons hot Rum-Raisin Applesauce over a scoop of low-fat vanilla ice milk or frozen yogurt. *Approximately 130 calories.*

## CHAMPAGNE-BAKED APPLES

4 baking apples
4 tablespoons golden raisins
2 teaspoons brown sugar
½ cup dry champagne (can be flat)
  Sugar substitute to equal 2 tablespoons sugar (optional)

Carefully core the apples without cutting through the bottom. Stand the apples in a baking dish just large enough to hold them. Fill the centers with raisins and sugar. Pour in the champagne. Bake in a preheated 350-degree oven for 30 to 45 minutes, basting frequently, until apples are tender but not mushy. Remove from oven and stir sugar substitute into juices in the pan, if desired. Serve apples warm or chilled. The wine forms a delicious sauce. *Four servings, 140 calories each.*

## APPLE CRISP

6 firm apples, cored, sliced
4 cups wheat cereal flakes, crushed
4 tablespoons sugar
1 teaspoon baking powder
1 egg
½ teaspoon cinnamon

Heat oven to 350 degrees. Place apple slices in a nonstick shallow 1½-quart baking dish. Crush cereal flakes in a blender or food processor, or by hand with a rolling pin. Mix crushed cereal, sugar, baking powder, and egg until crumbly; sprinkle over apples. Sprinkle with cinnamon. Bake 30 to 40 minutes. Serve warm. *Eight servings, 135 calories each.*

## APPLE-HONEY BAKED SOUFFLÉ

1 envelope plain gelatin
2 tablespoons sweet red wine or orange juice (or 1 tablespoon each)
¾ cup boiling water
1 cup unsweetened applesauce, homemade or canned
2 tablespoons honey
2 eggs, separated
  Cinnamon and sugar

Put gelatin in blender container with wine and/or juice. Let soften 2 minutes. Add boiling water. Blend until gelatin granules are dissolved. Add applesauce, honey, and egg yolks; blend.

*(continued)*

Beat egg whites stiff. Fold into gelatin mixture. Pour into casserole. Place casserole in a pan containing about 1 inch of water. Bake at 325 degrees 1 hour. (Soufflé will be liquid at this stage). Cool; then refrigerate until set, several hours. Sprinkle lightly with cinnamon and sugar. *Six servings, 75 calories each.*

## FRESH APPLE MINCE

How about some fresh "mincemeat"? Not the sugar-packed stuff that comes in a jar or a box (340 calories a cupful, or more, depending on the brand you buy!), but a spicy homemade mélange of raw chopped apples and raisins laced with brandy or rum and spiced with cinnamon and cloves. It's so good that you don't have to bury it in a heavy blanket of pie pastry, and you don't have to be waistline watching to enjoy it. But you'll enjoy it even more knowing that it's only 130 calories a serving, compared with about 350 calories for a slice of conventional mincemeat pie.

1 **unpeeled eating apple**
3 **ounces (6 tablespoons) raisins (3 small boxes)**
1 **tablespoon brandy or rum**
1 **tablespoon undiluted frozen orange-juice concentrate**
  **Pinch each of salt, cinnamon, cloves, and orange peel**
  **Whipped cream or low-calorie whipped topping (optional)**

Quarter and core the unpeeled apple. Slice very thin, then dice fine, into ⅛-inch cubes. Stir with remaining ingredients. Serve in stemmed glasses (with a dollop of whipped cream or low-calorie whipped topping, if desired). *Three servings, 130 calories each, without topping. Add 10 calories per tablespoon for pressurized whipped cream.*

**Apple Mince Jubilee—With Frozen Yogurt:** Set out 6 stemmed champagne glasses or dessert cups and place in each a scoop of low-fat frozen yogurt or vanilla ice milk. Return to freezer until serving time.

Prepare Fresh Apple Mince according to preceding directions, but substitute ½ cup orange juice for orange-juice concentrate. Combine juice with fruit and spices in a chafing dish or small flameproof glass saucepan. Heat to boiling. Increase brandy or rum to 2 tablespoons and add to simmering fruit. Light the brandy vapors with a long fireplace match. Spoon the flaming sauce over low-fat vanilla ice milk or frozen yogurt. *Six servings, 120 calories each.*

### Cranberry Treats

During the pre-holiday season, while cranberries are in the market, stock up! These tart and tangy native berries are useful year round. Few fruits freeze as easily and well as cranberries; they emerge from the deep freeze almost indistinguishable from the fresh-purchased variety.

The directions for freezing cranberries are simplicity itself: cover and freeze. They need no cooking, blanching, sugar, syrup, or any other treatment to survive months of zero storage. Simply overwrap with plastic or foil; then label and freeze. Or transfer the berries to plastic bags, or any container with cover. If you have a self-defrosting freezer that tends to dry the moisture out of foods, you might prefer to transfer the raw berries to covered glass jars.

Fresh or frozen cranberries are low-calorie, only 200 a pound; whole cranberries are high in food fiber. Keep in mind that commercial cranberry sauce strained of skins and seeds has been stripped of this valuable food fiber.

## CRANBERRY-STUFFED APPLES

**Baking apples**
**Fresh cranberries**
**Cinnamon or nutmeg**
**Honey or fructose syrup or liquid sugar substitute to taste**

With a sharp knife, remove the core from each apple; be careful not to cut through the bottom. Put each apple in the center of a square of foil, shiny side out. Put 1 tablespoon raw cranberries in the center of each apple. Sprinkle with spice if desired, and add 2 teaspoons honey or fructose syrup (not sugar substitute).

Bring foil loosely up around apples to retain juices, but don't cover tightly. Arrange foil-wrapped apples in a shallow baking pan. Bake in a preheated 350-degree oven 40 to 50 minutes, depending on size, until apples are tender but not mushy-soft. Serve warm, or close foil and refrigerate.

If using sugar substitute, sprinkle with liquid sweetener after apples are baked. *Each stuffed apple, approximately 105 calories; 20 calories less without honey or syrup.*

## CRANBERRIES JUBILEE

**1 cup raw whole cranberries**
**½ cup water or apple juice**
**3 or 4 tablespoons plain brandy or rum**
**4 scoops low-fat vanilla (or eggnog flavor) ice milk or frozen low-fat yogurt**

Combine cranberries and water or juice in a chafing dish or small saucepan. Simmer uncovered until cranberries pop open. Spoon liquor on top and heat gently. Carefully ignite vapors with a long fireplace match. Spoon the flaming berries over scoops of ice milk in dessert cups. *Four servings, 85 calories each with water; 110 calories with apple juice.*

## Pears

There's nothing more delightful than a pear at its moment of perfection. Trouble is, a pear's moment of perfection is just that—a day or so, no more. Pears are often rock hard and unsweet when purchased. They must wait a while, a few days perhaps, before reaching that gently-resistant state that signals perfect ripeness. Eat at once, or pears quickly turn mealy-textured.

To use pears imaginatively, consider them as a replacement for apples in any favorite fruit combination. How about a Pear Waldorf Salad with low-cal mayonnaise? Or make homemade chunky "pearsauce," no sugar needed. Or try these:

## CRANBERRY-PEAR COMPOTE

**1 cup whole-cranberry sauce**
**3 pears, peeled, cored, quartered**
**3 sweet eating oranges, peeled and cut in large chunks**
  **Pinch each of cinnamon, ginger, allspice**
**1 tablespoon honey, fructose, or equivalent sugar substitute (optional)**

Combine ingredients in baking dish. Cover and bake at 350 degrees for 35 to 40 minutes. Serve warm or cold. *Eight servings, 110 calories each; 10 additional calories per serving with honey or fructose.*

## BLUSHING POACHED PEARS

**8 fresh pears**
**1 cup Port, red sangría, or Concord grape wine**
**1 cup water, divided**
**5 whole cloves**
  **Pinch of cinnamon**
**1 tablespoon cornstarch (or arrowroot)**
  **Sugar substitute to equal ½ cup sugar (optional)**

Cut pears in half lengthwise but don't peel. Remove cores. Put cut side up in a shallow frypan and pour on the wine and ½ cup water; add cloves and cinnamon. Cover and simmer gently until just tender, about 8 to 10 minutes. Remove pears with a slotted spoon.

Stir cornstarch and remaining cold water together; mix into liquid in the skillet; cook and stir until thick. Remove from heat and add sugar substitute to taste, if desired. Pour over pears, serve warm or chilled. *Each pear half plus "syrup," approximately 115 calories.*

**Fruited Poached Pears:** Substitute unsweetened fruit juice (orange, pineapple, apple, apricot, grape) for the wine. For extra natural sweetness, add 1½ ounces golden raisins to the poaching liquid. *125 calories per serving.*

**Minted Poached Pears:** Substitute ¼ cup green crème de menthe and ¾ cup water for the wine. Garnish with sprigs of fresh mint, if you wish. *115 calories per serving.*

## ORANGE-POACHED PEARS

**4 firm-ripe fresh pears**
**¾ cup white wine (or substitute flat champagne)**
**½ cup water**
**Pinch of salt**
**½ teaspoon vanilla extract**
**4 tablespoons thawed undiluted orange-juice concentrate, divided**
**Cinnamon stick, or generous pinch of ground cinnamon**
**1 tablespoon orange liqueur (optional)**

Peel pears and slice in half; remove cores. Combine pear halves with wine, water, salt, and vanilla in a saucepan. Add 1 tablespoon undiluted orange-juice concentrate, cinnamon, and orange liqueur, if desired. Cover and simmer just until pears are tender-firm, about 8 to 10 minutes or longer, depending on type of pears used. Spoon poaching liquid over pears as they simmer.

With a slotted spoon remove pears to a dish. Uncover pan and continue to simmer the liquid until reduced by half. Stir in remaining 3 tablespoons orange-juice concentrate. Spoon the sauce over the pears. Serve warm or cold. *Eight servings, 70 calories each (orange liqueur adds about 5 calories per serving).*

## SANGRÍA POACHED PEARS

**1 cup red wine**
**¼ cup water or orange juice**
**4 tablespoons low-sugar orange marmalade**
**Pinch of cinnamon or allspice (optional)**
**4 firm-ripe fresh pears, peeled, halved, cored**

Over low heat in a saucepan, stir wine, water, marmalade, and spice, if desired, until blended. Add peeled pear halves. Cover and simmer until tender, turning the pears often in the poaching liquid.

Serve warm or cold, with the poaching liquid poured over the pear halves. *Eight servings, 75 calories each; 80 calories each if using orange juice in place of water.*

# PLUMS POACHED IN PINEAPPLE JUICE

Also known as Italian or prune plums, purple plums are a sweet treat for eating out of hand. But they offer a colorful—and flavorful—bonus when used in cooking. The natural "dye" of their skins dissolves into a rich ruby-red hue, Mother Nature's natural and nutritious nonchemical food coloring. For a pretty dessert, try plums poached in fruit juice or wine . . . or my Ruby Apple Cobbler, tinted to a rosy tone by the addition of fresh unpeeled purple plums. At only 10 to 20 calories a piece, depending on type, purple plums are a favorite.

1 pound (about 14–15) ripe fresh purple plums
1 cup unsweetened pineapple juice
¼ teaspoon cinnamon or mixed apple-pie spice
   Few drops honey, fructose, or sugar substitute to taste (optional)

Slash each plum on one side (along the "seam"). Remove the pits. Combine pitted plums, juice, and spice in a saucepan and heat to boiling. Simmer uncovered, just until plums begin to soften. Remove from heat and allow to cool. Sweeten to taste, if desired. Chill several hours. *Four servings, 120 calories each.*

**Plums in Port Sauce:** Substitute port wine for pineapple juice (alcohol calories evaporate).

# SLIM GOURMET RHUBARB

Rosy-hued rhubarb is really a vegetable. And it's vegetable-like about calories, too; only 60 per pound. Trouble is, rhubarb is so sour that it takes more than five times its calories' worth in sugar just to sweeten it up to an acceptable tang. That adds up to calories!

In our Slim Gourmet kitchen, we de-sour rhubarb with a little baking soda, to help neutralize its natural acid. Then we sweeten it with a combination of fruit sugar, sugar substitute, and vanilla. With its reduced sugar content, our rhubarb can be eaten with only a fraction of the calories.

1½ pounds fresh rhubarb
  4 tablespoons water
  4 tablespoons fructose
  1 teaspoon vanilla extract
 ¼ teaspoon bicarbonate of soda
   Sugar substitute to equal 4 tablespoons sugar, or to taste

Choose only young tender stalks (older rhubarb is tougher and more sour). Wash and cut in 1-inch lengths. Combine in a pan with remaining ingredients, except sugar substitute. Cover and simmer over very low heat only until just tender, 10 to 12 minutes. Remove from heat and stir in sugar substitute to taste. Chill thoroughly before serving (cold rhubarb tastes sweeter than warm rhubarb). *Six servings, 50 calories each.*

**Baked Rhubarb:** Omit water from preceding directions. Combine all ingredients, except sugar substitute, in a baking dish. Cover and bake 45 minutes at 300 degrees. Chill and sweeten to taste with no-calorie sweetener.

**Hot Rhubarb Sundaes:** Cook rhubarb by either of the preceding methods, eliminating both sweeteners. For each serving, spoon ½ cup hot rhubarb over a scoop of low-fat vanilla or strawberry ice milk. *Fewer than 100 calories.*

**Rhubarb-Yogurt Parfaits:** Cook rhubarb by directions in basic recipe or by baking. Omit vanilla, but include fructose and sugar substitute, sweetening to taste. Chill well. For each serving, layer vanilla low-fat frozen yogurt with chilled cooked rhubarb in tall parfait glasses. Add a grating of orange rind, if desired. *Fewer than 100 calories per serving.*

## Fruit Salads

When salad greenery looks winter-weary—as if it had walked to your supermarket cross-country—that's the time to Think Fruit. Fruit salads needn't be fattening if you're a calorie-wise cook.

You don't need a recipe to concoct a creative fresh fruit salad. The important determinant is what's available in your store. To our way of thinking, the more the merrier.

Add a different fruit for each person who will be eating the salad. A salad to serve six might be made up of six different fruits: apple, pear, orange, banana, and ½ cup each sliced strawberries and juice-packed pineapple chunks.

Other choices might be tangerines, fresh grapefruit sections, sliced pitted prunes, golden apple chunks, seedless grapes, even drained canned fruit cocktail, unsugared, of course. (Once you get beyond a dozen servings, your resourcefulness will really be put to the test!)

Citrus fruits are the most calorie-cheap choices, so include them liberally in diet-wise salads. Grapefruit sections, orange chunks, and tangerine pieces have the advantage of keeping other fruits from turning brown.

The most fattening part of any salad is likely to be the dressing. Many commercial dressings are 65 to 100 calories a tablespoon, but these do-it-yourself blends keep calories low:

# FRUIT SALAD DRESSING I

2 soft peeled bananas
  Juice of 1 lemon
½ cup skim milk
½ teaspoon salt
½ teaspoon prepared mustard
1 tablespoon salad oil
  Sugar substitute to equal 2 teaspoons sugar

In blender or electric mixing bowl, beat bananas smooth. Add remaining ingredients and beat until blended. *One cup, 25 calories per tablespoon.*

# FRUIT SALAD DRESSING II

½ cup low-fat mayonnaise
½ cup plain low-fat yogurt
  Few drops liquid sugar substitute
  Water

Blend ingredients smooth, adding only enough water to achieve desired consistency. *One cup, 25 calories per tablespoon.*

# FLUFFY FRUIT SALAD DRESSING

½ cup pressurized whipped cream
½ cup plain low-fat yogurt
½ cup low-fat mayonnaise

Spray whipped cream from an aerosol can into ½-cup measure. Combine yogurt and mayonnaise and fold in whipped cream. *One and a half cups, 20 calories per tablespoon.*

# 10
# ICE-CREAM-PARLOR AND SODA-FOUNTAIN TREATS: DRINKING "LIGHT"

**The Straight Scoop on Low-Calorie Ice Cream**

Here's the straight scoop on how various types of frozen desserts shape up. However, your best bet is to reach for a brand with a label that tells you what you want to know. Nutritional labeling is the maker's guarantee in writing that the product's calorie count actually matches its slim image. (Unfortunately, some frozen desserts are packaged and promoted in a way that implies a low calorie, fat, or sugar content, even though just the opposite may be true!)

Checking the nutrition label is especially important because different brands may vary widely in calories or fat content. Keeping track of brands is particularly troublesome in this food category because the ice-cream business is primarily regional; there are scores of local brands in each geographic area and a product in your store may have a considerably different calorie count from a similar product in another part of the country. Government nutrition information and calorie counts only reflect national averages.

With that in mind, let's take a look at how different desserts shape up in general:

ORDINARY VANILLA ICE CREAM averages around 250 to 270 calories a cupful, with a fat content ranging between 10 and 16 percent. The more "ordinary"' and low-priced the better, calorically speaking . . . because higher-priced ice cream usually has a higher fat content and proportionally more

## STRAWBERRY WALDORF SALAD

If you like Waldorf Salad, you'll love my strawberry version, a slim and nutritious mélange of colorful fruits in a tangy low-fat dressing. Simply delicious!

1 cup sliced fresh strawberries
1 seeded eating orange, peeled and diced
1 unpeeled diced yellow apple or ripe pear
2 cups diced celery
¼ cup plain low-fat yogurt
3 tablespoons low-fat mayonnaise
2 tablespoons defrosted orange-juice concentrate

Combine fruit and celery in a bowl. Combine remaining ingredients and stir into salad mixture. Chill. *Six servings, 75 calories each.*

## CALIFORNIA SPINACH SALAD

1 eating orange, peeled, seeded, diced
½ cup sliced strawberries
4 cups washed torn fresh spinach
¼ cup orange juice
1 tablespoon lemon juice
1 tablespoon corn oil
  Salt or pepper to taste

Arrange fruit on 3 beds of spinach. Shake remaining ingredients together and pour over salads. Season to taste. *Three servings, 100 calories each.*

## PEAR AMBROSIA SALAD

3 ribs celery, thinly sliced
2 eating oranges, peeled and diced
1 ripe fresh pear, unpeeled, cubed
2 tablespoons plain low-fat yogurt
2 tablespoons low-fat mayonnaise
1 tablespoon orange juice
  Lettuce leaves (optional)
2 tablespoons flaked coconut

Stir first 6 ingredients together. Mound on beds of lettuce, if desired, and sprinkle lightly with coconut. *Six servings, 65 calories each.*

calories. Fancy flavors are generally more fattening than plain vanilla. However, no product labeled "ice cream" has less than 10 percent fat, the legal minimum.

DIETETIC OR SUGAR-FREE ICE CREAM is usually sweetened with sorbitol, a slowly-absorbed caloric carbohydrate sweetener often used by diabetics, instead of sugar, and averages 250 to 270 calories a cupful, same as ordinary ice cream. Why? Because butterfat content is the same (legal minimum: 10 percent) and sorbitol has the same calories as sugar. (In fact, sorbitol is less sweet than sugar so it's necessary to use more calories' worth to get the same sweetness!) Some dietetic ice creams are sweetened with fructose (fruit sugar). Fructose also has the same calories as sugar. However, it's more sweet, so they may use less. Finally, there are dietetic sugar-free ice creams sweetened with no-calorie saccharin, which will save on sweetener calories. All these products are legally required to have full nutrition information, including calorie counts, on their labels.

PREMIUM, HIGH-PRICED, LUXURY ICE CREAM averages around 350 calories a cupful. Extra-dense, extra-rich, hand-packed ice cream in fancy flavors can have considerably more. The butterfat content averages 16 percent, may go up to 24 or 25 percent.

FROZEN CUSTARD is made with eggs as well as cream, a cholsterol catastrophe that can be 375 calories a cupful, and more in fancy flavors. The word to watch for is "custard," denoting the presence of eggs.

ICE MILK AND "LOW-FAT" FROZEN DESSERTS: The average vanilla ice milk contains 184 calories a cupful and has only 4 percent fat. But brands vary; some labeled "99 percent fat-free" may contain as little as 150 or 160 calories. However, some brands may have so much added sugar and thickener that the calories can go up to 225 or more. Soft-serve frozen ice cream, ice milk, and yogurt generally have fat and calorie contents similar to the hard-frozen product.

SHERBETS are frozen fruit-and-milk desserts that contain less butterfat than ice cream, between 3 and 4 percent, but they contain so much sugar that they average around 270 calories a cupful.

ICES are made with fruit juice, sugar, and water . . . no milk, cream, or butterfat, so their calorie counts average around 177 a cupful, while their fat content is virtually nil.

FROZEN YOGURTS average 180 calories a cupful for vanilla, 220 or more for fruit flavors. Most are around 2 percent butterfat but the sugar content may be considerably higher than that of either ice cream or ice milk.

What should *you* choose? If you have to count calories, look for the leanest, least-sweet vanilla ice milk (and serve it topped with fresh fruit). If you're cholesterol watching, your best bet is frozen ice. Stay away from frozen custard and high-priced ice cream. If you need to avoid sugar and calories, look for a dietetic frozen dessert sweetened with saccharin. If you have special diet needs, never buy any product without a nutritional label, and discuss your choice with your dietician or doctor.

## LOW-CALORIE FAST-FREEZE FRUIT CUSTARD

Low-calorie soft-serve fruit "ice cream" or "frozen custard," is easy to make with your blender. If using frozen fruit, it's ready to serve in only 15 or 20 minutes, because the icy fruit speeds up the chilling. With that in mind, you'll want to squirrel away the last of the season's fresh fruit harvest in your freezer, to make frozen desserts any time of the year. Here's the basic recipe:

1½ cups frozen unsweetened berries or diced fruit
 1 envelope plain gelatin
 1 egg
 ½ cup boiling water
 ⅔ cup instant nonfat dry milk powder
 3 tablespoons fructose or 5 tablespoons sugar or equivalent granulated
    sugar substitute
 1 teaspoon vanilla extract
   Pinch of salt
 4 ice cubes

Use blueberries, raspberries, whole hulled strawberries, diced or sliced peeled peaches or nectarines, mangos, melons, or any naturally-sweet fruit *except* pineapple. Fresh or canned fruit may be substituted (including canned pineapple) if you spread the fruit in metal ice-cube trays and freeze it solid before using it in this recipe.

Stir gelatin and egg together in your blender container. Wait 1 minute, then turn on the motor. Add the boiling water slowly through the small opening in the cover. Blend, scraping container frequently, until all gelatin granules are dissolved. Add dry milk, sweetener, vanilla, and salt; blend smooth. With blender running, add the ice cubes through the small opening, until ice is melted. Then add the fruit, a little at a time, until mixture is smooth.

Spoon the mixture into 6 dessert cups and place them in the coldest part of the freezer for about 15 minutes, until mixture is the consistency of frozen custard or soft-serve ice cream. *Six servings, approximately 90 calories each (with fructose and blueberries).*

## LOW-FAT "PHROZEN PHUDGICLES"

   4-serving low-calorie chocolate pudding mix
 3 cups skim milk
 ¼ teaspoon salt
 2 teaspoons vanilla extract
 ½ teaspoon instant coffee powder
 4 tablespoons granulated brown sugar or equivalent sugar substitute (op-
    tional)

Combine ingredients (except sugar substitute, if using) in a nonstick saucepan. Cook and stir until mixture comes to a full boil. Remove from heat. (At this point stir in sugar substitute if using.) Pour into a metal mixing bowl. Store, uncovered, in coldest part of freezer until edges of mixture are partly frozen.

Remove from freezer and quickly beat smooth with an electric mixer. Spoon into popsicle molds or small paper cups; insert a wooden stick into each "pop" and return to freezer until frozen firm. *Eight "phudgicles" 65 calories each with brown sugar; 50 calories each with sugar substitute.*

## POLYNESIAN ICE MILK

**13-ounce can evaporated skim milk**
**3 bananas**
**Sugar substitute to equal 5 tablespoons sugar**
**½ small (6-ounce) can unsweetened pineapple-juice concentrate (6 tablespoons), defrosted**

Pour canned milk into a metal mixer bowl and chill in a freezer until ice begins to form around the edges. Freeze beater blades, too. Whip until stiff peaks form. In another bowl, beat bananas, sugar substitute, and defrosted pineapple-juice concentrate together. Fold into whipped milk. Turn into refrigerator trays and freeze firm. Allow to soften slightly at room temperature before serving. *Eight servings, 105 calories each.*

## EASY LOW-CALORIE PUMPKIN ICE MILK

Before preparing this dessert, remove ice milk from freezer and place it in refrigerator for 30 minutes so it softens to a frozen-custard or soft-serve ice-cream consistency.

**Pinch of salt**
**2 egg whites at room temperature**
**Granulated brown or white sugar substitute to equal ⅓ cup sugar**
**2 teaspoons pumpkin-pie spice**
**1½ cups cooked or canned unsweetened pumpkin**
**1 pint vanilla ice milk**

Add salt to egg whites. Beat whites until stiff peaks form. In another bowl, stir sweetener and spice into pumpkin; then fold the pumpkin into the softened ice milk. Finally, gently but thoroughly fold in the egg whites. Freeze firm. Allow to soften before serving. *Eight servings, 70 calories each.*

# LOW-CALORIE CAPUCCINO "ICE CREAM"

1 envelope unflavored gelatin
¾ cup (6 ounces) cold brewed espresso
   13-ounce can evaporated skim milk
6 tablespoons granulated sugar or equivalent sugar substitute
1 teaspoon vanilla extract
½ teaspoon cinnamon
1 egg white, beaten

Soak gelatin in cold espresso 2 to 3 minutes; heat in small saucepan until gelatin melts. Add milk, sugar or substitute, vanilla, and cinnamon. Pour mixture into a 9-inch-by-5- by 4-inch loaf pan. Turn freezer control of refrigerator to coldest setting. Freeze mixture about 1 to 1½ hours, until frozen 1 inch around edge.

Break up the ice cream and put it into a large mixing bowl. Beat with electric mixer until smooth. Add the beaten egg white and continue beating until mixture is blended. Pour back into loaf pan and freeze again until mixture is frozen about 1 inch around edge. Beat again until smooth; return to pan and freeze until firm. *Eight servings (1 quart), 80 calories each serving with sugar; 50 calories each with sugar substitute.*

## No Need to Resist Tempting Cantaloupe

Ah, the sweet, seductive scent of muskmelon, how aptly named it is! You can allow yourself to be captivated by a cantaloupe, even if you're calorie-wary, because this sweet innocent of a fruit is one of the least-fattening, most-nutritious fruits there is. Only thirty calories a 3½-ounce serving (about ¼ of a melon), the cantaloupe is one of the richest sources of vitamin A. It's no laggard with vitamin C either, offering nearly as much vitamin C as that dieter's standby the grapefruit. And cantaloupe has even fewer calories! So have some with breakfast.

When it comes to cantaloupe, the nose knows. If you can't smell it, either you've got a cold or it isn't really ripe. Sniff the stem end, which should be slightly soft (but not punctured or mushy).

There's a lot more to do with cantaloupe than serve it for breakfast. Here are two ideas for Slim Gourmet cooks:

# MUSKMELON ICE

1½ cups water
½ cup granulated sugar
2 very ripe cantaloupes
¼ cup lemon juice

Combine water and sugar in a saucepan and simmer about 5 minutes. Remove from heat and cool.

Meanwhile, cut cantaloupes in half, remove the seeds and scoop the pulp and juice into a mixing bowl. Add the lemon juice and cooled sugar-water mixture; blend until smooth. Put the bowl into the freezer. When frozen around the edges, remove and beat smooth again. Spoon into a covered container and freeze firm. Soften briefly at room temperature before serving. *Six servings, 115 calories each.*

# CANTALOUPE-STRAWBERRY SUNDAE

1 ripe cantaloupe
2 scoops low-fat vanilla ice milk
1 cup cleaned and hulled fresh, ripe strawberries
2 teaspoons sugar, fructose, or equivalent sugar substitute
2 tablespoons orange juice

Have melon well chilled. Cut in half and remove seeds. Place a scoop of ice milk in each half. Puree or blend berries with sweetener and orange juice and spoon over ice milk. Serve immediately. *Two servings, 150 calories each with sugar; 135 calories each with sugar substitute.*

# FLAMING MINCEMEAT SUNDAES

4 scoops low-fat vanilla ice milk
1 raw apple, peeled and diced
1½ ounce box raisins
¼ teaspoon pumpkin-pie spice
¼ cup unsweetened orange juice
¼ cup plain brandy

Set out ice milk in 4 dessert cups or brandy glasses. In a small ovenproof saucepan heat apple, raisins, spice, and orange juice to boiling. Pour on brandy. With a long match, ignite the brandy vapors. Spoon the flaming fruit-brandy sauce over the ice milk. *Four servings, 125 calories each.*

*(continued)*

**Rum-Raisin Sundaes:** Follow the preceding recipe *but:* substitute apple-pie spice for pumpkin-pie spice; omit orange juice and, instead, use ¼ cup cider or apple juice; substitute rum for brandy. *Four servings, 125 calories each.*

## CHEATERS' "HOMEMADE" PEACH RIPPLE SHERBET

3 cups low-fat vanilla ice milk
2 very ripe sweet peaches, peeled and pitted
1½ teaspoons lemon juice
   Few drops almond flavoring (optional)

Transfer ice milk from freezer to refrigerator briefly, until it softens to the texture of soft-serve ice cream. Meanwhile, combine remaining ingredients in blender. Add ½ cup of the softened ice milk to the blender. Blend smooth. Quickly fold peach mixture into soft ice milk, with a marble effect. Cover and return to freezer. *Eight servings, 80 calories each.*

**Peach Ripple Frozen Yogurt:** Substitute low-fat frozen vanilla yogurt for the ice milk.

## BRANDIED FRUIT SHERBET

The small amount of alcohol in these recipes acts as a sort of antifreeze, keeping the mixture from freezing solid. However, the sherbet can also be made using brandy flavoring or, for an interesting change, orange-juice concentrate. In any case, homemade low-calorie sherbets are best if allowed to soften briefly before serving.

3 tablespoons peach or apricot brandy
1 envelope plain gelatin
   16-ounce can juice-packed peaches or apricots
1 teaspoon lemon juice
1 teaspoon grated lemon peel or orange peel (or a pinch of bottled peel)
   Pinch of salt
   Sugar substitute to equal 3 tablespoons sugar, or to taste (optional)

Put brandy in blender container. Sprinkle on gelatin granules and allow to soften. Drain fruit and measure juice. Add water to make 1½ cups. Heat the juice and water to boiling. Pour into blender. Cover and blend until all gelatin granules are dissolved. Add peaches, cover, and purée smooth. Add remaining ingredients and blend smooth.
   Pour mixture into a shallow metal tray and freeze until slushy. Break

up into mixing bowl; beat until fluffy. Return to freezer and freeze firm. Soften briefly before serving. *Eight servings, 45 calories each with peaches; 50 calories each with apricots.*

**With an Ice-Cream Machine:** Prepare the mixture according to above directions. Pour into an ice-cream machine and process according to manufacturer's directions.

**Orange-Apricot Sherbet:** Omit brandy. Substitute 3 tablespoons defrosted orange-juice concentrate (undiluted) for the brandy. Stir the concentrate with the gelatin granules before putting the mixture in the blender. *40 calories per serving with peaches, 45 with apricots.*

**Nonalcoholic Brandied Sherbet:** Omit brandy. Substitute 2 teaspoons brandy or rum flavoring and 2½ tablespoons water. *35 calories per serving.*

## Make Frozen Yogurt the Low-Calorie Way

Frozen yogurt is lower in fat than many ice creams, but still crammed with sugar calories. You can make it yourself at home, with less sugar and calories, by following these directions.

It's extra easy if you own one of those handy-dandy ice-cream machines that go *inside* your deep-freeze . . . no crushed ice or rock salt needed. Simply follow the manufacturer's directions.

Without an ice-cream machine, spoon the mixture into a metal mixing bowl (which conducts the cold) and put the bowl in direct contact with your freezer shelf. Wait 30 to 45 minutes, then remove bowl and beat mixture smooth again. Repeat one or more times, until the mixture is light and airy. Spoon mixture into a covered plastic container and freeze it firm. Allow it to soften slightly at room temperature before serving.

## PEACHY KEEN FROZEN YOGURT

1 envelope plain gelatin
¼ cup chilled orange juice
2 cups diced peeled ripe peaches
4 cups plain or vanilla low-fat yogurt
   Fructose or sugar substitute to taste (optional)

Sprinkle gelatin over orange juice in a small saucepan and wait 1 minute until softened. Meanwhile combine peaches and yogurt in blender; cover and blend smooth.

Heat the gelatin in the juice just until melted and add to yogurt mixture; cover and blend smooth.

*(continued)*

Sweeten to taste, if desired, and freeze the mixture in an ice-cream maker according to manufacturer's directions, or according to above instructions for freezing without ice-cream maker. *Twelve servings, 65 calories each with plain yogurt; 80 calories each with vanilla yogurt (fructose is 45 calories per table-spoon).*

## FROZEN FRUIT YOGURT

Here's how to make low-cal frozen yogurt from canned fruit:

    **8-ounce can unsweetened fruit packed in juice, undrained**
**1 envelope plain gelatin**
    **8-ounce container low-fat vanilla yogurt**
**1 cup skim milk**
**3 tablespoons fruit sugar (fructose) or 4 tablespoons sugar or equivalent**
    **granulated sugar substitute**
**¼ teaspoon salt**

Pour juice from canned fruit into a small nonstick saucepan. Sprinkle on the gelatin. Wait 1 minute, then heat gently, until gelatin melts.

Combine with remaining ingredients in blender. Cover and blend smooth. Pour into an ice-cream machine and freeze according to manufacturer's directions, or according to above instructions for freezing without ice-cream maker.

*Eight servings, 70 calories each (with canned peaches and fruit sugar).*

## FROZEN CRANBERRY YOGURT

    **Pinch of salt**
**2 egg whites**
**1 cup whole cranberry sauce**
    **8-ounce container low-fat plain or vanilla yogurt**
    **Sugar substitute to equal ¼ cup sugar (optional)**
**1 cup vanilla ice milk (regular or dietetic)**

NOTE: Soften ice milk in the refrigerator 20 to 30 minutes before using in this recipe.

Add salt to egg whites and beat until stiff. In another bowl, stir cranberry sauce, yogurt, and sweetener together. Stir in the softened ice milk. Gently but thoroughly fold in egg whites. Freeze firm. Allow to soften slightly before serving. *Eight servings, under 100 calories each.*

## PINEAPPLE LOW-FAT FROZEN YOGURT

1 cup juice-packed crushed pineapple, including juice
1 envelope plain gelatin
5 tablespoons fructose or honey
1 cup ice-cold skim milk
    8-ounce container low-fat vanilla yogurt

Drain the pineapple juice into a saucepan and sprinkle on the gelatin. Wait 1 minute to soften, then heat gently, just until gelatin is dissolved. Combine with remaining ingredients in blender, cover, and blend smooth. Process in an ice-cream machine, according to manufacturer's directions, or according to instructions for freezing without ice-cream maker (page 209). *Six servings, 110 calories each; honey adds 15 calories per serving.*

**Sugar-Free Dietetic Version:** Omit honey or fructose. Replace with sugar substitute equal to ½ cup sugar, or to taste. Substitute plain low-fat yogurt and 2 teaspoons vanilla extract for the sweetened vanilla yogurt. *Six servings, 70 calories each.*

## Try a True-Fruit "Spritz"

These homemade diet sodas are actually true fruit spritzers . . . a nonalcoholic, no-sugar-added blend of real fruit juice and sparkling water. The fun of spritz making is to invent your own combinations, but here are some basic ideas to start you thinking:

## CRANBERRY-ORANGE SPRITZER

1 tablespoon undiluted defrosted orange-juice concentrate
¼ cup cranberry-juice cocktail
    Club soda or seltzer
    Fresh fruit garnish (optional)

Combine; serve over ice. *70 calories (garnish approximately 10 calories additional).*

**Fresh-Squeezed Orange Spritz:** Combine the juice of 1 orange, with 6 to 8 ounces sparkling water over ice cubes in a tall glass. *65 calories.*

**Purple Passion Spritz:** Combine ¼ cup undiluted bottled grape juice with 2 tablespoons lemon juice and 6 to 8 ounces sparkling water over ice. *45 calories.*

**Nectar Spritz:** Combine ⅓ cup unsweetened canned pineapple, apricot, peach, or mango juice with 6 to 8 ounces sparkling water; serve over ice. *Under 50 calories.*

*(continued)*

**Apple Spritz:** Combine 2 tablespoons undiluted defrosted apple or cider concentrate with 6 to 8 ounces sparkling water over ice. *60 calories.* (Store remaining defrosted concentrate in refrigerator and use as needed.) Other fruit spritzes to make with juice concentrate: pineapple, *65 calories;* orange or tangerine, *60 calories;* grape, *65 calories;* grapefruit, *50 calories* . . . any true juice concentrate, *not* frozen sugar-sweetened punches or fruit "ades."

**Polynesian Passion Spritz:** Combine 2 tablespoons undiluted defrosted pineapple-juice concentrate and ¼ cup fresh orange juice with ½ cup sparkling water over ice. *90 calories.* Or substitute orange-juice concentrate and canned unsweetened pineapple juice, *95 calories).*

**Pink Grapefruit Spritz:** Combine 3 tablespoons bottled red grape juice and 1 tablespoon undiluted defrosted grapefruit-juice concentrate with 6 to 8 ounces sparkling water over ice. *55 calories.*

**Citrus Tea Spritz:** Combine 2 tablespoons defrosted undiluted orange- or tangerine-juice concentrate and ¼ cup strong cold tea with 6 to 8 ounces sparkling water over ice. *60 calories.*

**Peach-Pineapple Spritz:** Combine 1 tablespoon defrosted undiluted unsweetened pineapple-juice concentrate and ¼ cup peach nectar with 6 to 8 ounces sparkling water over ice. *60 calories.*

## DO-IT-YOURSELF "DIET SODA"

Diet sodas are nutritional neuters—no calories, no vitamins, nothing of value. But nondiet sodas are even worse: nothing of value plus sugar! Why not make your own "diet sodas" by flavoring no-cal club soda or seltzer with small amounts of fruit juice lightly sweetened with sugar substitute. Not calorie-free, but not as fattening as undiluted fruit juice or sugar-sweetened soda pop. You can even save storing or shopping for diet soda by making your own carbonated water with a siphon bottle, sold in housewares or appliance departments. No deposit, no return!

**Homemade Diet Soda I:** Pour ½ cup chilled, unsweetened orange or grapefruit juice (or apple, grape, pineapple, apricot,—any unsweetened favorite) into a tall glass. Add 1 packet sweetener (or sweeten to taste.) Fill with ice cubes. Add carbonated water and stir. *About 65 calories.*

**Homemade Diet Soda II:** Keep small cans of defrosted unsweetened fruit juice concentrate in your refrigerator as a "syrup base" for homemade diet sodas. For Real Orange Soda, combine 2 tablespoons defrosted unsweetened orange juice with a can of club soda. Sweeten to taste and add ice cubes. Substitute or blend other juices. *60 calories.*

### Easy Blender Milkshakes

What's the perfect pick-me-up for waistline watchers? A milkshake! Not the kind they serve in the sweet shoppe, however. Soda-fountain milkshakes generally contain more junk calories than they do milk.

Nonfat dry milk, the kind you mix with water, is a protein bargain. Five tablespoons (⅓ cup) of the dry stuff offers 8 grams of appetite-appeasing protein. Combined with ice cubes, water, and other low-cal ingredients in a blender, dry milk whips up into a thick, foamy shake with a palate-pleasing chill.

To make a shake, first take a measuring cup and fill it with ice cubes. Then add tap water until it's full. Pour cubes and water into blender container and add remaining ingredients. Cover and blend on high speed until the ice stops chinking. The volume will have doubled; you'll have enough to fill a milk-shake-size glass.

Frozen unsweetened fruit juice straight from the freezer can replace ice cubes. Add an egg to any milkshake drink and you've got a light meal-in-a-glass that can replace breakfast or lunch. Milk plus egg equals 14 grams of protein, almost 30 percent of your daily needs. Strawberries add vitamin C plus all-important fiber. Don't use sugar, it adds *nothing* (but calories). If you have an unreformed sweet tooth, add a little honey (20 calories per teaspoon) or fructose (15 calories per teaspoon) or sugar substitute to taste. Both fructose and the low-calorie aspartame sugar substitute help bring out the flavor of fruit shakes.

## BANANA SHAKE FOR TWO

 1 **very ripe banana**
 2 **teaspoons fructose or equivalent sugar substitute**
   **Few drops vanilla extract**
   **Ice cubes and water—enough to reach 2-cup measure on blender cup**
10 **tablespoons nonfat dry milk powder**

Combine in blender, cover, and blend on high speed until ice stops chinking. Serve immediately. *Two servings, 145 calories each with fructose; 130 calories each without fructose.*

# BANANA BREAKFAST NOG

If you're running late, a banana eggnog whizzed up in the blender can serve as a speedy eye opener that sends you out with some lean protein under your belt.

**1 very ripe banana, peeled**
**1 egg**
**1 cup cold fresh nonfat milk**
   **Vanilla extract to taste**
   **Dash of cinnamon or nutmeg**
   **Granulated sugar substitute to taste (optional)**

Combine ingredients in blender. Cover and blend until frothy. Serve immediately. *275 calories.*

**Orange Nog Instant Breakfast (or Lunch):** In blender, replace banana with 1 tablespoon defrosted undiluted orange-juice concentrate. Omit vanilla extract and spices. Add ½ cup ice cubes. Cover and blend smooth. *200 calories.*

**Frosty Banana Nog:** For a very cold banana nog or milkshake, store the unpeeled banana overnight in the refrigerator. Peel and blend with above ingredients. Or substitute ⅓ cup dry milk powder, ½ cup cold water and 3 or 4 ice cubes for the milk. *270 calories.*

# BANANA-STRAWBERRY FLOAT

**1 cup ice-cold skim milk**
**5 or 6 frozen whole unsweetened strawberries**
**1 small very ripe banana**
   **Sugar substitute to taste (optional)**

Blend milk, strawberries, half the banana, and sugar substitute in covered blender until smooth. Slice remaining banana into a tall glass. Pour in milkshake. Serve with a straw and a tall spoon. *190 calories.*

## NONALCOHOLIC BRANDIED EGGNOG

A meal-in-a-glass.

1 raw egg
1 cup ice cubes and water
5 tablespoons nonfat dry milk powder
1 teaspoon fructose or equivalent sugar substitute
  Pinch of salt
  Dash of vanilla extract (optional)
  Dash of nutmeg
¼ teaspoon brandy flavoring

Break egg into blender. Add remaining ingredients. Cover and blend smooth. *One serving, 175 calories with fructose, 160 calories without fructose.*

## BERRY SHAKE

½ cup frozen strawberries, raspberries, blueberries, or other unsweetened
    fruit
1 cup water
½ teaspoon vanilla extract
5 tablespoons nonfat dry milk solids
  Dash of salt
1 teaspoon fructose or equivalent sugar substitute

Combine in covered blender on high speed. *One serving, 135 calories with fructose; 120 calories without fructose.*

## CAFÉ AU LAIT SHAKE

1 teaspoon instant coffee
  Sugar substitute to equal 2 teaspoons sugar
¼ cup boiling water
1 cup ice cubes and water
¼ teaspoon vanilla extract
5 tablespoons nonfat dry milk powder

Combine coffee, sugar substitute and boiling water in blender, cover, blend. Add remaining ingredients to blender, cover, and blend on high speed. *One serving, 80 calories.*

**Mocha Shake:** Follow preceding recipe, but substitute liquid chocolate flavoring for vanilla extract.

*(continued)*

**Milk-Chocolate Shake:** Substitute 1 to 2 tablespoons unsweetened plain cocoa powder for the instant coffee. Sweeten with one packet sugar substitute (or to taste). *One serving, 105 calories.*

**Carob Coffee Shake:** Follow the basic recipe, including instant coffee powder. Add 1 to 2 tablespoons carob powder to the mixture before blending. *One serving, 110 calories.*

## FRACTURED FRUIT FROST

½ cup canned juice-packed unsweetened fruit cocktail, including juice (or
    substitute canned peaches)
½ cup dry nonfat dry milk powder
    Dash of salt (optional)
1 cup ice cubes and water

Combine all ingredients, except ice cubes, in blender. Cover and purée smooth. Add cubes a few at a time with water, until dissolved. *One serving, 170 calories.*

**Punched Peaches (or Pears):** Substitute ½ of an 8-ounce can unsweetened juice-packed peaches (or pears) for the fruit cocktail. *One serving, 175 calories.*

## FRESH PEACH MILKSHAKE

2 small (or 1 large) very ripe peaches, pitted, peeled
½ cup cold water
1 envelope low-calorie vanilla milkshake mix, or ⅓ cup non-fat dry milk
1 cup ice cubes
    Sugar substitute to taste (optional)
    Few drops vanilla extract (optional)

Blend smooth in covered blender. *One serving, approximately 160 calories.*

## SMASHED STRAWBERRY SHAKE

¾ cup frozen whole unsweetened strawberries (other frozen fruit may be
    substituted)
1 cup cold fresh skim milk
    Dash of salt (optional)
½ teaspoon vanilla extract (optional)
    Few drops honey to taste (optional)

Combine in blender, cover, and process smooth. *One serving, 125 calories; honey adds 5 calories per ¼ teaspoon.*

### Skinny Yogurt Drinks That Really Cool You Off

Thick yogurt shakes can be as calorie-heavy as a hot fudge sundae—filling, fattening, and oppressively heat making. Remember, calories *are* heat!

What are needed when the weather warms up are light, lean yogurt drinks that cool you off. Here are some easy ideas:

## YOGURT SHERBET SODA

Naturally sweet and light, in pretty pastel shades.

FOR EACH SERVING
  3 tablespoons plain unsweetened low-fat yogurt
1½ tablespoons undiluted defrosted unsweetened fruit-juice concentrate (orange, tangerine, pineapple, etc.)
    Sugar substitute equal to 1 teaspoon sugar, or to taste (optional)
 ½ cup chilled seltzer, club soda, or sparkling water
    Ice cubes

Stir yogurt, fruit-juice concentrate and sugar substitute smooth. Combine with soda and ice in a tall glass. (Garnish with fresh fruit, if desired.) *Each serving, approximately 70 calories (without garnish).*

## FRESH-FRUIT YOGURT FLOAT

1 cup ice cubes and skim milk
  Sugar substitute to equal 2 teaspoons sugar (optional)
1 cup low-fat plain or vanilla yogurt
1 cup fresh blueberries, pitted sweet cherries, or small strawberries

Fill a 1-cup measure with ice cubes; then pour in skim milk to the top. Combine the ice cubes, milk, and sugar substitute if using with yogurt in blender. Cover and blend on high speed until ice is completely melted. Put ½ cup fruit in each of 2 glasses. Pour yogurt mixture over fruit; serve with tall spoons. *Two servings, 130 calories each with blueberries; 140 calories each with cherries; 100 calories each with strawberries (vanilla yogurt adds 25 calories per serving).*

# LUNCHTIME PEACH-YOGURT SHAKE-TO-GO

1 large or 2 small peaches, peeled, pitted
1 cup plain or vanilla low-fat yogurt
3 or 4 ice cubes
  Sweetener to taste, if using plain yogurt (optional)

Puree peaches or mash thoroughly. Combine with remaining ingredients in an unbreakable 1-quart insulated container, tightly sealed. By lunchtime the ice cubes will have melted and diluted the yogurt to drinking consistency, while keeping the mixture chilled.

Before opening, shake the container vigorously to blend ingredients thoroughly. *One large serving, 225 calories with plain yogurt; 275 calories with vanilla yogurt (caloric sweetener additional).*

# CRUSHED CRANAPPLE FRAPPE

1 apple, peeled and quartered
½ cup plain or vanilla low-fat yogurt
¼ cup canned whole-berry cranberry sauce
1 cup ice cubes and water

Combine all ingredients, except ice cubes and water in blender. Cover and process smooth. Add ice cubes and water, a few at a time, until melted. *One serving, 250 calories with plain yogurt; 275 calories with vanilla yogurt.*

# BASHED BANANA NOG

½ small ripe banana
½ cup plain or vanilla low-fat yogurt
  Dash of salt (optional)
1 cup ice cubes and water
  Cinnamon or nutmeg (optional)

Combine peeled banana, yogurt, and salt in blender. Cover and puree smooth. Fill 1-cup measure with ice cubes, then fill to the top with ice water. Pour the water into the blender and run on high speed. Add the cubes a few at a time through top or small opening in cover. Continue to blend until clinking stops and ice cubes are melted. Sprinkle with spice, if desired. *One serving, 115 calories (25 calories more with vanilla yogurt).*

**Busted Blueberry:** Substitute ½ cup blueberries (or other berries) for the banana. *One serving, 115 calories.*

**Shook-up Pineapple Nog:** Substitute ½ cup canned crushed unsweetened pineapple for the banana. *One serving, 135 calories.*

### No-Calorie Espresso

Flavor doesn't have to be fattening; in fact, it can have no calories at all. Consider coffee. The heady fragrance is so rich it smells fattening! Even the most flavorful coffee—deep, dark espresso—is virtually calorie-free.

Today, expensive espresso-making machines are all the rage among gadget collectors, but you don't really need special equipment to capture espresso flavor. The flavor comes from the bean, not the machine! The most widely available espressos on the American market are ground to work with conventional coffee-making equipment. That means you can brew espresso in whatever you use to make ordinary coffee.

How? Plan to use more espresso than you would ordinary coffee, because espresso is supposed to be strong. However, the "rules" are happily adjustable for suit-yourself American tastes. The standard, if you want to be authentic, is to use 2 coffee measures (4 tablespoons) ground espresso for every 6 ounces of water (or ⅔ cup espresso to 2 cups water) . . . in other words, double the amount you would usually use for regular coffee.

That's a touch too assertive for some American tastes. Many prefer to use less: 1½ coffee measures (3 tablespoons) for each 6 ounces of water (or ½ cup espresso to 2 cups water). If you're a traditionalist, you'll drink it straight and unsweetened, but with a twist of lemon peel. If you like it sweet but still calorie-free, you can sweeten it to taste with sugar substitute. (The deep flavor of espresso completely masks the bitter aftertaste of sweeteners that some people are sensitive to, so there's no reason to waste calories.)

Better than wasting calories on sugar, some people prefer to add its equivalent in flavorful liqueurs: 1 or 2 teaspoons of anisette or anise-flavored Sambucca, for example, or Amaretto, Vandermint, Kahlua, curaçao, Grand Marnier, etc. Most are about 18 to 20 calories per teaspoon. If you add them to the water before the coffee is brewed, some of the alcohol calories will vaporize. Another, less fattening, idea is to flavor espresso brews with a teaspoon or two of undiluted fruit-juice concentrate. Or spice it with cinnamon, nutmeg, cloves, or allspice; they cost you virtually nothing in calories.

Cold espresso can be recycled into flavorful sweets and treats. Here are some to try:

## ESPRESSO MILK SHAKE I

¾ cup cold brewed espresso, or very strong coffee
⅓ cup nonfat dry milk powder
2 or 3 ice cubes
1 teaspoon sugar or equivalent no-calorie sweetener
¼ teaspoon vanilla, rum, or brandy, extract, or ½ teaspoon chocolate extract
  (optional)
  Pinch of cinnamon, nutmeg, cloves, allspice, apple-pie spice or pumpkin-pie
  spice (optional)

Combine in blender until ice is dissolved. *One serving, under 100 calories (15 calories less without sugar).*

**Jamaica Banana Shake:** Omit sugar, substitute ½ small very ripe banana. Use ½ teaspoon rum flavoring and a pinch of allspice. *125 calories.*

**Espresso Milkshake II:** For brewed espresso and dry milk powder substitute 1 cup cold skim milk and 2 rounded teaspoons instant espresso coffee powder. *Makes a very large (about 2-cup) shake, 105 calories.*

Iced espresso can also be treated to low-calorie sweetener and perhaps a twist of lemon peel, just like hot espresso.

### Try Nonfattening Hot Chocolate

Hot chocolate is fattening. Consider jolly ol' St. Nicholas. Despite all the exercise, Santa Claus also gets a cup of cocoa at nearly every stop.

If you'd like to avoid a roly-poly North Pole figure—without passing up hot cocoa—try our "decalorized" variations:

## LOW-CAL HOT CHOCOLATE I

FOR EACH SERVING
 2 teaspoons unsweetened cocoa
¼ teaspoon arrowroot or cornstarch
 Pinch of salt or butter-flavored salt
 2 teaspoons sugar or equivalent sugar substitute
 1 cup skim milk, heated

Put dry ingredients in blender container. Add hot milk, cover, blend until frothy. Serve immediately. One serving, 135 calories with sugar; *105 calories with sugar substitute.*

## HOT CHOCOLATE II

FOR EACH SERVING
 2 teaspoons unsweetened cocoa
 Sugar substitute to equal 2 teaspoons sugar
⅓ cup dry skim-milk powder
 Dash of salt or butter-flavored salt
 1 cup boiling water

Put dry ingredients in blender container. Add the boiling water and cover. Blend until frothy. Serve immediately. *105 calories per 1-cup serving.*

## HOT SPICED MOCHA COCOA

FOR TWO SERVINGS
  1 tablespoon plain cocoa
  1 tablespoon instant coffee
    Dash salt
  ½ cup water
  2 cups skim milk
  1 teaspoon noncaloric liquid sweetener
  ½ teaspoon vanilla extract
    Cinnamon sticks

Combine cocoa, coffee, salt, and water in a saucepan. Cook over medium heat, stirring constantly until mixture comes to a boil. Add skim milk, liquid sweetener, and vanilla extract. Heat just to boiling. Serve with a cinnamon-stick stirrer. *Five ½-cup servings, 40 calories each.* (From *The Kid Slimming Book* by Audrey Ellis, published by Regnery).

## SUGAR-FREE LOW-FAT HOT COCOA MIX

Enough for 24 cups.

8 cups nonfat dry milk powder
1 cup unsweetened cocoa
1 cup granulated sugar substitute
1 tablespoon salt or butter-flavored salt

Stir together thoroughly and store in a tightly covered container.
  For 1 serving, combine 5 heaping tablespoons mix with 1 cup boiling water in blender. Cover and blend until frothy. *95 calories per serving.*

**Mocha Cocoa:** Follow the preceding directions, but add ¼ teaspoon instant coffee powder for each serving.

**Spiced Cocoa:** Add a few drops of vanilla extract and a dash of cinnamon to each serving.

### Party-Goers' Calorie Guide: Beer, Wine, Liquors, and Mixes

Here's the news on booze for calorie-wary merrymakers:
  SLIM GIN? No such thing! There is no real calorie difference among hard liquors of the same proof. Ninety-proof gin, vodka, scotch, rum, whiskey, and tequila are all 74 calories an ounce. Eighty-proof booze is 65 calories while

100-proof is 83 calories. The alcohol percentage of hard liquor is half the proof. In other words, 100-proof vodka is 50 percent alcohol!

MAKE MINE WINE: The alcohol percentage in wine ranges from a low of 7 or 8 percent for some of the "light" wines and popular Italian imports to a high of 12 or 13 percent for some of the strong sherries or fortified wines like vermouth. The lower the alcohol content of the wine, the lower the calorie count is likely to be: about 20 calories an ounce for an 8- or 9-percent-alcohol wine, compared to about 42 calories for sweet vermouth.

A word about finding "light" wine: look for the alcohol content on the label; the word "light" is no guarantee. In wine talk the word "light" can also mean color, depth, or body. Double whammy drinks such as martinis and manhattans, that combine vermouth with hard liquor, are especially calorific. For the least calories, combine light low-alcohol wine with club soda in a tall glass with ice cubes.

LOOK OUT FOR LIQUEURS: Drinks like Amaretto, Kahlua, Curaçao, creme de menthe and crème de cacao combine both alcohol and sugar syrup and are especially devastating. Calories differ, depending on proof and sweetness, but 60-proof liqueurs average around 100 calories an ounce. Combining them with cream pushes them into the hot-fudge-sundae class, calorically speaking.

EGGNOG IS A HEAVYWEIGHT, even without liquor added. Most commercially cartoned brands range between 300 and 350 calories a cupful, without liquor added. And homemade eggnog can be even heavier on the cream and hard stuff. A cup of holiday cheer can cost you more calories than seven-layer cake.

NIX ON SUGARY MIXERS: Even those that don't seem very sweet can be sour about calories. Would you believe bitter lemon soda is 128 calories for 8 ounces? By comparison, lemon-flavored Sprite and Seven-Up are 100 calories. But sugar-free Seven-Up and Fresca have only a trace. Tonic water and ginger ale have 85 calories. Club soda and mineral water are calorie free.

FATTENING FRUIT JUICES, used as mixers, can have as many calories as soda, or more. Orange juice is 112 calories an 8-ounce glass; unsweetened pineapple is 138. But tomato juice, plain or spicy-seasoned, is only 46 calories a cupful. Packaged drink mixes range from a low of 20 to 25 for old-fashioned and bloody mary mixes to 70 or more for margarita and whiskey sour. Unsweetened coconut cream, used in making piña coladas, is a whopping 800 calories per cupful because of its high fat content. Most canned products also contain several tablespoons of sugar.

GO LIGHT ON BEER: Beers can range from light to heavy in calories as well as taste. Even among the calorie-reduced "light" alternatives, there's a considerable range: 70 calories or less per 12 ounces for some extra-light brands, up to 134 for Michelob Light. Regular beer is 150 calories per can, but some of the newly-popular dark imports can weigh in at much more than that. "Light" can also refer to color or flavor as well as calorie count, so look for calorie information on the label before you assume that a "light" import is what you want.

## Any Alcoholic Drink Can Be a Spritzer

Need help turning short, fat drinks into tall, skinny ones? Get first aid from club soda and ice cubes. Any favorite-but-fattening concoction can be rescued from its high calorie count by turning it into a spritzer.

A traditional spritzer is white wine diluted with club soda or seltzer water, and lengthened into a tall glass with lots of ice. Cuts the calories, too!

You can apply the spritzer remedy to any high-calorie or alcohol-heavy beverage merely by cooling it down with lots of ice cubes and sparkling water, seltzer, or club soda. Don't waste money on high-priced imported mineral waters when making spritzers; their salty taste actually detracts from the flavor.

Some ideas to try:

# SUNRISE SPRITZER

**2 tablespoons 80-proof tequila**
**1 tablespoon undiluted defrosted orange-juice concentrate**
**1 tablespoon bottled red grape juice**
   **Club soda or seltzer**

Combine; serve over ice. *105 calories.*

# WHISKEY SOUR SPRITZER

**2 tablespoons 80-proof whiskey**
   **Juice of ½ lime or lemon**
**1 teaspoon fine sugar, honey, or fructose syrup (optional)**
   **Club soda or seltzer**

Combine; serve over ice. *70 calories (90 calories with sweetener).*

# MANHATTAN SPRITZER

**2 tablespoons 80-proof whiskey**
**¼ cup sweet or dry vermouth**
   **Dash of bitters (optional)**
   **Club soda or seltzer**

Combine; serve over ice. *130 calories.*

# MARTINI SPRITZER

2 tablespoons 80-proof gin
¼ cup dry vermouth
  Club soda or seltzer
  Olive (optional)

Combine gin, vermouth, and club soda or seltzer; serve over ice, garnished with olive (about 5 calories), if desired. *130 calories.*

# BLOODY MARY SPRITZER

2 tablespoons 80-proof gin or vodka
¾ cup plain or seasoned tomato juice
2 teaspoons lemon juice
  Dash of hot pepper sauce and Worcestershire (optional)
  Club soda or seltzer

Combine; serve over ice (add a rib of celery as a stirrer, if desired). *105 calories.*

# SHERRY-NECTAR SPRITZER

1 tablespoon undiluted defrosted pineapple-juice concentrate
¼ cup canned apricot or peach nectar
3 tablespoons dry sherry (or dry vermouth)
  Club soda or seltzer

Combine; serve over ice. *120 calories.*

# IRISH COFFEE OR ESPRESSO SPRITZER

¼ cup very strong cold coffee, espresso or American, or instant coffee
2 tablespoons 80-proof whiskey
  Pinch of cinnamon (optional)
2 teaspoons superfine sugar or equivalent sugar substitute or to taste (optional)
  Club soda or seltzer
  Skim milk (optional)

In a tall glass mix together coffee, whiskey and cinnamon and sugar if used. Add soda or seltzer to fill halfway. Fill with ice cubes. Add milk, if desired.

If using instant coffee, put a rounded teaspoon in a tall tempered glass or clear glass coffee mug. Add cinnamon and sweetener, if desired. Stir in ¼ cup boiling water, until dissolved. Proceed as before. *65 calories; with sugar and milk, 105 calories.*

## WINE-APPLE SPRITZER

2 tablespoons undiluted apple juice or cider concentrate, defrosted
3 tablespoons white wine
  Club soda or seltzer
  Diced apple (optional)

Combine; serve over ice with a stirrer. Add some diced apple—5 calories per ¼ cup—if desired. *155 calories.*

## EXTRA-LIGHT WINE SPRITZER

3 ounces any low-alcohol light white wine (under 9 percent alcohol)
  Club soda, seltzer, or charged water (*not* mineral water)
  Twist of lemon or lime

Fill a tall glass or footed water goblet with ice cubes. Add wine and soda; garnish with a twist of lemon or lime. Approximately 60 calories, depending on the sweetness of the wine.

## KIR SPRITZER

¼ cup any low-alcohol white wine (9 percent alcohol or less)
1 tablespoon crème de cassis (black currant liqueur)
  Club soda, seltzer, or charged water (not mineral water)
  Twist of lemon

Combine liquid ingredients over ice cubes in a tall glass or footed water goblet. Garnish with lemon peel. Approximately 85 calories.

**Grape Kir Spritzer:** Substitute 2 tablespoons bottled unsweetened grape juice for the crème de cassis. *Approximately 65 calories.*

**Cranberry Kir Spritzer:** Substitute 3 tablespoons cranberry-juice cocktail for the crème de cassis. *Approximately 75 calories.*

## LIGHT SANGRÍA SPRITZER

¼ cup any low-alcohol red wine (9 percent alcohol or less)
1 tablespoon undiluted frozen orange-juice concentrate
  Club soda, seltzer, or charged water (not mineral water)
  Fruit garnish (optional)

Combine liquid ingredients in a tall glass or footed water goblet. Garnish with orange slices, seedless grapes, hulled whole strawberries, blueberries, etc., if desired. Approximately 70 calories (excluding fruit garnish).

**White Sangría Spritzer:** Substitute light (low-alcohol) white wine.

**Light Sangría:** For a still (nonsparkling) sangría, combine ¼ cup low-alcohol red wine with ½ cup fresh or reconstituted orange juice; omit club soda. *Approximately 95 calories.*

**Sangría Screwdriver:** Substitute low-alcohol white wine for the red wine. Garnish with orange slices.

## LOWER-CALORIED PARTY EGG NOG

One-third less calories than the standard kind.

4 **eggs, separated**
2 **cups low-fat vanilla ice milk**
1 **cup skim milk**
1 **cup 80-proof whiskey**
2 **tablespoons 80-proof rum**
4 **tablespoons sugar**
   **Nutmeg**

Beat egg yolks until light. Beat in ice milk, then milk, whiskey, and rum. Set aside.

Using clean beater and bowl, beat egg whites until stiff but not dry. Gradually beat in sugar. Fold beaten egg whites into egg-yolk mixture. Pour into serving bowl and sprinkle with nutmeg. *Twenty servings, 80 calories each.*

# 11
# NONSWEET NIBBLES, NOSHES, AND OTHER SAVORY SNACKS, DECALORIZED

## Light Peanut Butter . . . and Other Nutty Ideas

If you have to count your calories, one item that's sure to be on your forbidden-foods list is peanut butter. At 94 calories a tablespoon, peanut butter's calorie count is topped only by such mega-calorie items as butter, margarine, mayonnaise, and salad oil.

Commercial peanut butter, even the low-salt dietetic kind, is one of the most-fattening foods there is. This decalorized version contains less than half the calories, far less fat, and much more protein. Two tablespoons of our Slim Gourmet peanut butter has eight grams of protein . . . that's more than an egg. How about our peanut butter on your breakfast toast?

## SLIM GOURMET "LIGHT" PEANUT BUTTER I

**9-ounce jar (2 cups) dry-roasted peanuts**
**1¼ cups cold water (approximately)**
**2 teaspoons sugar or sugar substitute (optional)**

Put peanuts in blender container, cover, and blend on high speed until peanuts are reduced to a powder. Uncover and add the water, a little at a time, blending after each addition, until the proper peanut-butter consistency is reached. Sweeten to taste, if desired.

Scrape down frequently with a rubber scraper. Spoon into a jar and store in the refrigerator. (Homemade peanut butter, without preservatives, should be refrigerated.) *Makes 2¼ cups, 43 calories per tablespoon, with sugar; 42 calories per tablespoon without sugar.*

Calorie-wise, here's how it compares:

**Peanut Butter Calories**

| 1 Tablespoon | Calories |
| --- | --- |
| Slim Gourmet | 43 |
| Commercial brands | 95 |
| Dietetic brands | 95 |

When a peanut shortage caused the price to soar almost as high as the calorie count, butters from other nuts and seeds became popular. Many wondered if these other butters were a better bargain. Can you save calories with cashew butter? Is sesame or sunflower butter less fattening?

Most peanut-butter competitors don't list calorie counts, but the labels do indicate if the product is "pure" or if it contains other ingredients. One pound of pure cashew butter will have the same calorie count as the cashews did before they were ground. The same is true of other nuts and seeds ground into butters without additives. Because most nuts and seeds have similar fat contents, the differences among them are slight:

| 1 Pound | Calories |
| --- | --- |
| Peanuts | 2,558 |
| Almonds | 2,713 |
| Cashews | 2,545 |
| Sesame | 2,554 |
| Sunflower | 2,540 |

Can you save calories on nut and seed butters? A quick way to remove some of the calories is simply to drain them away . . . by pouring off the oil that separates to the top. Each tablespoon of oil you drain off has about 115 to 125 calories, while the nut residue has considerably less. Keep in mind that fat has more than twice the calories of protein, carbohydrate, or fiber. The ability to pour off oil (and calories) is one good reason for buying pure peanut butter rather than brands with added hard fats that keep them from separating.

# "LIGHT" PEANUT BUTTER II

Another way to cut the calories of peanut or other nut and seed butters is to blend them into a protein-rich spread made with the dieter's friend: cottage cheese. This "light" spread is particularly tasty when made with ground sesame-seed "butter" (also known as "tahini").

½ **cup pure peanut, sesame, or other nut butter**
½ **cup uncreamed low-fat cottage cheese**
  **Pinch of salt (optional)**

Pour off surface oil from the nut butter. Have the cottage cheese firmly packed when measuring it. Combine butter, cheese, and salt, if using, in blender or food processor; process until completely smooth. Scrape down the sides of the container with a rubber scraper. Blend again. Transfer to a 1-cup container. Cover and keep stored in the refrigerator. *One cup, 55 calories per tablespoon.*

**Mock Walnut Butter:** Follow the preceding recipe, using sesame "butter." Add walnut flavoring (to taste) and blend smooth. Store in the refrigerator. *55 calories per tablespoon.*

## Low-Calorie Breadspreads

In search of a better breadspread? Discover part-skim ricotta.

It makes a delicious breadspread straight from the container, although it's not as smooth or salty as butter. You can make it more butterlike by beating it smooth in your blender or food processor. Season it with salt or butter flavoring, if you like. Whether you use it straight from the container or blended and salted, ricotta makes a delicious spread for your breakfast toast. Try topping it with raisins (instead of jelly) and a sprinkle of cinnamon.

Here are some ideas to try:

# LOW-CALORIE BREADSPREAD

7½ **ounces (½ container) part-skim ricotta**
3 **tablespoons butter**
  **Salt or butter-flavored salt, or butter flavoring, to taste**

Blend ricotta smooth in a covered blender or in a food processor, using the steel blade. Add room-temperature butter and blend smooth. Season to taste with salt, butter-flavored salt, a few drops butter flavoring, or 2 or 3 teaspoons powdered butter flavoring. *10 calories per tablespoon.*

# CHEDDAR CHEESE "BUTTER"

Here's a zesty breadspread that's great on pumpernickel or Swedish rye crisp bread. It's equally good as a topping for baked potatoes, rice, or hot fresh vegetables. Or try tossing it with hot drained pasta. Use a yellow cheese for buttery color, and be sure the cheese is extra sharp. Add more mustard, if you like, for a spicier flavor.

3 ounces extra-sharp yellow Cheddar cheese
  15-ounce container part-skim ricotta
  Salt to taste
1 teaspoon prepared mustard (optional)
  Shake of cayenne pepper (optional)

Shred or grate Cheddar (use metal shredding disk in food processor, or use steel blade in processor or blender). Beat ricotta smooth in blender or food processor, using the steel blade. Add Cheddar, salt to taste, mustard and cayenne, if desired; beat smooth. Spoon into 2 half-pound margarine containers; cover and store in refrigerator. It will keep 2–3 weeks, depending on the freshness of the ricotta (check label). Will become firmer when chilled. *Approximately 1 pound, 20 calories per tablespoon.*

# HERBED PARMESAN "BUTTER"

7½ ounces (½ container) part-skim ricotta cheese
¼ cup grated Parmesan cheese
¼ cup fresh parsley
¼ teaspoon dried basil or oregano
  Salt or onion or garlic salt, to taste

Blend ricotta smooth in blender or food processor, using the steel blade. Add remaining ingredients and blend smooth. Store in a covered container in the refrigerator. Use on French or Italian bread, toss with pasta, or add to broccoli or zucchini. *Approximately 1¼ cups, 15 calories per tablespoon.*

# LOW-FAT DIP BASES

Instead of sour cream at nearly 1,000 calories a pint—or cream cheese at 800 or more an eight-ounce package—whip up a decalorized dip base in your blender or food processor at only one-half or one-third the calories. Avoid most "nondairy" synthetic sour cream, or cream cheese substitutes made with oil. The fat is usually highly-saturated coconut oil and these products may be as fattening and cholesterol-causing as the "real thing." Try these:

**Mock Sour Cream I:** Combine in a blender or food processor, using the steel blade: 2 cups small-curd low-fat cottage cheese and ½ cup buttermilk. Cover and process smooth. *10 calories per tablespoon.*

**Mock Sour Cream II:** Process 2 cups small-curd low-fat cottage cheese with 2 tablespoons lemon juice, ½ cup skim milk. *10 calories per tablespoon.*

**Mock Sour Cream III:** Process 2 cups dry-curd low-fat cottage cheese with 1 cup plain yogurt. *10 calories per tablespoon.*

**Mock Sour Cream IV:** Put plain low-fat yogurt in a paper coffee filter cone (over a container) and allow it to drain in the refrigerator several hours until it is the right thickness. *10 calories per tablespoon.*

**Mock Sour Cream V:** Combine 1 cup sour half 'n' half and 1 cup plain low-fat yogurt. *15 calories per tablespoon.*

**Mock Cream Cheese Base I:** Combine softened 3-ounce package low-calorie ("light") cream cheese with 1 cup part-skim ricotta cheese in blender. Cover and blend smooth. *25 calories per tablespoon.*

**Mock Cream Cheese Base II:** Combine in blender an 8-ounce package low-calorie ("light") cream cheese at room temperature with 1 cup skim milk. Cover and blend smooth. *15 calories per tablespoon.*

**Mock Cream Cheese Base III:** Combine an 8-ounce package Neufchâtel cheese with 1 cup skim milk in blender. Cover and blend smooth. *20 calories per tablespoon.*

**Mock Cream Cheese Base IV:** Combine a 3-ounce package low-calorie ("light") cream cheese with 1 cup large-curd creamed cottage cheese and ½ cup skim milk in blender. Cover and blend smooth. *15 calories per tablespoon.*

## STIR AND SERVE DIPS

To each cup of mock sour cream or cream cheese base, prepared according to any of the above directions, add any of the following:

**Garlic Dip:** 1 minced clove garlic or ⅛ teaspoon instant garlic, plus 1 teaspoon salt and 2 tablespoons chopped fresh parsley.

**Instant Onion Dip:** 1 tablespoon dry onion flakes and 1 envelope (or teaspoon) instant beef broth.

**California Dip:** ½ envelope dry onion-soup mix.

**Chili "Christmas" Dip:** 1 tablespoon minced green pepper, 1 tablespoon minced sweet red pepper, 1 tablespoon chili sauce, ½ teaspoon onion salt.

**Blue Cheese Dip:** Partially freeze a chunk of blue cheese, then grate. Stir in 2 tablespoons grated cheese, 1 teaspoon Worcestershire sauce, 1 teaspoon garlic salt.

**Cheddar Dip:** Partially freeze a chunk of extra-sharp Cheddar, then grate. Add 5 tablespoons grated Cheddar, 2 tablespoons minced red or green bell pepper, 1 tablespoon minced onion, ½ teaspoon salt.

**Shrimp Dip (for shrimp or cold seafood):** Add 5 tablespoons low-fat mayonnaise, 1 tablespoon chili sauce, 2 tablespoons lemon juice, 1 tablespoon grated onion, 1 or more teaspoons prepared horseradish, ½ teaspoon garlic salt (optional).

**Curried Fruit Dip (for apple cubes, other fresh fruit):** Add 5 tablespoons low-fat mayonnaise, 1 tablespoon granulated sugar substitute or 2 teaspoons honey, ½ teaspoon salt, 1 teaspoon curry powder.

**No-Work Dips:** Combine your favorite dip base with ½ packet of dry salad-dressing mix (Green Goddess, Garlic French, Cheese-Italian, Bleu Cheese, Smokey Bacon, etc).

## Easy, Low-Calorie Homemade Crock Cheeses

Why not "process" your own more-flavorful cheese spreads? Home-processed soft cheese can be a lot less fattening than the commercial kinds with their artificial flavors and fatty fillers. During the garden season, you can make your homemade cheese spreads really special by using fresh herbs instead of the dried variety.

Home-processed cheeses are a snap if you have a food processor . . . or a blender.

The basis of homemade low-calorie cheese spreads is 1 cup low-fat fresh cheese (ricotta, cottage, farmer) to 2 ounces very sharp, *very* flavorful aged cheese. Since the hard aged cheese has most of the fat (and calories), it's imperative that you choose only the strongly-flavored varieties. There's little point in wasting calories on bland-but-fattening cheeses like Swiss or Jarlsberg!

Your low-calorie homemade cheese blend is then further seasoned with strongly flavored accents: fresh herbs, onion, garlic, mustard, horseradish, for example. You can vary the seasonings to suit your taste; a little more or less won't alter the calorie count very much. The only high-calorie ingredient in these blends is the full-fat hard cheese . . . so don't use more than 2 ounces.

**Processed Cheese:** For best results, the hard cheese should first be grated or shredded, using a hand shredder or the shredding disk of a food processor. Or cut the hard cheese into cubes, then process the cubes into a fine powder in the blender or food processor, using the steel blade.

Once the hard cheese is shredded or grated, combine it with the soft fresh cheese and other ingredients in either the blender or the food processor, using the steel blade. Puree the mixture smooth. At this point, the spread will be very soft and creamy. However, it will become firmer once it's chilled.

Scoop the spread into covered containers or crocks and store in the refrigerator. (It should keep until the expiration date on the package of fresh cheese from which it was made.) Use as a spread for flatbread, crackers, saltines, pretzels, or raw vegetables. Crisp bread, homemade cheese, and raw vegetables make a healthy, nutritious, low-calorie lunch.

## TEX-MEX CHEESE SPREAD

2 ounces extra-sharp aged Cheddar cheese
1 cup part-skim ricotta cheese
1 clove garlic
2 tablespoons minced onion or 2 teaspoons onion flakes
2 tablespoons minced fresh parsley
1 tablespoon minced fresh oregano or 1 teaspoon dried oregano
2 teaspoons whole cumin seeds or 1 teaspoon ground cumin
1 teaspoon chili powder (or more, to taste)
  Butter flavoring, salt, to taste (optional)

Follow How-to directions  (see page 232). *About 1½ cups, approximately 25 calories per tablespoon.*

## ITALIAN CHEESE SPREAD

2 ounces grated sharp Romano cheese
1 cup part-skim ricotta cheese
1 small clove garlic, chopped
2 tablespoons minced onion or 2 teaspoons onion flakes
2 tablespoons minced fresh parsley
1 tablespoon minced fresh oregano or 1 teaspoon dried oregano
1 tablespoon minced fresh basil or 1 teaspoon dried basil
  Butter flavoring, salt, pepper, to taste (optional)

Follow How-to directions (see page 232). *About 1½ cups, approximately 25 calories per tablespoon.*

# GREEK CHEESE SPREAD

2 ounces crumbled part-skim feta cheese
1 cup farmer cheese or uncreamed low-fat cottage cheese
3 tablespoons plain low-fat yogurt
2 teaspoons lemon juice
1 small clove garlic
3 tablespoons chopped fresh parsley
1 tablespoon fresh or 1 teaspoon dried mint or marjoram
⅛ teaspoon nutmeg
2 teaspoons fresh or ½ teaspoon dried oregano or basil (optional)
 Butter flavoring, salt, pepper, to taste (optional)

Follow "How-to" directions (see page 232). *About 1½ cups approximately 20 calories per tablespoon with farmer cheese; 15 calories per tablespoon with cottage cheese.*

# LOW-CAL APPLE-CURRY PARTY DIP

12 ounces (1½ cups) low-fat cottage cheese
1 cup unsweetened applesauce
1 envelope onion-soup mix
 Sugar substitute to equal 3 tablespoons sugar (optional)
2 teaspoons curry powder or more, to taste

In covered blender, beat cottage cheese and applesauce smooth. Stir in soup mix; season to taste with sugar substitute and curry. Serve with raw vegetables, fresh fruit, or cubes of lean cooked cold meat on picks. *Approximately 2⅔ cups, 10 calories per tablespoon.*

# APPLE CURRY DIP

1 cup part-skim fresh ricotta
1 cup unsweetened applesauce
2 to 3 teaspoons curry powder (to taste)
½ teaspoon pumpkin- or apple-pie spice or a pinch each of cinnamon, nutmeg,
 cloves, ginger
 Salt and pepper to taste

If using unwhipped ricotta or chunky applesauce, combine all ingredients in blender or food processor and blend smooth. If using already-whipped ricotta and smooth applesauce, simply stir ingredients together until blended. Chill until serving time. Surround with fresh fruit or vegetable "dippers." *Approximately 2 cups, 14 calories per tablespoon.*

## FRUITED CHEESE SPREAD

**8-ounce package low-calorie ("light") cream cheese (or Neufchâtel cheese)**
**2 tablespoons defrosted orange- or pineapple-juice concentrate**
**Few drops vanilla extract**

Have cheese at room temperature. Beat in remaining ingredients. Use as a spread on toasted protein or high-fiber bread. *Approximately 30 calories per tablespoon.*

### Farmer Cheese: Easy Base for Nonfattening Spreads

If you entertain the Slim Gourmet way, it's always a good idea to have a package or two of low-calorie farmer cheese on hand in your refrigerator. Be sure to use *fresh* farmer cheese, the kind with the soft texture of cream cheese or dry cottage cheese—not the aged farmer cheese, with a firm texture similar to mozzarella. It's easy to whip up a nonfattening dip or spread in seconds. Here are some ideas to try:

## MEXICAN CHEESE BALL

**7½-ounce package fresh farmer cheese**
**1 or 2 hot red cherry peppers, fresh or canned**
**1 teaspoon dried oregano**
**1 clove garlic, peeled**
**1 tablespoon cumin seeds or 1½ teaspoons ground cumin**
**About 5 tablespoons toasted sunflower seeds**

Combine ingredients (except sunflower seeds) in blender or food processor, using the steel blade. Blend smooth. Sprinkle some sunflower seeds on a sheet of aluminum foil. Pile cheese mixture on top of seeds and gently shape into a ball. Pat remaining sunflower seeds onto the surface of the cheese, until covered with seeds. Gently fold over aluminum foil to cover. Refrigerate until serving time. Serve with corn chips, celery scoopers or thin crackers. *Cheese ball: 35 calories per tablespoon.*

**With Sweet Pepper:** Substitute 4 tablespoons minced sweet red bell pepper or drained canned pimiento for the hot cherry pepper. Add chili powder, cayenne pepper, or Tabasco to taste.

*(continued)*

**Mexican Crock Cheese:** Omit sunflower seeds. Pile mixture into a cheese crock or other covered container and refrigerate. *20 calories per tablespoon.*

## FARMER'S LOW-FAT "CREAM CHEESE"

**8-ounce package regular or salt-free fresh farmer cheese or dry pot cheese**
**Salt or butter-flavored salt to taste or 1 envelope butter-flavored granules**
**  (optional)**

Combine ingredients in blender or food processor, using the steel blade. Process on high speed 2 to 3 minutes, until every bit of graininess disappears and mixture has the texture of very thick cream. Transfer to a covered container and store in the refrigerator. When chilled, it will have the taste and texture of spreadable cream cheese. *Sixteen tablespoon-size servings, under 20 calories each; 3 calories more per serving with granulated butter substitute.*

### More Entertaining Ideas with Farmer Cheese

Blend or process farmer cheese with commercial bottled low-calorie salad dressing. The higher the ratio of salad dressing, the more liquid the dip will be. Try Bleu Cheese *(about 12 calories per tablespoon)* or Italian *(about 8 calories per tablespoon,* depending on the brand).

Or blend farmer cheese with a packet of dry salad-dressing mix for a firm spread. For a more liquid dip, thin with a little lemon juice, yogurt, skim milk, buttermilk, or water.

For a sweet spread, blend or process farmer cheese with mixed minced dried fruit and a few tablespoons fruit juice or cider. Season with spices or curry powder, if desired, and top with dry-roasted nuts.

Try the old onion-soup trick (California Dip) using farmer cheese instead of sour cream: blend or process 1 package farmer cheese with 1 envelope dry onion-soup mix, to make a firm spread. For a thinner dip, add plain low-fat yogurt, skim milk, or buttermilk.

## MONTEREY PEPPER CHEESE

**  1  very large well-shaped green bell pepper**
**  4  tablespoons minced red pepper (sweet bell pepper or canned pimiento)**
**7½  ounces fresh farmer cheese**
**1½  ounces extra-sharp Cheddar, diced**
**  2  teaspoons prepared mustard (mild or spicy)**
**  1  to 2 teaspoons chili powder (optional)**

Slit off the top of the green pepper to form a cup. Remove and discard seeds and membranes. Trim off and discard stem from pepper top; mince the edible part of the pepper top and add it to the minced red pepper. Combine remaining ingredients in blender or food processor (using the steel blade) and blend smooth. Fold in minced pepper. Pile the mixture into the pepper cup. Refrigerate until serving time. To serve, surround with thin crackers, vegetable scoopers, or corn chips. *Makes about 1¼ cups. 25 calories per tablespoon (cheese only).*

## SPANISH OLIVE DIP

7½ ounces fresh farmer cheese
¼ cup liquid from olive jar
¼ cup minced green olives with pimiento
   Paprika, sliced olives for garnish (optional)

For this recipe, use the less-expensive "salad olives"—cut-up green olives and red pimiento pieces.

Put cheese and olive liquid in blender or food processor and blend until smooth and fluffy. Add olives and blend with quick on-off motions, just until olives are minced. Sprinkle with paprika and garnish with sliced olives, if desired. Refrigerate until serving time. *One and a quarter cups, 16 calories per tablespoon.*

## FARMER CHEESE-PINEAPPLE BALL

1 cup juice-packed crushed pineapple
16 ounces fresh farmer cheese (2 packages, 8 ounces each)
¼ cup minced bell pepper
3 tablespoons chopped chives or scallions
½ cup salted dry-roasted sunflower seeds

Drain pineapple, pressing out moisture well. Combine with remaining ingredients, except sunflower seeds, until well blended. Shape mixture into a ball and roll in sunflower seeds until well coated. 32 servings, 35 calories each.

**Smooth Pineapple-Pepper Spread:** Omit sunflower seeds. Combine remaining ingredients in blender or food processor, using the steel blade. Process smooth. Spoon into a crock and refrigerate until serving time. *25 calories per serving.*

# PINEAPPLE-CHEESE DESSERT SPREAD

½ cup juice-packed crushed pineapple
8 ounces fresh farmer cheese
1 teaspoon vanilla extract
2 tablespoons honey, fructose, or equivalent sugar substitute (optional)
   Cinnamon

Press out moisture from pineapple; combine pineapple with remaining ingredients, except cinnamon, in blender or food processor, using the steel blade. Blend smooth. Spoon into a crock; sprinkle with cinnamon and refrigerate until serving time.

Use as a spread for graham crackers or thin vanilla wafers, topped with raw apple wedges, whole strawberries, or other fresh fruit—tastes like miniature cheesecakes! *Spread for 16 crackers, 25 calories each (spread only); if using honey or fructose 35 calories each.*

# CURRIED FRUIT CROCK CHEESE

7½ ounces fresh farmer cheese or Neufchâtel cheese or low-calorie ("light")
   cream cheese
2 teaspoons curry powder (or to taste)
   Salt, if needed, or butter-flavored salt
6 tablespoons diced dried fruit bits

Combine ingredients, except fruit, in food processor (using the steel blade) or in blender or electric mixer bowl. Beat until fluffy. Fold in fruit. Spoon into a covered crock and store in the refrigerator. Serve with saltines or thin wheat crackers. *About 1⅓ cups crock cheese, 20 calories per tablespoon with farmer cheese, 30 calories per tablespoon with Neufchâtel, 25 calories per tablespoon with low-calorie cream cheese.*

## Calorie-Cheap Chips and Dippers:

Raw carrot sticks; celery scoops; mushroom slices; cauliflorets; broccoli buds; radish disks; baby carrots; white radish icicles; sliced canned water chestnuts; red or green bell-pepper rings; cucumber, zucchini, or dill pickle chips; pared sliced jicama or sunchokes; pineapple fingers; apple or pear cubes; orange sections or melon cubes.

## Quick Pickles in the Refrigerator

Peter Piper's plenty picky about pickles, so he was tickled pink when Penny Potter pickled her own for their picnic. Previously, Peter had picked up the pickles, but they proved perilously pound-provoking, because the processed pickles Peter purchased were packed with sugar.

Here are my favorite homemade pickle recipes. These are super-simple "new" or "green" pickles you make in the refrigerator . . . no elaborate canning techniques necessary. If you like your pickles fresh and crispy, more like marinated than processed, you'll love these.

# NEW GREEN REFRIGERATOR PICKLES

4 cups small whole pickling cucumbers
1 tablespoon mixed pickling spices
1 clove garlic, mashed
4 tablespoons non-iodized salt
¼ cup white or cider vinegar
1 quart club soda or seltzer (not mineral water, as minerals add unwanted flavors)

Wash unpeeled cucumbers and put them in a nonmetal container. Combine remaining ingredients and boil 5 minutes. Pour over cucumbers. Cover and refrigerate. Wait 2 to 3 days before serving. Store in refrigerator. *Each pickle, approximately 7 calories.*

# CIDER-MARINATED ZUCCHINI PICKLES

4 cups sliced raw unpeeled zucchini
2 tablespoons non-iodized salt
 Ice cubes
¼ cup cider vinegar
1½ cups unsweetened cider or apple juice
1 onion, thinly sliced
1 clove garlic, mashed, or pinch of instant garlic
1 tablespoon dill seeds
 A few sprigs fresh dill leaves (optional)

Slice zucchini into pickle-size chips. (Cut larger zucchini into strips or cubes.) Place in a non-metallic bowl. Sprinkle with salt and stir in a tray of ice cubes. Leave at room temperature until ice is melted. Drain off ice water.

Combine drained zucchini with remaining ingredients in a jar, crock, or other nonmetal container. Cover and refrigerate 2 days before serving. Store in refrigerator. *Approximately 15 calories per ¼ cup.*

**Cider Cucumber Pickles:** Slice fresh medium-size cucumbers into slices or spears and substitute for zucchini.

# FRUCTOSE-SWEETENED
# BREAD-AND-BUTTER PICKLES

**4 cups sliced cucumbers**
**1 cup sliced onion**
**½ cup diced red bell pepper**
**3 tablespoons non-iodized salt**
**1 cup unsweetened cider or apple juice**
**7 tablespoons fructose (fruit sugar) or fructose syrup**
**½ teaspoon ground turmeric**
**1 teaspoon celery seeds**
**1 teaspoon dry mustard**

Stir cucumbers, onion, and bell pepper with salt until well coated. Refrigerate 2 to 3 hours. Remove from refrigerator and rinse off salt. Combine remaining ingredients and heat to boiling. When mixture boils, stir in vegetables; then reheat to boiling. Allow to cool, then pour into a nonmetallic container. Cover and store in the refrigerator. Wait 2 or 3 days before serving. *Approximately 25 calories per ¼ cup.*

**Sugar-Free Bread-and-Butter Refrigerator Pickles:** Omit fructose. After the vegetables are heated to boiling, remove from the heat and stir in noncaloric sugar substitute equal to ¾ cup sugar (36 quarter-grain saccharin tablets or 18 packets granulated sweetener). *Approximately 10 calories per ¼ cup.*

### "Homemade" Low-Fat Slicing Cheese

Here's the secret for combining low-calorie fresh farmer cheese with hard grating cheese to make a "homemade" cheese that's really sharp and flavorful, all natural, firm enough to slice for sandwiches or serve on crackers . . . yet it's 39 calories less per ounce than sharp Cheddar.

You say it can't be done? Well, you're partially right . . . *unless* you have a food processor or a top-quality blender. You really need the muscle of a powerful motor to combine the two cheeses to a smooth firm texture. This is *not* a project that can be done by hand, or even with an electric mixer. With a food processor, however, it's easy. While a powerful blender can also do the job, it's very difficult to extract the thick mixture from a blender container, unless it's the type with a removable base.

The basic idea is to process together equal amounts of finely-grated well-aged hard cheese and soft, low-fat fresh farmer cheese until thoroughly amalgamated. Then you shape the mixture into a loaf, and chill it until it becomes firm.

Here are some tips before you begin:

• For best flavor, use a well-aged, very flavorful hard grating cheese such as imported Parmigiano Reggiano or Locatelli Romano. The sharper the hard cheese, the better the flavor of your homemade cheese. Be sure to use a hard grating cheese, not Cheddar, American, or any other slicing cheese. Regular cheese is too soft.

• Be sure to use a loaf of firm-textured fresh farmer cheese, not a container of pot cheese or cottage cheese (these have too much moisture).

• Unsalted farmer cheese is preferred, because the hard grating cheeses are usually quite salty.

• The hard cheese must be very finely grated, almost to a powdery texture. Commercially packaged Parmesan and Romano are fine enough, but grated-to-order hard cheeses may be too coarsely shredded. If so, process the shredded cheese in the food processor, using the steel blade, or in the blender, until powdery.

• If using solid hard cheese, grate it before you begin. Here's how: Cut the hard cheese into 1-inch cubes. Put them through the shredding disk of the food processor. Remove the cheese. Replace the shredding disk with the steel blade. Now process the coarsely shredded cheese to a fine powder.

## SLIM GOURMET LOW-CAL SHARP SLICING CHEESE

**7½-ounce loaf unsalted fresh farmer cheese**
**7½ ounces aged hard grating cheese (Parmigiano, Romano, etc.), finely grated**

For best results, have both cheeses at room temperature before you begin.

Put the fresh farmer cheese into the food processor, using the steel blade, or the blender. Cover and process until completely smooth and creamy, with no graininess . . . until the texture of thick cream.

With the motor running, add the finely grated hard cheese, a few tablespoons at a time. Scrape down container frequently. Continue to process until the mixture becomes smooth, soft, thick and warm—the texture of a heavy dough. Taste the mixture. If any grittiness or graininess remains, continue to process. (The heat generated by the churning action helps to blend the cheeses together.)

To shape the cheese: Line a square or rectangular refrigerator container with plastic wrap, then press the soft cheese into the container. (The container must be lined, otherwise you won't be able to remove the cheese once it hardens.) Fold over the plastic and press down firmly. Chill several hours. The cheese becomes firm as it chills.

To use: Lift out by the plastic wrap. Unwrap, then slice thin to serve on sandwiches or crackers, or dice into cubes for salad. Rewrap and store in the refrigerator. *Each half-ounce slice only 40 calories.*

## Some Variations

If you prefer a milder, softer, lower-caloried cheese, decrease the amount of hard grating cheese. For example, 7½ ounces fresh farmer cheese processed with 4 ounces hard grating cheese creates a well-flavored soft cheese that's only 65 calories an ounce.

For a soft, mild, low-calorie cheese spread that can be processed in a blender, combine 7½ ounces fresh farmer cheese with only 1 or 2 ounces sharp grating cheese. (Your spread will be only 25 or 30 calories per tablespoon.) Spoon into a covered crock and store in the refrigerator.

If you prefer a yellow cheese, add a pinch of ground turmeric (available on the spice shelf). Or use yellow food coloring or butter-flavored buds. Curry powder or powdered saffron will also add yellow color, as well as an interesting flavor accent.

Caraway seeds, dried herbs, ground mustard, cumin seeds, and pepper flakes are some of the other seasonings you might like to experiment with.

To turn your homemade cheese into a quick dip, combine 2 ounces of it with 8 ounces of plain low-fat yogurt in the blender or food processor.

Money-saving idea: Hard, dry, bargain-priced cheese ends on sale in the supermarket can be grated and processed with farmer cheese to make a potluck blend.

## LOW-CALORIE POPCORN

Popcorn is the waist watcher's most calorie-safe snack. Even the two-fisted snack snatcher finds it hard to scoop up more than 25 calories' worth at once!

Consider this:

Plain popcorn is less than 25 calories a cupful (and you'd need two hands cupped together to collect that much at once!). Oil added is about 40 calories. Buttered popcorn? That depends on who does the buttering, but even so, it's rarely more than 150 calories a cupful, and less fattening than most alternatives.

Differing from chips and dippers, popcorn is "self-contained." It doesn't collect calories in the form of cheese spread or sour-cream dip on its way from the cocktail table to your mouth.

Popcorn is even high fiber.

Popcorn is more than a spectator snack, it's something to do. Popcorn making is fun for all ages. It is an unpretentious, friendly food that goes best with fireside floor-sitting.

Speaking of fireplaces, that's the least-fattening place to make popcorn . . . in one of those wire baskets specifically designed for popping corn. No fats or oils needed!

**Popping Corn with Little or No Fat:** To make popcorn with no fat added, the best appliance is an electric hot-air popcorn pumper designed for the job. Next best: an electric popcorn maker with a nonstick finish to minimize the risk of sticking or burning. (There are even models with a revolving inner arm to keep the kernels moving as they pop . . . better yet.)

Lacking a corn popper, choose a big, heavy, deep pot with a nonstick finish. It should be covered, with the lid slightly off-center. That allows the steam to escape and prevents sogginess.

To make popcorn with little or no fat, spray the inside well with cooking spray for no-fat frying. If you wish, add 1 tablespoon (no more is needed) cooking oil (not butter or margarine). Add 2 or 3 kernels of corn and turn heat high. When the kernels pop, add ½ cup fresh popping corn.

Shake the pot or popcorn maker to keep the corn moving. When the popping stops, it's ready. Empty immediately into a bowl and season with salt or butter-flavored salt (no butter needed).

**Seasoned Popcorn:** If you prefer, sprinkle the hot popcorn with seasoned salt, hickory-smoked salt, garlic salt, or salt substitute, for folks on low-salt diets. Or toss the hot popcorn with butter-flavored granules.

**Leftover Popcorn:** should be allowed to cool, then bagged in plastic. It can be reheated and recrisped by spreading it on a cookie tin and putting it in a 325-degree oven for 5 minutes or so.

## NO OIL, NO SUGAR GRANOLA

**2½ cups quick oats**
**3 tablespoons shredded coconut**
**3 tablespoons dry-roasted almonds or cashews, chopped**
**3 tablespoons raisins**
**1 teaspoon cinnamon**

Spray a shallow nonstick pan or cookie tin with baking spray. Combine oats, coconut, and nuts; sprinkle them on the pan in a shallow layer. Bake uncovered, in a preheated 350-degree oven, stirring occasionally, until crisp and golden, about 20 minutes. Remove from the oven and stir in raisins and cinnamon. Allow to cool thoroughly, then store in a covered jar. Use as a snack or serve as breakfast cereal with skim milk and sliced fresh fruit. *Three cups granola, 185 calories per ½-cup serving.*

# FRENCH-BREAD PIZZA

**1-pound loaf French or Italian bread, long or round**
**½ pound shredded part-skim mozzarella cheese**
   **Garnishes: sliced peppers, mushrooms, onions, etc. (optional)**
**2 jars or cups Homemade Pizza Sauce (recipe given)**

Check the bread label; be sure to use a brand with no added fat or sugar.
With a serrated bread knife, slice the loaf in half, separating the top from the bottom. Pull out and set aside the soft bready center, reducing the calories by half. (Save the excess bread for homemade breadcrumbs.) Fill the center evenly with cheese and vegetables, if desired. Top with sauce; spread evenly. Bake the pizza in a preheated 375-degree oven about 10 to 12 minutes, until sauce is bubbling. Slice each half into 6 pieces to serve. *Twelve pieces, 120 calories each.*

# ENGLISH-MUFFIN PIZZA

FOR EACH "PIZZA"
**½ ounce part-skim mozzarella cheese**
**½ English muffin**
**2 tablespoons Homemade Pizza Sauce (recipe given)**

Spray a nonstick baking sheet (or the tray of a toaster oven) well with cooking spray for no-fat baking. Preheat the toaster-oven or oven to 500 degrees while you assemble the pizzas. Arrange cheese on muffin halves (with the cut sides up). Spoon the sauce over the cheese, smoothing it with the back of the spoon so that all the muffin is covered. Arrange the individual pizzas in a single layer on the baking sheet and bake uncovered 4 to 5 minutes, until cheese and sauce are bubbling hot. *Each pizza, 120 calories.*

# HOMEMADE PIZZA SAUCE

**2 cups well-crushed Italian tomatoes, undrained**
**1 cup water (or fat-skimmed beef broth)**
   **6-ounce can tomato paste**
**2 teaspoons dried oregano**
**1 cup chopped onion (optional)**
**1 or 2 cloves garlic, minced (optional)**
**2 or 3 minced black olives or ¼ cup olive liquid from can of olives (optional)**

Crush tomatoes and stir well with remaining ingredients in a heavy nonstick saucepan. (Add olives or olive liquid for a low-calorie olive-oil flavor without oil.) Cover and simmer 12 to 15 minutes. Uncover and continue to simmer 5 or 6 minutes, stirring often, until mixture is very thick. Allow to cool. Spoon into 1-cup jars. Store in the refrigerator, or label and freeze. *About 3¾ cups, 5 calories per tablespoon.*

**Mushroom-Flavored Pizza Sauce:** Substitute chopped or sliced mushrooms for all or part of the onion. Or use a 4-ounce can mushroom stems and pieces, undrained.

**Sweet-Pepper Pizza Sauce:** Remove the top and seeds from a large green bell pepper. Chop the pepper fine and add it to the ingredients before cooking.

**Pizza Sauce with Sausage Seasonings (meatless):** Replace 1 teaspoon of the oregano with 1 teaspoon dried basil. Add ½ teaspoon sage or mixed poultry seasonings and 1 teaspoon anise or fennel seeds. If desired, add a pinch of red pepper flakes. (These are the seasonings that give high-fat Italian pork sausage its distinctive flavor.)

# INDEX

acid foods, sweeteners in, 7
After-School Fruit Cups, 180–181
aftertaste of sweeteners, 11
  of saccharin, 15
alcoholic beverages, calories in, 221–222
allergies, 14
All-Season Fruit Medley, 177
Almond Glaze, 41
Almond-Cinnamon Mini-Macaroons, 46
Ambrosia, Apple, 192
Ambrosia Flan, 126
Ambrosia Jel-low, 99
Ambrosia Salad, Pear, 201
American Journal of Clinical Nutrition, 8
Angel Pie Shell, 49–50
  Bavarian fillings for, 62–63
apple(s), 191
  ambrosia, 192
  baked, rum-raisin, 192
  bread, high-fiber fruit, 82
  bread pudding, rum-raisin, 107
  calorie content of, 173
  champagne-baked, 193
  cheesecake, Cheddar-apple, 142
  cobbler, ruby apple, 52
  compote, winter orchard, 178
  cranberry-stuffed, 195
  crisp, 193
  filling, rum-raisin, 89
  frappe, crushed cranapple, 218

apple(s) (cont.)
  to freeze, 188
  glazed, 104
  insulin response to, 8
  jel-low, ambrosia, 99
  loaf, banana fruit, 82
  McIntosh, 12, 13, 47, 51
  mince, 194
  mincemeat, 55
  muffins, 79–80
  omelet, fruit and cheese, 95–96
  pie:
    brandied apricot apple, 52–53
    cheese-apple Danish, 134–135
    mince, 55
    orange spiced fruit, 56–57
    pineapple-apple strudel, 68–69
    pineapple-apricot-apple, 53
    rum-raisin-apple, 54
    spiked fruit, 54–55
    sugar substitutes in, 12, 13, 51
    sugarless, 51
    sweetened with raisins, 50
  pudding cake, 34
  quiche, honey-apple, 136–137
  sangría fruit cups, 187
  soufflé, honey baked, 193–194
  streusel, extra-easy, 39
  tart, French apple-cheese, 134
  yogurt banambrosia, 183

apple juice:
  cider, 102
  frozen concentrate:
    applesauces, 166–167
    gelatin desserts, 103
    glazes, 64–65, 103–104, 179
    jelly, grownup cider, 171
    spritz, 212
    spritzer, wine-apple, 225
    "hard sauce", apple cream, 155
applesauce, 86, 166–167
  chunky rum-raisin, 192
  cupcakes, 35
  dip, apple curry, 234–235
  mousse, apple-wine, 119
  pancakes, orange-flavored, with, 85
  topping, apple-cream, 155
apricot(s):
  calorie content of, 173
  dried, 37–38
    sauce, brandied sundae, 161
    squares, brandy cheese, 150–151
  to freeze, 188
  pie:
    brandied apple-apricot, 52–53
    peach and apricot cheese, 67
    pineapple-apple-apricot, 53
  sherbet, orange-apricot, 209
arrowroot, pies thickened with, 48
ascorbic acid, fruit frozen with,
    188
aspartame, 11–14
  cooking with, 9, 11, 13
  with saccharin, 10
  stability of, 9

baby food, blueberry, 159
bacon, 83
  substitutes for, 91
Baked Apple Mince Pie, 55–56
Baked Cranberry Sauce, 165
baked foods:
  aspartame in, 13
  egg substitutes in, 18
  fructose in, 7
  honey-sweetened, 6
  sugar in, 9
  sweeteners in, 15
Baked Rhubarb, 199
baking of pies, 48
Banambrosia, Yogurt, 183
banana(s), 181–182
  Apple Ambrosia, 192
  bread, high-fiber, 82
  in bread batter, 81
  cake, quick layer, 32–33
  coconut-baked, 184
  compote, 177
  flan, ambrosia, 126
  freeze, tropical, 182–183

banana(s) *(cont.)*
  Fruit Salad Dressing I, 200
  gelatins:
    Ambrosia Jel-low, 99
    Banana-Blueberry Jel-low, 98
    Brandied Banana-Peach Jel-low, 99
    Cranberry-Banana Jel-low, 100–101
    Real Peach-Banana Jel-low, 105
    Strawberry-Banana-Orange Jel-low, 100
    Strawberry-Orange Jel-low, 98
  glazed, 103–104
  gingerbread, light, 29–30
  ice milk, Polynesian, 205
  jubilee, 163
  loaf, banana fruit, 82
  muffins, golden fruit, 79
  muffins, orange banana, 77–78
  nog, bashed banana, 218
  nog, breakfast, 214
  oven-fried, 184
  pancakes, 87
  parfaits, Fourth of July, 158
  pie, pronto banana yogurt, 66
  pops, tropical, 182
  quickbread, orange banana, 81
  Rosanna, 183
  shake, Jamaica, 220
  shake for two, 213
  split, cottage-cheese peachy, 160
  strata, chocolate-banana, 147
  strawberry-banana float, 214
  trifle, banana-rum, 126
  Yogurt Banambrosia, 183
Bashed Banana Nog, 218
basting sauce, Oriental, 161
batters, egg substitutes in, 18
Bavarians:
  Buried Berries Bavarian, 63
  Double Berry Bavarian, 62–63
beer, calorie content of, 222
berry(ies):
  breakfast, favorite, 175
  crisp, no-bake, 174–175
  to freeze, 188
  sauce, smashed berry, 159
  shake, 215
  *See also* blueberry(ies); cranberry(ies);
    strawberry(ies)
Best Ever Strawberry Sauce, 157–158
between-meal snacks, 2
beverages:
  alcoholic, calories in, 221–222
  aspartame in, 13
  Banana Breakfast Nog, 214
  Banana Shake for Two, 213
  Banana-Strawberry Float, 214
  Bashed Banana Nog, 218
  Berry Shake, 215
  Bloody Mary Spritzer, 224
  Busted Blueberry Nog, 218

beverages *(cont.)*
Café au Lait Shake, 215–216
Chocolate, Hot, 220
cocoa mix, 221
coffee, 219
Cranberry Kir Spritzer, 225
Crushed Cranapple Frappe, 218
diet sodas, homemade, 212
Espresso Milkshakes, 219–220
Extra-Light Wine Spritzer, 225
Fractured Fruit Frost, 216
Fresh Peach Milkshake, 216
Fresh-Fruit Yogurt Float, 217
Grape Kir Spritzer, 225
Hot Spiced Mocha Cocoa, 221
Irish Coffee Spritzer, 224
Jamaica Banana Shake, 220
Kir Spritzer, 225
Lower-Caloried Party Egg Nog, 226
Lunchtime Peach-Yogurt Shake-to-go, 218
Manhattan Spritzer, 223
Martini Spritzer, 224
milkshakes, 213
Nonalcoholic Brandied Eggnog, 215
Sangria Screwdriver, 226
Sangria Spritzer, 225–226
Sherry-Nectar Spritzer, 224
Shook-up Pineapple Nog, 218
Smashed Strawberry Shake, 216
sodas, calories in, 8
Spritzers, 211–212, 223
Sunrise Spritzer, 223
Whiskey Sour Spritzer, 223
Wine-Apple Spritzer, 225
yogurt, 217
Yogurt Sherbert Soda, 217
biscuit bread, Irish, no-knead, 72
Biscuit Shortcake, 28–29
biscuits, 73
drop, stir-and-bake, 74
variations, 75
bitterness of saccharin, 15, 16
Bittersweet Chocolate Cream Sauce for
Fresh Fruit, 156
Bittersweet Chocolate Sauce, 156
Black Forest Coupe, 157
Black Forest Parfaits, 113
Black Forest Roll with Cherry Filling, 25–26
blackberries, calorie content, 173
Blender-Easy Pineapple Preserves, 170–171
blintzes, 93
blood sugar, 6
Bloody Mary Spritzer, 224
Blue Cheese Dip, 232
blueberry(ies), 33, 58
baby food, 159
biscuit or muffin variation, 75
calorie content, 173
cake, cinnamon-blueberry, 33–34
cake, pineapple-crush, 34

blueberry(ies) *(cont.)*
cookies, blueberry-filled, 152
cornbread, 77
dessert, raw blueberry, 59
flummery, 121
to freeze, 188
glazed, 103–104
jam, 169
jam with gelatin, 170
jel-low, banana-blueberry, 98
mousse, easy, 120
nog, busted blueberry, 218
pancakes, 85
parfaits, Fourth of July, 158
pie, windowpane, 64–65
sauce, hot blueberry wine, 162
shortcake, strawberries on, 34
shortcake, sugarless, 29
smashed, 159
spread, easy, 169
strata, blueberry-pineapple, 187
syrup, low-sugar, 92
tarts, "cream cheese", 151–152
tarts, honey blueberry, 58
Blushing Poached Pears, 196–197
Bottomless Orange Spiced Fruit Pie, 56–57
bottomless pies, 49
bran cereal:
biscuit and muffin variation, 75
Granny's Brannies, 110
muffins, prune, 80
Brandied Apple-Apricot Pie, 52–53
Brandied Banana-Peach Jel-low, 99
Brandied Eggnog, Nonalcoholic, 215
Brandied Fresh Peaches with "Italian
Cream", 180
Brandied Fruit Sherbert, 208–209
Brandied Peach Sauce, 163
Brandy Chocolate Pudding, 111
Brandy-Apricot Cheese Squares, 150–151
bread puddings:
orange-raisin, high-fiber, 107–108
rum-raisin-apple 107
spiced chocolate, 108–109
Bread-and-Butter Pickles, 240
breads:
Apple-Raisin Muffins, 79–80
Banana Fruit Loaf, 82
Blueberry Cornbread, 77
Buttermilk Bannock, 73
Dot's Low-Calorie Cranberry Bread,
80–81
Easy Stir-and-Bake Low-Calorie Muffins,
74
Fabulous High-Fiber Fruit Bread, 82
Fiber-Bread Orange Muffins, 78
Food Processor Whole-Grain Corn-bread,
75–76
Golden Fruit Muffins, 79

breads *(cont.)*
  Moist Orange Banana Breakfast Muffins, 77–78
  No-Fat-Added Cornbread, 76–77
  One-a-Day Prune Breakfast Muffins, 80
  Orange Banana Quickbread, 81
  Quick and Easy Country Toasting Bread, 71
  Soy-Enriched Bannock Bread, 73
  Stir-and-Bake Low-Cal Drop Biscuits, 74
  Super-Speedy Irish No-Knead Biscuit Bread, 72
  Whole-Kernel Corn Muffins, 76
  Whole-Wheat Bannock Bread, 73
  Yeast Bread, 70–71
  *See also* pancakes; waffles
Breadspreads, Low-Calorie, 229
  *See also* spreads
breakfast cereals:
  aspartame and, 14
  berries and, 175
  cookies, 110
  cookies, raisin-bran drop, 45
  muffins, orange banana, 77–78
  muffins, prune, 80
  Protein Puffs, 46
breakfast muffins:
  orange banana, 77–78
  prune, 80
breakfast squares, pineapple-cheese, 151
Broken Cookie Pie, 140
brown sugar, 4–5
browning of baked foods, 15
Brownulated sugar, 5
buckwheat pancake mixes, 84
Buckwheat Pancakes, 85
Buried Berries Bavarian, 63
Buried-Treasure Cream Cheese Pie, 66–67
Busted Blueberry Nog, 218
butter, bananas substituted for, 81
Butter, Blender Fruit, 168
  *See also* spreads
buttermilk:
  bannock (Irish Soda Bread), 73
  pancake variation, 85
  shortcake, sugarless, 28

Café au Lait Shake, 215–216
cake mixes, 31
cakes, 19
  aspartame in, 12
  Apple Pudding Cake with Self-Making Sauce, 34
  Applesauce Cupcakes, 35
  Black Forest Roll, 25–26
  Blueberry-Pineapple-Crush Cake, 34
  Carrot Chiffon Cake, 22–23
  Chocolate Sour-Cream Icebox Cake, 37
  Christmas Slimmer Stollen, 41
  Cinnamon-Blueberry Cake, 33–34
  Devil's Fridge Cake, 37

cakes *(cont.)*
  Double Chocolate Roll, 25
  Extra-Easy Apple Streusel, 39
  Ginger Squares, 31
  Ginger-Peach Upside-Down Cake, 31–32
  Honey Spongecake, 21
  Hot Ginger-Peach Winter "Shortcakes", 32
  Lady Finger Layer Cake, 27
  Light Carrot Torte, 22
  Light Gingerbread, 29–30
  Low-Calorie Peaches 'n' Cream Cake, 35
  No-Bowl No-Egg Chocolate Cake, 26
  Passover No-Bake Fruit Cake, 40
  Pineapple Cassata, 24–25
  Quick Banana Layer Cake, 32–33
  Skinny Biscuit Shortcakes, 28–29
  Slim Cinnamon Streusel, 38
  Slim Peach Kuchen, 36
  Slim Peach Melba Cake, 21
  Slim Spongecake, 20–21
  Slimmer Chiffon Cake, 19–20
  Spiced Apricot Cupcakes, 37–38
  Stir-Crazy Light Fruitcake, 29
  Sugarless Blueberry Shortcake, 29
  Sugarless Buttermilk Shortcake, 28
  Sugarless Strawberry Shortcake, 28
  Strawberry Russe Fridge Cake, 36–37
  Strawberries on Blueberry Shortcake, 34
  Yogurt Strawberry Cake, 37
California Dip, 231
California Spinach Salad, 201
calorie content:
  of alcoholic beverages, 221–222
  of bananas, 81, 181
  of blueberries, 33, 58
  of breakfast meats, 91
  of brown sugar, 5
  of Cheddar cheese, 142
  of confectioners' sugar, 4
  of egg substitutes, 18
  of eggs, 18
  of fruits, 173
  of gingerbreads, 29–30
  of honey, 6
  of ice creams, 143, 202–203
  of molasses, 5
  of nuts, 228
  of peanut butter, 228
  of pumpkin, 59
  of raisins, 44
  of ricotta, 153
  of sugar, 4
  of Sweet 'n' Low, 14
Calorie-Cheap Chips and Dippers, 238
Calorie-Reduced Maple Syrup, 92
Canadian bacon, 91
candies:
  dietetic, sorbitol sweetened, 9
  Granny's Brannies, 110
  low calorie, 109

candies *(cont.)*
 Phruit Phudge, 109
 Pinenibbles, 110
canned fruits, streusel with, 39
Cannoli Pies, 146–147
cantaloupe, 206
 calorie content of, 173
 to freeze, 188
 sundae, cantaloupe-strawberry, 207
 *See also* melons
Capuccino, 117–118
 "ice cream", 206
carbohydrates, 8
carob, chocolate substitute, 10, 16
Carob Coffee Shake, 216
carrot(s):
 chiffon cake, 22–23
 kugel, nondairy light, 124–125
Cassata, Pineapple, 24–25
ceramic cookies, 42–43
cereals, *see* breakfast cereals
Champagne-Baked Apples, 193
Charlotte Russe, Strawberry-Orange, 117
Cheaters' "Homemade" Peach Ripple
  Sherbet, 208
Cheddar cheese, 142
 biscuit and muffin variation, 75
 "butter", 230
 dip, 232
 Monterey pepper cheese, 236–237
 spread, Tex-Mex, 233
cheese:
 ball, Mexican, 235–236
 biscuit and muffin variation, 75
 omelet, fruit and cheese, 95–96
 for slicing, 240–242
 spreads, 232–233
  Greek, 234
  Italian, 233
  Tex-Mex, 233
 *See also* name of cheese
cheesecakes:
 apple-cheddar, 142
 cottage cheese in, 130
 nectarine-filled, 132–133
 peach-filled, 131–132
 Philly cream-cheese cake, 140–141
 pineapple, speedy, 141–142
 pineapple-topped strawberry, 133–134
 parfaits, 150
Cheesecake-Flavored Pineapple Parfaits, 106
cherry(ies):
 calorie content of, 173
 coupe, Black Forest, 157
 filling, Black Forest roll with, 25–26
 to freeze, 188
 sauce, cherry-cranberry, 164
 sauce, Jubilee, 162–163
 topping, for cheesecake, 141
chiffon cake, 19–20
 carrot, 22–23

chiffon pie, pumpkin, 61–62
children, desserts for, 17
Chile "Christmas" Dip, 231
Chinese Fortune Cookies, 43
chips, 238
chive-parsley biscuit and muffin variation, 75
chocolate:
 aspartame and, 12
 bread pudding, spiced, 108–109
 cake, no-bowl no-egg, 26
 cake, sour-cream icebox, 37
 cookies, raisin, 44–45
 filling, chocolate cream, 42
 fondue, fresh fruit, 157
 hot, 220
  aspartame in, 13
  spiced mocha cocoa, 221
 meringues, 45
 mousses, 114
  saccharin in, 16
  spicy, 115
  world's easiest, 113–114
 pie:
  Cannoli, 146–147
  cinnamon chocolate cheese, 138
  cookie pudding, 139–140
  double chocolate chip, 68
  orange, 139
 "Phrozen Phudgicles", 204–205
 pudding, 110–111
  rice, spiced, 128
  spice, 112
 roll, 25
  with cherry filling, 25–26
  pineapple-filled, 26
 sauce, bittersweet, 156
 sauce, flaming fruit, 162
 strata, banana, 147
 swirl, Jamocha, 119–120
 syrup, chocolate-orange, 161–162
cholesterol:
 in eggs, 18
 to reduce in pancakes, 85
Chomocha Mousse, 114
Christmas Slimmer Stollen, 40
Chunky Rum-Raisin Applesauce, 192
cider, *see* applesauce
Cider-Marinated Zucchini Pickles, 239–240
Cider-Spiced Applesauce, 166
cinnamon, 48
Cinnamon Chocolate Cheese Pie, 138
Cinnamon Streusel, 38
Cinnamon-Almond Mini-Macaroons, 46
Cinnamon-Blueberry Cake, 33–34
cinnamon-raisin biscuit and muffin variation,
  75
citrus fruits, 199
 *See also* name of fruit
Citrus Tea Spritz, 212
cobblers, 47
 Ruby Apple Cobbler, 52

cocoa, hot, see chocolate, hot
Coconut-Baked Bananas, 184
Coconut-Pineapple-Orange "Cream" Pie, 136
Coeur à la Crème, 148
coffee:
    aspartame in, 12, 13
    cocoa, hot spiced mocha, 221
    decaffeinated, 16
    espresso, 219
    ice cream, Capuccino, 206
    milkshakes, espresso, 219–220
    mousse, Chomocha, 114
    mousse, Jamocha rum, 114
    mousse, quick Capucchino, 117–118
    pie, Continental, 64
    sauce, bittersweet chocolate cream, 156
    shake, café au lait, 215
    swirl, Jamocha, 119–120
cold foods:
    aspartame in, 12
    sweeteners in, 7, 10
compote:
    banana, 177
    winter orchard, 178
confectioners' sugar, 4
constipation prevented by prunes, 190
Continental Coffee Pie, 64
cookies, 42–43
    Chinese Fortune Cookies, 43
    Chocolate Meringues, 45
    Cinnamon-Almond Mini-Macaroons, 46
    cooky-crumb crust, 64
    Healthier Sandwich Cookies, 114
    Protein Puffs, 46
    Raisin Bars, 44
    Raisin-Bran Drop Cookies, 45
    Raisin-Chocolate Chip Cookies, 44–45
    sugar substitutes in, 13, 15
    See also Squares
corn, fresh, pancakes, 85
corn oil, pastry made with, 49
cornbreads:
    Blueberry Cornbread, 77
    Food Processor Whole-Grain Cornbread,
        75–76
    No-Fat-Added Cornbread, 76–77
    sweetening of, 75
    Whole-Kernel Corn Muffins, 76
Cornmeal Pancakes, 85
cornstarch, pies thickened with, 48
cottage cheese, 130–131
    blintz filling, 93
    breakfast squares, pineapple, 151
    cheesecake:
        nectarine-filled, 132–133
        peach-filled, 131–132
        pineapple-topped strawberry, 133–134
    Coeur à la Crème, 148–149
    dip, apple-curry, 234
    fondue, peach-cheese, 149

cottage cheese (cont.)
    fruited, 190
    lunch, peachy banana-split, 160
    mousse, chocolate-orange, 114
    mousse, creamy orange, 115–116
    pancakes, 87
    parfaits, "cheesecake", 150
    parfaits, cheesecake-flavored pineapple, 106
    parfaits, strawberry creme, 150
    peanut butter, 229
    pie:
        apple-cheese Danish, 134–135
        chocolate cooky pudding, 139–140
        chocolate orange, 139
        cinnamon chocolate cheese, 138
        orange-pineapple-coconut, 136
        pineapple "cream", 135–136
        pumpkin-cheese, 137
    pudding, chocolate spice, 112
    quiche, honey-apple, 136–137
    sauce, orange strawberry crush, with, 27
    spread, Greek, 234
    tart, French apple-cheese, 134
    winter peaches and, 149
    See also pot cheese
cranberry(ies), 194–195
    apples, cranberry-stuffed, 195
    bread, Dot's low-calorie, 80–81
    compote, cranberry-pear, 196
    frappe, crushed cranapple, 218
    frozen yogurt, 210
    jel-low, banana, 100–101
    Jubilee, 195
    mousse, cranberry yogurt, 121–122
    sauce, 164–165
        baked, 165
        pineapple-cranberry, 165
        sugar-free orange-cranberry, 164–165
    spritzer, Kir, 225
    spritzer, orange-cranberry, 211
Crazy Pineapple Pie, 68
cream, whipped:
    Heartless Coeur à la Crème, 148–149
    Tangy Topping II, 156
cream cheese, low-fat, 140–141
    cake, slimmed down, 140–141
    cheesecake, apple-Cheddar, 142
    cottage cheese substituted for, 131
    Crème Frâiche III, 155
    custard, one-egg, 148
    pie:
        buried-treasure, 66–67
        hidden-pineapple, 67–68
        no-bake, 143
        pineapple, 143–144
        pumpkin, 62
        refrigerator, 144
        winter peaches 'n' cream, 145–146
    substitutes for, 231
    tarts, blueberry-topped, 151–152

cream puffs, orange, 116–117
Creamy Orange Mousse, 115–116
Crème Chantilly, yogurt, 175
Crème de Cacao, Pots de, 117
Crème Fraîche, 154–155
crêpes, 94
    cottage cheese filling for, 131
    orange-strawberry crush filling for, 27
    strawberry-filled, 94–95
Crocked Fruit, 176–177
crush sauce, orange-strawberry, 27
Crushed Cranapple Frappe, 218
cucumber pickles, 239, 240
cupcakes:
    applesauce, 35
    spiced apricot, 37–38
Curried Fruit Crock Cheese, 238
Curried Fruit Dip, 232
curry dip, apple, 234–235
custard pie, pumpkin, 60–61
custards:
    Ambrosia Flan, 126
    Fast-Freeze Fruit Custard, 204
    frozen, 203
    One-Egg Cream-Cheese Custard, 148
    Pumpkin Custard, 122
cyclamate:
    cooking with, 9
    government regulation of, 14–15, 16
    importation of, 10
    with saccharin, 10
    stability of, 10, 11

decaffeinated coffee, 16
demerara sugar, 5
Devil's Fridge Cake, 37
diabetics:
    fructose used by, 7
    sugar substitutes used by, 9
diet margarine, 39, 74
    pastry made with, 48, 49
diet soda, homemade, 13, 212
Dieter's Apple-Cream "Hard Sauce", 155
Dieter's Mincemeat Without Pie, 55
dietetic candies, sorbitol sweetened, 9
dietetic ice cream, 203
diets, failure of, 1–2, 17
dips, 231–232
    apple-curry, 234–235
    farmer cheese, 236
    low fat bases for, 230–231
    Spanish olive, 237
Dot's Low-Calorie Cranberry Bread, 80–81
Double Applesauce, 166
Double Berry Bavarian, 62–63
Double Chocolate Chip Pie, 68
Double Chocolate Roll, 25
dressings, salad, 199, 200
dried fruit, *see* fruit, dried

Easy Applesauce, 166–167
Easy Blender Pumpkin-Cheese Pie, 137
Easy Blueberry Mousse, 120
Easy Blueberry-Pineapple Strata, 187
Easy Chocolate Orange Mousse, 114
Easy Low-Calorie Pumpkin Ice Milk, 205
Easy No-Bake Pumpkin Pies, 122
Easy Pumpkin Pudding, 122
Easy Refrigerator Cheese Pie, 144
Easy Rum-Raisin Yogurt, 174
Easy Stir-and-Bake Low-Calorie Muffins, 74
Easy Upper-Crust Sugarless Apple Pie Plus, 51–52
eclairs, low-calorie, 41–42
Eggbeaters, 18
eggnog, 226
    banana, 214
    calorie content of, 222
    nonalcoholic brandied, 215
Eggnog Mousse, 125–126
eggs, 18
English Trifle, 23
English-Muffin Pizza, 244
Equal (aspartame), 11
    cooking with, 12–13, 39
    packaging of, 11–12
espresso coffee, 117–118, 219
Espresso Milkshakes, 219–220
Espresso Spritzer, 224
Extra-Easy Apple Streusel, 39
Extra-Light Wine Spritzer, 225

Fabulous High-Fiber Fruit Bread, 82
Fall Fruited Yogurt or Cottage Cheese, 190
farmer cheese, 235, 236
    ball, Mexican, 235–236
    ball, pineapple, 237
    "cream cheese", low-fat, 236
    crock cheese, curried fruit, 238
    dip, Spanish olive, 237
    frosting, light orange, 29
    Monterey Pepper Cheese, 236–237
    slicing cheese, 240–242
    spread, pineapple-cheese, 238
Fast-Freeze Fruit Custard, 204
fats, refined, 2
FDA (Food and Drug Administration), sweeteners banned by, 14–15
feta cheese spread, 234
Fiber-Bread Orange Muffins, 78
fillings:
    for blintzes, 93
    cherry, Black Forest Roll with, 25–26
    chocolate cream, 42
    chocolate mousse as, 114
    peach ambrosia, 88
    pineapple, 88
    rum-apple-raisin, hot, 89
    strawberry, 95
Flaming Mincemeat Sundaes, 207–208

flour, 70
  self-rising, 71–72
Fluffy Fruit Salad Dressing, 200
flummery, blueberry, 121
fondue, berry, 175
fondue, peach-cheese dessert, 149
Food and Drug Administration (FDA),
    sweeteners banned by, 14–15
food processor, pancakes made in, 85
Food Processor Whole-Grain Cornbread,
    75–76
Fortune Cookies, 43
Fourth of July Parfaits, 158
Fractured Fruit Frost, 216
freezing instructions:
  bananas, 182
  cottage cheese, 130
  cranberries, 195
  Buttermilk Bannock, 73
  fruit, 187–189
  Orange Banana Breakfast Muffins, 78
  pancakes, 86
French Apple-Cheese Tart, 134
French Fruited Fromage Dessert, 190
French toast, 18, 91–92
  accompaniments for, 91
  high-fiber, 92
  toppings for, 92
French-Bread Pizza, 244
frostings, 153–154
  chocolate mousse as, 114
  cottage cheese, 131
  orange, 29
Frosty Banana Nog, 214
frozen custard, 203
frozen desserts:
  aspartame in, 13
  Brandied Fruit Sherbet, 208–209
  Capuccino "Ice Cream", 206
  Cheaters' "Homemade" Peach Ripple
    Sherbet, 208
  Fast-Freeze Fruit Custard, 204
  Frozen Chocolate Pudding, 111
  Frozen Cranberry Yogurt, 210
  Frozen Fruit Yogurt, 210
  frozen yogurt, 209
  Muskmelon Ice, 207
  Peachy Keen Frozen Yogurt, 209–210
  "Phrozen Phudgicles", 204–205
  Pineapple Low-Fat Frozen Yogurt, 211
  Polynesian Ice Milk, 205
  Pumpkin Ice Milk, 205
  Tropical Banana Freeze, 182–183
  Tropical Banana Pops, 182
  See also ice cream; sundaes
frozen yogurt, 203, 209
fructose, 6–8, 39
  ice cream with 203
  in pies, 47

fructose (cont.)
  with saccharin, 10
  substituted for honey, 57
fruit(s), 172
  All-Season Medley, 177
  and aspartame, 11, 12, 14
  bread, high-fiber, 82
  butter, 168
  calorie content, 173
  canned, in streusel, 39
  cooking of, 174
  in cream-cheese pies, 66–67
  crocked, Polynesian, 176–177
  custard, fast-freeze, 204
  dried, see fruit, dried
  fondue, 157
  freezing of, 187–189
  frost, 216
  frozen, low-cal jam with, 168
  frozen fruit yogurt, 210
  fruit cups, 180–181
    sangria, 187
  gelatin desserts, 97, 101–102, 104
  glazed, 103–104
  loaf, banana fruit, 82
  mousse, layered, 118–119
  muffins, golden fruit, 79
  omelet, fruit and cheese, 95–96
  pancake, German, 89–90
  pies, 47, 48
    baked with sugar substitutes, 12,
      13
    orange spiced, 56–57
    raw fruit, 179
    spiked, 54–55
  salads, 199
    dressings for, 199, 200
  sauce for, chocolate cream, 156–157
  sauces, 158
    chunky, to freeze, 189
  sherbet, brandied, 208–209
  substituted for blueberries, 59
  topping for, 155
  yogurt, 174
  yogurt float, 217
  See also name of fruit
fruit, dried, 189
  apricots, 37–38
    sauce, brandied, 161
    squares, brandy cheese, 150–151
  crock cheese, curried fruit, 238
Fall Fruited Yogurt or Cottage Cheese,
    190
French Fruited Fromage, 190
Granny's Brannies, 110
peach(es):
  cream cheese pie, 145–146
  and creamed cottage cheese, 149
  rice pudding, 128

fruit juice:
  apple, frozen concentrate, 102, 103–104
    cranberry sauce, 164
    in pies, 51
  apple cider, 102
  calorie content of, 222
  frozen concentrates, 154
    applesauce, 166, 167
    candy, 109
    crocked fruit, Polynesian, 176–177
    diet soda, 212
    fruit cups, 180
    gelatin desserts, 97–103
    jelly, orange, 168
    mousse, 118–119
    in pies, 47
    in sauces, 160
    spritzers, 211–212
    yogurt, fruit-flavored, 173
    yogurt sherbet soda, 217
  gelatin desserts, 99–100
  glaze, 64–65
  insulin response to, 8
  orange, frozen concentrate:
    compote, 178
    gelatin desserts, 98, 99, 100
    marmalade, sugarless, 171
    mousses, 114, 115–116
    muffins, orange banana, 77–78
    pie, chocolate orange, 139
    pie, orange spiced fruit, 56–57
    quickbread, orange banana, 81
    sauce, strawberry Romanoff, 158–159
    strawberries and, 185
    syrup, chocolate-orange, 161–162
  rice pudding, 129
  spritzers, 211–212
fruit sugar, *see* fructose
fruitcake, no-bake, 40
fruitcake, stir-crazy light, 29
Fruited Cheese Spread, 235
Fruited Poached Pears, 197

Garlic Dip, 231
gelatin, with aspartame, 13
gelatin candies:
  Granny's Brannies, 110
  Phruit Phudge, 109
  Pinenibbles, 110
gelatin desserts, 97
  Ambrosia Jel-low, 99
  apple juice concentrate in, 102
  Apple-Honey Baked Souffle, 193–194
  Apple-Wine Refrigerator Mousse, 119
  Banana-Blueberry Jel-low, 98
  Brandied Banana-Peach Jel-low, 99
  Buried Berries Bavarian, 63
  Cheesecake-Flavored Pineapple Parfaits,
    106

gelatin desserts *(cont.)*
  Chocolate Cooky Pudding Pie, 139–140
  Chocolate Spice Pudding, 112
  Cinnamon Chocolate Cheese Pie, 138
  cottage cheese in, 130
  Cranberry Yogurt Mousse, 121–122
  Cranberry-Banana Jel-low, 100–101
  Creamy Orange Mousse, 115–116
  Double Berry Bavarian, 62–63
  Easy Blueberry Mousse, 120
  Easy Blueberry-Pineapple Strata, 187
  Easy Chocolate-Orange Mousse, 114
  Easy Pumpkin Pudding, 122
  Easy Refrigerator Cheese Pie, 144
  Eggnog Mousse, 125–126
  Fresh Orange-Pineapple-Coconut "Cream"
    Pie, 136
  Fresh Peach Pie, 185–186
  Fruit Under Glass, 103–104
  glaze, for fruit pie, 179
  Italian Chocolate-Banana Strata, 147
  Jamocha Swirl, 119–120
  Layered Fruit Mousse, 118–119
  mixes, 104
  Nesselrode Pudding, 126
  No-Bake Cream Cheese Pie, 143
  One-Egg Cream-Cheese Custard, 148
  Orange-Peach Jel-low, 98
  Peach and Apple Jel-low, 103
  Peach Jel-low, 161
  Pineapple-Topped Strawberry Cheesecake,
    133–134
  Pots de Crème de Cacao, 117
  Pronto Pineapple-Cream-Cheese Pie,
    143–144
  Pumpkin Chiffon Pie, 61–62
  Pumpkin-Gingersnap Layered Mousse,
    123
  Quick Capuccino Mousse, 117–118
  Quick Pineapple Yogurt Blender
    "Pudding", 105–106
  Real Apple Jel-low, 102
  Real Peach-Banana Jel-low, 105
  Real Strawberry Jel-low, 99–100
  Speedy Pineapple Cheesecake, 141–142
  Spicy Chocolate Mousse, 115
  Strawberry-Banana-Orange Jel-low, 100
  Strawberry-Orange Jel-low, 100
  Sugarless Fruit Jel-low, 97
  Sugarless Strawberry Strata, 101
  Tangy Pineapple "Cream" Pie, 135–
    136
  Three-Layer Low-Cal Gelatin with Fresh
    Fruit, 101–102
  Yogurt Peach Mousse, 121
German Fresh-Fruit Pancake, 89–90
German pancake, oven-baked, 88
Ginger Peachy Sundaes, 160
Ginger Squares, 31

gingerbread, 29–30
  brandied peach sauce for, 163
  shortcake, hot ginger-peach, 32
Ginger-Peach Upside Down Cake, 31–32
gingersnaps:
  crisp, gingersnappy peach, 175
  mousse, pumpkin layered, 123
  sundaes, ginger peachy, 160
glazes:
  fruit juice, 64–65, 179
  lemon gelatin, 179
glucose, 6
glucose tolerance levels, 8
Golden Fruit Muffins, 79
Golden-Raisin Applesauce, 167
government regulation of sugar substitutes,
      14–15, 16
Graham crackers:
  crust, 133, 138
  pie, rum-raisin-apple, 54
  substituted for gingersnaps, 123
  trifle, banana-rum
Granny's Brannies, 110
granola, no oil, no sugar, 243
grape(s):
  calorie content of, 173
  insulin response to, 8
  compote, winter orchard, 178
  yogurt banambrosia, 183
grape juice:
  gelatin desserts, 99–101
  glaze, 64–65
  spritzer, Kir, 225
  strata, strawberry, 101
grapefruit, calorie content of, 173
Grapefruit Pudding, 108
Greek Cheese Spread, 234
Grownup Cider Jelly, 171
Grownup Grape Jelly, 171
Guildford Strawberry Trifle, 24

hangover, fructose as cure for, 7
Hawaiian Yogurt Sundae, 176
Healthier Sandwich Cookies, 114
Heartless Coeur à la Crème, 148–149
heat, and sweeteners, 9
Herbed Parmesan "Butter", 230
herbs, Italian, biscuit and muffin variation,
      75
Hidden-Pineapple Cheese Pie, 67–68
high-fiber bread puddings, 107–108
  spiced chocolate, 108–109
High-Fiber French Toast, 92
High-Protein High-Fiber-Bread Pancakes,
      90
High-Protein Sugar-Free Rice Pudding, 127
holiday desserts:
  Christmas Slimmer Stollen, 41
  Honey Spongecake, 21
  Light Carrot Torte, 22

holiday desserts (cont.)
  Nondairy Light Carrot Kugel, 124–125
  Passover No-Bake Fruit Cake, 40
honey, 6, 47, 136
  marmalade, orange-cranberry, 165
  pie, nectarine, 57–58
  pie, peach deep-dish, 57
  quiche, 136–137
  souffle, apple-honey, 193–194
  spongecake, 21
  syrup, honey-maple, 92
  tart, blueberry, 58
honeydew melon, calorie content of, 173
hot drinks, aspartame in, 12
hypoglycemia, 8

ice cream, 144, 202–203
  with aspartame, 13
  calorie content of, 143
ice milk, 143, 144, 203
  Polynesian, 205
  pumpkin, 205
iced espresso, 220
ices, 203
Irish Coffee Spritzer, 224
Irish No-Knead Biscuit Bread, 72
Irish Soda Bread, 73
Italian Cheese Spread, 233
Italian Chocolate-Banana Strata, 147
Italian Chocolate-Chip Cannoli Pie, 146
"Italian Cream", Brandied Fresh Peaches
      with, 180
Italian herbs, biscuit and muffin variation, 75
Italian Layer Cake, 24–25

Jamaica Banana Shake, 220
Jamocha Rum Mousse, 114
Jamocha Swirl, 119–120
jam:
  aspartame in, 13
  blueberry, 169, 170
  frozen fruit, 168
  peach, 167–168
  pineapple, 170
  refrigerator, 167
jelly, 171
  aspartame in, 13
  cider, 171
  grape, 171
  orange, 168

Key Lime Parfaits, 66
Key Lime Pie, 65–66
Kir, peach wine, 161
Kir Spritzer, 225
kuchen, peach, 36

labels, information on, 17, 202
Lady Finger Layer Cake, 27
laxative effect of prunes, 190–191

Layered Fruit Mousse, 118–119
Lemon Gelatin-Glaze, 179
lime parfaits, 66
lime pie, 65–66
liqueurs, calorie content of, 222
lunch, berry favorite, 175
lunch, surfside salad, 177
Lunchtime Peach-Yogurt Shake-to-go, 218

macaroons, cinnamon-almond, 46
Manhattan Spritzer, 223
mannitol, 9
maple sugar, 5–6
maple syrup, 92
margarine, *see* diet margarine
marmalade:
   honey orange-cranberry, 165
   sugarless, 171
Martini Spritzer, 224
measuring of flour, 71–72
Melba, fresh peach, 178
melon(s), 173, 206
   cantaloupe-strawberry sundae, 207
   to freeze, 188
   muskmelon ice, 207
Melon Melange, 173
meringue(s):
   angel pie shell, 49–50
   chocolate, 45
   pie, pumpkin, 61
Mexican Cheese Ball, 235–236
milk, in chocolate pudding, 111
milk, pink, 175
milkshakes, 213
   Banana Shake for Two, 213
   berry, 215
   café au lait, 215–216
   carob coffee, 215
   chocolate, 216
   espresso, 219–220
   Fractured Fruit Frost, 216
   mocha, 215
   peach, 216
   strawberry, 216
   yogurt, 217
mincemeat, 55
   fresh apple, 194
   sundaes, flaming, 207–208
Minted Poached Pears, 197
Miriam's Orange Pudding, 108
mocha cocoa, hot, spiced, 221
mocha pudding, 111
Mocha Shake, 215
Mock Cream Cheese, 231
Mock Mango Pie, 65
Mock Mango Sauce, 160
Mock Sour Cream, 231
Mock Walnut Butter, 229
Moist Orange Banana Breakfast Muffins,
   77–78

molasses, 5
molds, superfruit, 105
Monterey Pepper Cheese, 236–237
mousses:
   apple-wine refrigerator, 119
   with aspartame, 13
   blueberry, easy, 120
   chocolate orange, 114
   chocolate pineapple, 114
   chomocha, 114
   cranberry yogurt, 121–122
   eggnog, 125–126
   Jamocha rum, 114
   layered fruit, 118–119
   orange, creamy, 115–116
   pumpkin-gingersnap layered, 123
   pumpkin-yogurt marbled, 124
   quick capuccino, 117–118
   spicy chocolate, 115
   world's easiest chocolate, 113–114
   yogurt peach, 121
MSG (monosodium glutamate), 14
muffins, 73–74
   apple-raisin, 79–80
   easy stir-and-bake, 74
   fiber-bread orange, 78
   golden fruit, 79
   orange banana, 77–78
   prune, 80
   spiced apricot, 37–38
   variations, 75
   whole-kernel corn, 76
Mushroom-Flavored Pizza Sauce, 245
Muskmelon Ice, 207

Nectar Spritz, 211
nectarine(s):
   cheesecake, nectarine-filled, 132–133
   crisp, gingersnappy, 175
nectarine(s), continued
   to freeze, 188
   parfaits, "cheesecake", 150
   pie, honey nectarine, 57–58
   with raspberry sauce, 178
Nesselrode Pudding, 126
New Green Refrigerator Pickles, 239
Nonalcoholic Brandied Eggnog, 215
Nondairy Light Carrot Kugel, 124–
   125
nutmeg, 48
NutraSweet (aspartame), 11
nuts, calorie content of, 228

oil, pastry made with, 49, 50
olive dip, Spanish, 237
omelet, fruit and cheese, 95–96
omelets, cottage cheese filling for, 131
One-a-Day Prune Breakfast Muffins, 80
One-Egg Cream-Cheese Custard, 148
Onion Dip, 231

orange(s):
  ambrosia, apple, 192
  ambrosia filling, peach, 88
  compote, cranberry-pear, 196
  frosting, 29
  insulin response to, 8
  marmalade, sugarless, 171
  Mephistopheles, 157
  muffins, fiber-bread, 78
  Peachsauce, 160
  pie, pineapple-coconut "cream", 136
  pie, Polynesian, 56
  relish, cranberry, uncooked, 165
  salad, California spinach, 201
  salad, pear ambrosia, 201
  sauce, pineapple-orange, 158
  sauce, strawberry-crush, 27
  and strawberries, 184–185
  topping, marmalade "cream", 30
  topping, strawberry, 20
  yogurt banambrosia, 183
orange juice:
  bread pudding, 107–108
  Charlotte Russe, strawberry, 117
  gelatin desserts, 98, 100
  jelly, 168
  mousse, chocolate-orange, 114
  mousse, creamy, 115–116
  muffins, banana, 77–78
  nog, instant breakfast, 214
  pancakes, with applesauce, 86
  pears, orange-poached, 197
  pie, chocolate orange, 139
  pie, spiced fruit, 56–57
  preserves, raspberry-orange, 169–170
  pudding, Miriam's orange, 108
  quickbread, banana, 81
  sauce, orange-cranberry, 164–165
  sherbet, orange-apricot, 209
  spritzer, cranberry-orange, 211
  sundae, strawberry yogurt, 186
  syrup, chocolate-orange, 161–162
Oriental Basting Sauce, 161
Oven-Baked German Pancake, 88
Oven-Baked Rum-Raisin-Apple
    Graham-Cracker Pie, 54
Oven-Fried Bananas, 184
overripe fruit:
  bananas, 182
  sauces made from, 159–160

pancakes, 83–84
  accompaniments for, 91
  banana, 87
  German, 88, 89–90
  high-protein high-fiber-bread, 90
  main-course, 90
  pineapple, 86
  "shortcakes", 87
  variations, 85

pancakes (cont.)
  yogurt cottage-cheese, 87
  See also blintzes; crêpes
parfaits:
  apple ambrosia frozen yogurt, 192
  Black Forest, 113
  "cheesecake", 150
  cheesecake-flavored pineapple, 106
  Fourth of July, 158
  Key lime, 66
  rhubarb-yogurt, 199
  strawberry crème, 150
  yogurt strata, 177
Parmesan cheese:
  biscuit and muffin variations, 75
  herbed Parmesan "butter", 230
Passover No-Bake Fruit Cake, 40
pastry, 47–50
  cream puff, 41–42, 116–117
peach(es), 178
  brandied, 180
  cake, Melba, 21
  cake, peaches 'n' cream, 35
  calorie content of, 173
  cheesecake, 131–132
  crisp, gingersnappy, 175
  filling, peach ambrosia, 88
  fondue, peach-cheese, 149
  to freeze, 188
  frozen yogurt, 208, 209–210
  gelatins, 98, 99, 103, 105
  German pancake, 89–90
  glazed, 64–65, 103–104
  jam, 167–168
  Kir, 161
  kuchen, 36
  Melba, 178
  milkshake, 216
  mousse, yogurt peach, 121
  pie, 179, 185–186
  pie, cream-cheese, 66–67
  pie, deep-dish, 57
  sauce, 159–161
    brandied, 163
  shake-to-go, yogurt, 218
  sherbet, 208
  "shortcake", ginger-peach, 32
  spritz, peach-pineapple, 212
  substituted for blueberries, 59
  toppings, 144–145, 161
  upside-down cake, ginger, 31–32
peaches, dried:
  rice pudding, 128
  pie, cream cheese, 145–146
Peachsauce, 159–161
Peachy Keen Frozen Yogurt, 209–210
Peachy Keen Spritzer, 160–161
peanut butter, 227–229
pear(s), 196
  calorie content of, 173

pear(s) *(cont.)*
   compote, cranberry-pear, 196
   compote, winter orchard, 178
   to freeze, 188
   fruit cups, sangría, 187
   glazed, 104
   Helène, 157
   pie, sweeteners for, 50, 51
   poached, 196–197
   salad, ambrosia, 201
pectin, 166
   orange-cranberry sauce, 164–165
"Phrozen Phudgicles", 204–205
Phruit Phudge, 109
pickles:
   cider-marinated zucchini, 239–240
   fructose-sweetened, 240
   refrigerator, 239
pie crust:
   cookie crumb, 64
   graham-cracker, 133, 138
   meringue, 49–50
   pastry, 47–50
pies:
   Apple-Pineapple Strudel, 68–69
   Apple-Pineapple-Apricot Lattice-Top, 53
   Baked Apple Mince, 55–56
   Blueberry Mousse, 120
   Bottomless Orange Spiced Fruit, 56–57
   Brandied Apple-Apricot, 52–53
   Buried-Treasure Cream-Cheese, 66–67
   Cannoli, 146–147
   Chocolate Cookie Pudding, 139–140
   Chocolate Orange, 139
   Cinnamon Chocolate Cheese, 138
   Continental Coffee, 64
   Crazy Pineapple, 68
   Decalorized Pumpkin, 59–60
   Double Chocolate Chip, 68
   Easy Blender Pumpkin-Cheese, 137
   Easy No-Bake Pumpkin, 122
   Easy Refrigerator Cheese, 144
   Easy Upper-Crust Apple, 51
   French Apple-Cheese Tart, 134
   Fresh Peach, 185–186
   Fresh-Fruit Windowpane, 64–65
   fruit, sweeteners for, 12, 50, 51
   Fruit Medley, 67
   Hidden-Pineapple Cheese, 67–68
   Honey Blueberry Topless Tart, 58
   Honey Nectarine, 57–58
   Honey Peach Deep-Dish, 57
   Italian Chocolate-Chip Cannoli, 146
   Mock Mango, 65
   No-Bake Cream-Cheese, 143
   No-Sugar-Added Raw Peach, 179
   Orange-Pineapple-Coconut "Cream", 136
   Oven-Baked Rum-Raisin-Apple
      Graham-Cracker, 54
   Peach and Apricot Cheese, 67

pies *(cont.)*
   Peach Medley, 67
   Peach-Pineapple Cheese, 67
   Pear, 50, 51
   Pronto Banana Yogurt, 66
   Pronto Pineapple-Cream-Cheese, 143–144
   Pumpkin Chiffon, 61–62
   Pumpkin Cream-Cheese, 62
   Pumpkin Meringue, 61
   Quick and Easy Spiked Fruit, 54–55
   Quick-Bake Sugar-Reduced Pumpkin
      Custard, 60–61
   Raw Blueberry Filling for, 59
   Raw Fruit, with Apple-Juice Glaze, 179
   to reduce calories in, 47–48
   Ruby Apple Cobbler, 52
   Slimmed Down Key Lime, 65–66
   sugar substitutes in, 13
   sugar-free, cream-cheese, 67
   Tangy Pineapple "Cream", 135–136
   Topless Polynesian, 56
   Winter Peaches 'n' Cream Cheese,
      145–146
pineapple:
   ball, farmer cheese-pineapple, 237
   breakfast squares, 151
   cake, blueberry-crush, 34
   calorie content of, 173
   cassata, 24–25
   cheesecake, 141–142
      strawberry, pineapple-topped, 133–
         134
   cobbler, ruby apple, 52
   filling, 88
   flan, ambrosia, 126
   to freeze, 189
   frozen yogurt, 211
   in gelatin, 97
   jam, 170
   mousse, chocolate, 114
   nog, 218
   pancakes, 86
   parfaits, cheesecake-flavored, 106
   pies:
      apple-pineapple strudel, 68–69
      apple-pineapple-apricot, 53
      cheese, 67–68
      "cream", 135–136
      cream-cheese, 143–144
      orange spiced, 56–57
      Polynesian, 56
      spiked fruit, 54–55
   preserves, 170–171
   pudding, yogurt, 105–106
   roll, chocolate, 26
   sauce, 162, 166
      orange-pineapple, 158
      pineapple-cranberry, 165
   spread, pineapple-cheese, 238
   strata, blueberry-pineapple, 187

pineapple *(cont.)*
  topping, for pancakes, 86
  yogurt banambrosia, 183
pineapple juice:
  pie, orange-coconut "cream", 136
  plums poached in, 198
  sauce, 160
  spritz, peach-pineapple, 212
Pineapplesauce, 166
Pinenibbles, 110
Pink Grapefruit Spritz, 212
Pink Milk, 175
pizza, 244
  sauce, 244–245
plums:
  calorie content of, 173
  cobbler, ruby apple, 52
  to freeze, 189
  glazed, 103–104
  poached in pineapple juice, 198
  pyromaniac's, 163
poached pears, 196–197
poached plums, 198
poly-dextrose, 9
Polynesian Crocked Fruit, 176–177
Polynesian Ice Milk, 205
Polynesian Passion Spritz, 212
Polynesian Sangría, 177
popcorn, 242–243
port sauce, plums poached in, 198
pot cheese:
  fruited fromage, 190
  pie, cannoli, 146
  pie, double chocolate chip, 68
  squares, brandy-apricot, 150–151
Pots de Crème de Cacao, 117
preservative, sugar as, 9
preserves:
  aspartame in, 13
  pineapple, blender-easy, 170–171
  raspberry-orange, 169–170
  strawberry, sugarless, 169
Pronto Banana Yogurt Pie, 66
Pronto Pineapple-Cream-Cheese Pie,
    143–144
Protein Puffs, 46
Prunes, 190–191
  muffins, 80
  sponge squares, 191
puddings:
  with aspartame, 13
  Chocolate Spice, 112
  Easy Pumpkin, 122
  Fruit-Juice Rice, 129
  Grapefruit, 108
  High-Protein Sugar-Free Rice, 127
  Low-Calorie Chocolate, 110–111
  Miriam's Orange, 108
  Nesselrode, 126
  Nondairy Light Carrot Kugel, 124–125

puddings *(cont.)*
  Orange-Raisin High-Fiber Bread, 107–
    108
  Quick Lo-Cal Rice, 127
  Rum-Raisin-Apple Bread, 107
  Spiced Chocolate Bread, 108–109
  Spiced Chocolate Rice, 128
  Sugar-Free Refrigerator Rice, 129
  Winter Peach Rice, 128
pumpkin, 59
  custard, 122
  filling, chiffon, 61–62
  ice milk, 205
  mousse, gingersnap layered, 123
  mousse, yogurt marbled, 124
  pie:
    cheese, 137
    cream-cheese, 62
    custard, 60–61
    decalorized, 59–60
    meringue, 61
  pudding, easy, 122
Punched Peaches, 216
Purple Passion Spritz, 211
Pyromaniac's Plums, 163

quiche, cottage cheese in, 130
Quick and Easy Country Toasting Bread, 71
Quick and Easy Spiked Fruit Pie, 54–55
Quick Banana Layer Cake, 32–33
Quick Capuccino Mousse, 117–118
Quick Lo-Cal Rice Pudding, 127
Quick Pineapple Yogurt Blender "Pudding",
    105–106
Quick-Bake Sugar-Reduced Pumpkin
    Custard Pie, 60–61

raisin(s), 44
  apple pie sweetened with, 50
  applesauce, rum-raisin, 192
  baked apples, rum-raisin, 192
  bars, 44
  biscuit and muffin variation, 75
  bread pudding, orange, 107–108
  bread pudding, rum-apple, 107
  cobbler, ruby apple, 52
  cookies, chocolate chip, 44–45
  cookies, drop, 45
  filling, hot rum-apple, 89
  mincemeat, 55
  muffins, apple-raisin, 79–80
  pie, baked apple mince, 55–56
  pie, rum-apple graham-cracker, 54
  in pies, 47, 51
  yogurt, rum-raisin, 174
raspberry(ies):
  calorie content of, 173
  Melba, peach, 178
  preserves, raspberry-orange, 169–170
  sauce, nectarines with, 178

refrigerator cakes:
Chocolate Sour-Cream Icebox Cake, 37
Devil's Fridge Cake, 37
Strawberry Russe Fridge Cake, 36–37
refrigerator jams, 167
refrigerator pickles, 239
relish, cranberry-orange, 165
rhubarb, 198–199
rice pudding, 127
cottage cheese in, 130
Fruit-Juice, 129
High-Protein Sugar-Free, 127
Quick Lo-Cal, 127
Spiced Chocolate, 128
Sugar-Free Refrigerator, 129
Winter Peach, 128
ricotta, 153–154
"butter", Cheddar cheese, 230
"butter", herbed Parmesan, 230
Coeur à la Crème, 148–149
Crème Fraîche, 154–155
dip, apple curry, 234–235
"Italian Cream", brandied peaches with,
180
mousse:
chocolate, 113–114
creamy orange, 115–116
eggnog, 125–126
pumpkin-gingersnap, 123
pie, cannoli, 146–147
sauce, chocolate cream, 156
spreads, 229, 232–233
strata, chocolate-banana, 147
swirl, 119–120
topping, apple-cream, 155
topping, orange "cream", 30
whipped, 154
Romano cheese, spread, 233
Romanoff, strawberries, 185
Rosanna, bananas, 183
Rosh Hashanah, 124
Ruby Apple Cobbler, 52
Rum Chocolate Pudding, 111
Rum-Apple-Raisin Filling, hot, 89
Rum-Raisin Apple Sundae, 192
Rum-Raisin Baked Apples, 192
Rum-Raisin Sundaes, 208
Rum-Raisin Yogurt, 174
Rum-Raisin-Apple Bread Pudding, 107
Rum-Raisin-Apple Graham-Cracker Pie,
54

saccharin, 10, 14–16
cooking with, 9, 11
ice cream sweetened with, 203
salad dressings, 199, 200
salads:
California Spinach, 201
fruit, 199
Pear Ambrosia, 201

salads *(cont.)*
Strawberry Waldorf, 201
Surfside, 177
salt, in bread, 71
salty foods, 17–18
Sangría, Polynesian, 177
Sangría Fruit Cups, 187
Sangría Poached Pears, 197
Sangría Screwdriver, 226
Sangría Spritzer, 225–226
sauces:
Applesauce, 166–167
Baked Cranberry, 165
Best Ever Fruit, 158
Best Ever Strawberry, 157–158
Bittersweet Chocolate, 156
Bittersweet Chocolate Cream, 156
Brandied Apricot Sundae, 161
Brandied Peach, 163
Cherries Jubilee, 162–163
Cherry-Cranberry, 164
Chocolate Flaming Fruit, 162
Chocolate-Orange, 161–162
Cranberry, 164–165
fruit, to freeze, 189
Hot Blueberry Wine, 162
Hot Pineapple, 162
Orange-Pineapple, 158
Pineapple-Cranberry, 165
Pyromaniac's Plum, 163
Raspberry, Nectarines with, 178
Smashed Berry, 159
Strawberry Romanoff, 158–159
sausage, 83, 91
sausage seasonings, pizza sauce with,
248
self-rising flour, 71–72
self-rising pancake mix, 85
sherbets, 203
Brandied Fruit, 208–209
Orange-Apricot, 209
Peach Ripple, 208
Sherry-Nectar Spritzer, 224
Sherry-Spiked Applesauce, 166
Shook-up Pineapple Nog, 218
shortcakes, 26–27, 74
biscuit, 28–29
sugarless, 28–29
Trader's, 177
Shrimp Dip, 232
Smashed Berry Sauce, 159
Smashed Strawberry Shake, 216
snacking, 2
soda (beverage):
calorie content of, 8, 222
diet, 13, 212
Yogurt Sherbet, 217
soft drinks, and aspartame, 10
sorbitol, 9, 203
souffle, apple-honey baked, 193–194

sour cream:
  Crème Fraîche I, 154
  filling, strawberry, 95
  substitutes for, 131, 231
South Seas Sundae, 176
Soy-Enriched Bannock Bread, 73
Spanish Olive Dip, 237
Spiced Apricot Cupcakes, 37–38
Spiced Chocolate Rice Pudding, 128
spices, in pies, 48
Spicy Carrot Torte, 22
Spicy Chocolate Mousse, 115
spinach salad, 201
spongecakes, 20–21
  Honey Spongecake, 21
  Light Carrot Torte, 22
  Peach Melba Cake, 21
spreads, 229–230
  Cheddar cheese "butter", 230
  cheese, 232–233
  Easy Blueberry, 169
  farmer cheese, 236
  Fruited Cheese, 235
  herbed Parmesan "butter", 230
  marmalade, sugarless, 171
  peach, 161
  pineapple-cheese, 238
  pineapple-pepper, 237
  sweet, aspartame in, 13
Sprinkle Sweet, 39
spritzers, 211–212, 223
  Bloody Mary, 224
  Extra-Light Wine, 225
  Irish Coffee, 224
  Kir, 225
  Manhattan, 223
  Martini, 224
  Peachy Keen, 160–161
  Sangría, 225–226
  Sherry-Nectar, 224
  Sunrise, 223
  Whiskey Sour, 223
  Wine-Apple, 225
squares:
  Brandy-Apricot Cheese, 150–151
  Ginger, 31
  Pineapple-Cheese Breakfast, 151
  Prune Sponge, 191
Stollen, Christmas Slimmer, 40
strata:
  Easy Blueberry-Pineapple, 187
  Peach-Cheese, 149
  parfait, yogurt, 177
  strawberry, sugarless, 101
strawberry(ies):
  Bananas Rosanna, 183
  Bavarian, 63
    Double Berry, 62–63
  cake, Russe fridge, 36–37
  cake, yogurt, 37

strawberry(ies) *(cont.)*
  calorie content of, 173
  Charlotte Russe, orange, 117
  cheesecake, pineapple-topped, 133–134
  Coeur à la Crème, 148–149
  crepes filled with, 94–95
  float, banana-strawberry, 214
  to freeze, 189
  gelatin desserts, 98, 99–100
  jubilee, orange, 186
  and oranges, 184–185
  parfait, strawberry creme, 150
  pie, windowpane, 64–65
  preserves, sugarless, 169
  Romanoff, 185
  salads, 201
  sauce, 157–158
    orange-strawberry crush, 27
    Romanoff, 158–159
  shake, smashed, 216
  shortcake, blueberry, strawberries on, 34
  shortcake, sugarless, 28
  strata, sugarless, 101
  substituted for blueberries, 59
  sundaes, cantaloupe-strawberry, 207
  sundaes, orange-strawberry yogurt, 186
  Swiss-style yogurt, 174
  topping, peach ambrosia, 88
  topping, strawberry-orange, 20
  trifle, 24
streusel, apple, 39
streusel, cinnamon, 38
substitutes:
  honey, for sugar, 6
  for maple sugar, 5–6
  for sugar, *see* sweetners, artificial
sucrose, 4, 6
sugar, 2, 16–17
  in baked foods, 3
  brown, 4–5
  confectioners', 4
  demerara, 5
  maple, 5–6
  substitutes for, *see* sweetners, artificial
  turbinado, 5
  white, 4
"sugar alcohols", 9
Sugar Twin, 39
Sugar-Free Bread-and-Butter Pickles, 240
Sugar-Free Chocolate Mousse, 114
Sugar-Free Chocolate Pudding, 111
Sugar-Free Chocolate Spice Pudding, 112
sugar-free ice cream, 203
Sugar-Free Low-Fat Hot Cocoa Mix, 221
Sugar-Free Orange-Cranberry Sauce,
    164–165
Sugar-Free Refrigerator Rice Pudding, 129
  high-protein, 127
Sugar-Free Superfruit Gelatin, 104
Sugarless Blueberry Shortcake, 29

Sugarless Buttermilk Shortcake, 28
Sugarless Strawberry Shortcake, 28
Sugarless Strawberry Strata, 101
Sundaes:
  Brandied Apricot Sauce for, 161
  Cantaloupe-Strawberry, 207
  Flaming Mincemeat, 207–208
  Ginger Peachy, 160
  Hawaiian Yogurt, 176
  Hot Rhubarb, 199
  Orange-Strawberry Crush Sauce for, 27
  Orange-Strawberry Yogurt, 186
  Rum-Raisin, 208
  Rum-Raisin Apple, 192
  South Seas, 176
Sunrise Spritzer, 223
Superfruit Gelatin, 104
Super-Speedy Irish No-Knead Biscuit Bread, 72
Surfside Salad Lunch, 177
Sweet 'n' Low, 14
Sweet 'n' Natural Fruit Sugar, 7
Sweet-Pepper Pizza Sauce, 245
sweeteners, artificial, 3
  cooking with, 9, 12
  pies sweetened with, 47–48, 67
  stability of, 9, 10
sweetening power:
  of aspartame, 11, 12
  of brown sugar, 5
  of confectioners' sugar, 4
  of fructose, 6, 7, 47
  of honey, 6, 47
  of mannitol, 9
  of maple sugar, 5
  of molasses, 5
  of saccharin, 14
  of sorbitol, 9
  of xylitol, 9
sweetness, perception of, 15
Swiss-style yogurt, strawberry, 174
synergistic effect of sweetener combinations, 10
syrups:
  Calorie-Reduced Maple, 92
  Chocolate-Orange, 161–162
  Low-Sugar Blueberry, 92
  maple, substitutes for, 5–6
  molasses, 5
  Slim Honey-Maple Syrup, 92

tangerine juice, substituted for orange juice, 115
tangerines, Sangria Fruit Cups, 187
Tangy Pineapple "Cream" Pie, 135–136
Tangy Whipped Topping, 155–156
tarts:
  Blueberry-Topped "Cream Cheese", 151–152
  Honey Blueberry Topless, 58

tarts *(cont.)*
  Raw Fruit, with Apple-Juice Glaze, 179
  sugar substitutes in, 13
tea, aspartame (Equal) in, 12, 13
temperature:
  aspartame and, 12
  fructose affected by, 7
  sweeteners and, 9
  for yeast, 71
Tex-Mex Cheese Spread, 233
Three-Layer Low-Cal Gelatin With Fresh Fruit, 101–102
tomato juice, calorie content of, 222
topless pies, 49
Topless Polynesian Pie, 56
toppings:
  Almond Glaze, 41
  Apple-Cream, Whipped, 155
  Cherry, for cheesecake, 141
  Crème Fraîche, 154–155
  for French toast, 92
  fruit, to freeze, 189
  Orange "Cream", 30
  peach, 161
  Peach Ambrosia, 88
  pineapple, 89, 133
    for pancakes, 86
  Strawberry-Orange, for cake, 20
  Tangy Whipped, for fruit, 155–156
  Winter Peach, 144–145
  Yogurt Cream, 23
torte, carrot, light, 22
Trader's Shortcake, 177
trifle, 23
  Banana-Rum, with Graham crackers, 126
  Guildford Strawberry, 24
  with Orange-Strawberry-Crush Sauce, 27
  Yogurt English, 23–24
triglyceride levels, and fructose, 8
Tropical Banana Freeze, 182–183
Tropical Banana Pops, 182
turbinado sugar, 5
turkey sausage, 91
turmeric, egg whites colored with, 18

Upside-Down Cake, Ginger-Peach, 31–32

vanilla, 48
vitamin A:
  in cantaloupe, 206
  in pumpkin, 59
vitamin C, 158
  in cantaloupe, 206
vitamin C tablets, fruit frozen with, 188

Whipped Apple-Cream Topping, 155
Whipped Ricotta, 154
Whiskey Sour Spritzer, 223
white sugar, 4
Whole Cranberry Sauce, 164

Whole-Berry Cranberry Sauce, 164
Whole-Kernel Corn Muffins, 76
Whole-Wheat Bannock Bread, 73
Whole-Wheat Pancakes, 85
Windowpane Pie, 64–65
wine:
    calorie content of, 222
    port, Blueberry Flummery, 121
    red:
        Apple-Wine Refrigerator Mousse, 119
        Hot Blueberry Wine Sauce, 162
    white, Peach Wine Kir, 161
Wine-Apple Spritzer, 225
Winter Orchard Compote, 178
Winter Peach Rice Pudding, 128
Winter Peach Topping, 144–145
Winter Peaches and Creamed Cottage
    Cheese, 149
Winter Peaches 'n' Cream Cheese Pie,
    145–146
World's Easiest Chocolate Mousse, 113–114

X-Rated Cookie Pie, 140
xylitol, 9

yeast, use of, 70–71
yogurt:
    Apple Mince Jubilee with, 194
    Banambrosia, 183
    breads made with, 71, 72
    cake, strawberry, 37
    Coeur à la Crème, 148–149
    cream, 24
    Crème Chantilly, 175

yogurt (cont.)
    Crème Fraîche II, 155
    Fall Fruited, 190
    filling, 95
    float, fresh-fruit, 217
    frozen, 203, 209, 210
        cranberry, 210
        mousse, spicy chocolate, 115
        parfait, apple ambrosia, 192
        peach, 208, 209–210
        pineapple, 211
    fruit, 173, 174
    jel, superfruit 'n' yogurt, 105
    mousse, cranberry, 121–122
    mousse, peach, 121
    mousse, pumpkin, 124
    pancakes, 85, 87
    parfaits, pineapple, 106
    parfaits, rhubarb, 199
    parfaits, strata, 177
    pie, banana, 66
    pie, brandied apricot-apple, 53
    "pudding", pineapple, 105–106
    rum-raisin, 174
    shake, 177
    shake-to-go, peach, 218
    sherbet soda, 217
    sundae, Hawaiian, 176
    sundae, orange-strawberry, 186
    Swiss-style, strawberry, 174
    topping, whipped, 155–156
    trifle, English, 23–24

zucchini pickles, cider-marinated, 239